G000022395

PSYCHOLOGY SURVEY
No. 3

Other works by Professor Jeeves

THINKING IN STRUCTURES, with Z. P. Dienes, Hutchinson

THE EFFECTS OF STRUCTURAL RELATIONS ON TRANSFER, with Z. P. Dienes, Hutchinson

EXPERIMENTAL PSYCHOLOGY – AN INTRODUCTION FOR BIOLOGISTS, Edward Arnold

Note on Series

The first volume of the *Psychology Survey* was published under the editorship of Professor Brian M. Foss and the second under the editorship of Professor Kevin Connolly. Lists of the chapters and their authors are provided at the end of this book.

Psychology Survey No. 3

edited by

MALCOLM A. JEEVES
Professor of Psychology, St Andrews University

London
GEORGE ALLEN & UNWIN
Boston Sydney

First published 1980

This book is copyright under the Berne Convention. All rights are reserved. Apart from any fair dealing for the purpose of private study, research, criticism or review, as permitted under the Copyright Act, 1956, no part of this publication may be reproduced, stored in a retrieval system, or transmitted, in any form or by any means, electronic, electrical, chemical, mechanical, optical, photocopying, recording or otherwise, without the prior permission of the copyright owner. Enquiries should be sent to the publishers at the undermentioned address:

GEORGE ALLEN & UNWIN LTD
40 Museum Street, London WC1A 1LU

© Malcolm A. Jeeves, 1980

British Library Cataloguing in Publication Data

Psychology survey.
No. 3
1. Psychology
I. Jeeves, Malcolm Alexander
150 BF121 80-40965

ISBN 0-04-150073-3
ISBN 0-04-150074-1 Pbk

Set in 10 on 11 point Times by Red Lion Setters, London, W.C.1
and printed in Great Britain
by Biddles Ltd, Guildford, Surrey

Foreword

Sufficient time has elapsed since the appearance of *Psychology Survey No. 1* for the first comments and reactions of reviewers to be published. Two comments in particular impressed me as noteworthy. In welcoming the series some readers felt that its usefulness would be increased if, in each volume, selected topics were given more extensive treatment. Other reviewers recognized that no one volume could begin to do justice to the range of contemporary psychology and that a three year cycle would be necessary to fulfil the aims and objectives of the series. In deciding whom I should ask to contribute to *Psychology Survey No. 3*, I kept these two points in the forefront of my mind.

Readers of *Psychology Surveys Nos 1* and *2* will notice that Chapters 3 and 8 of this volume are appreciably longer than contributions to the earlier volumes. In each case the authors have been given space to adduce arguments for why they believe that their particular approach to enduring problems in cognitive and in social psychology remain important, if at times controversial. As regards the second general observation made above, I have directed rather more space than hitherto to the biological bases of behaviour and to the abnormal functioning of memory and language processes. Thus, Chapters 7 and 9 focus upon the neural and hormonal bases of behaviour, while Chapters 4 and 5 deal with disorders of memory and language.

In addition, I felt it appropriate to include two chapters on issues of very contemporary and topical interest. One of these relates to the concern of Governments in several countries about the shortage of an adequate supply of mathematicians and scientists. It therefore seemed appropriate to survey the field of mathematical thinking concentrating on what psychologists can contribute to a better understanding of the processes involved and of how mathematical skills originate, develop and grow. The other contemporary issue is the psychology of unemployment dealt with in Chapter 12. Inevitably this topic is handled more speculatively than others, thus highlighting the lack of firm evidence and the need for more research initiatives in this field.

The primary objectives stated by Professor Foss in his Foreword to No. 1 remain unchanged. Accordingly the 'mix' of this volume includes aspects of the core topics of perception, learning, memory and thought aimed at a target readership of students studying psychology for a first degree. At the same time, as Professor Connolly intimated, an effort has been made to include material of interest to teachers and researchers, as well as to non-psychologists curious to know what psychologists are up to.

I am grateful to Mrs Estelle Johnston who has patiently handled the stream of correspondence with contributors and publishers. Professors Brian Foss and Kevin Connolly read through the first drafts of the chapters and offered many perceptive and uninhibited comments and criticisms. I thank them most warmly, as I do the already busy people who were prepared to respond to my invitation to contribute to this volume. It began under the guidance of John Churchill and was completed by Roger Jones. Two pleasanter and more patient publishers would be hard to find.

MALCOLM JEEVES
St Andrews

Contents

Chapter 1

Handedness

MARIAN ANNETT

Questions about handedness can be posed at several levels of generality. At the most general handedness can be considered as one of a multitude of asymmetries in the physical and natural world. The directions in which crystals rotate light, radioactive particles decay, DNA molecules coil, the stems of climbing plants twist, the bathwater escapes down the drain and many other asymmetries are entertainingly reviewed by Martin Gardner (1967). There are right- and left-sided species of flounders, fish spending their adult life lying on the ocean floor, one eye having migrated from the other side of the head; in some species the adults may be right- *or* left-sided. Among male fiddler crabs one or other of the front claws develops into a large pincer. In the mollusc, *Limnaea peregra*, most shells are twisted in a dextral spiral but there are occasional sinistral individuals; the latter have been shown to depend on a recessive gene following the rules of Mendelian inheritance, with the interesting qualification that the direction of coil depends not on the genes of the individual but those of its mother. An asymmetry which man shares with other vertebrates is a displacement of the heart to the left side which is normally associated with a typical arrangement of the visceral organs and asymmetries of the circulation to the arms and to the cerebral hemispheres. Speculations relating handedness to visceral and circulatory laterality have a long history. This was one of the vulgar errors exposed by Sir Thomas Browne, the seventeenth-century country doctor who pointed out that, 'the seat of the liver on the left side is monstrous and rarely to be met with in the observation of physicians' and hence could not be the cause of a trait as common as left-handedness. Recent attempts to link handedness with phylogenetically ancient asymmetries are to be found in Corballis and Morgan (1978). In my view, the most important things to be explained about human handedness are the characteristics man does *not* share with his nearest primate cousins. These are a bias to right hand preference and an associated bias to left-sided representation of speech in the brain. Despite assiduous search for 'precursors' of these human asymmetries in primates no convincing evidence has been found. This suggests that the bias to right hand and left brain are recently evolved human asymmetries.

In contrast to the broad perspective above, questions can be posed by the individual who would like to know why and how one hand is more skilful than the other and if the skilled hand were impaired by injury or stroke, would the other hand be trainable to a similar level of skill? Recovery of function probably depends mainly on individual differences in the original level of skills and on personal motivation in retraining. Research on the nature of the preferred hand advantage suggests that it does not depend on reaction time, the ability to apply a precise pressure, or the capacity to make separate movements of the fingers (Kimura and Vanderwolf 1970; Provins 1956). The preferred hand is better at hitting small targets, especially as the task difficulty increases (Sheridan 1973). Analysis of film records of the hands placing pegs in holes found that both hands make many errors, and correct them at about the same rate; the preferred hand is more likely to make a 'hole in one' and the non-preferred hand is more likely to need four of five attempts (Annett, Annett, Hudson and Turner 1979).

Between the broader perspective of asymmetry in nature and the narrower perspective of individual skill, handedness can be examined as a characteristic of *Homo sapiens*. How does handedness vary between individuals and how is this variability distributed in the population? Answers to these questions must be sought before we can ask how handedness relates to other asymmetries such as eyedness, footedness, and above all, the representation of speech in the cerebral hemispheres.

THREE METHODS OF ASSESSMENT

Self-classification

The simple question, 'Are you right-handed or left-handed?' is probably sufficient for records of schoolchildren, recruits, and hospital entrants. Only about 3 in 1000 will reply, 'I can write with either hand'. True ambidexterity in the sense of equal skill *and* equal practice in both hands is rare enough to be disregarded in most samples. The fact that everyday experience suggests that people can be easily classified into one of two discrete categories has been one of the main stumbling blocks in the psychological analysis of handedness. Investigators expect to make generalizations about 'the left-hander'. When self-classified right- and left-handers are questioned more closely, or asked to perform skilled actions with each hand, the category 'left-hander' becomes decidedly fuzzy.

Preference

The most widely used method of assessment is an enquiry into the hand used for several actions, usually presented as a questionnaire for written response. If people are asked to *perform* the actions: using matches, playing cards, scissors and other tools, they are sometimes surprised to find that they do things the 'other' way, not having attended to their own handedness before. This lack of awareness is a small but real source of inaccuracy in questionnaire findings. Among 113 students who completed a 12 item questionnaire and performed the same actions a few weeks later, only 2.7% of responses changed between 'right' and 'left'. Other changes, 4.9%, involved 'either hand' responses. Demonstrations of performance are necessary, of course, in assessments of children.

With demonstration of performance, 'either' will be recorded for some items and a decision must be made whether to treat this response as evidence of sinistral tendencies. Table 1.1 shows the percentages of young adults giving 'left' and 'either' responses for each of 12 actions.

Table 1.1 *Percentages of 2321 subjects responding 'left' and 'either' to 12 items of a hand preference questionnaire (from Annett 1970a).* (*letters refer to order of presentation of items.)

	'Left' responses			*'Either' responses*	
I*	dealing cards	17.0	L	unscrewing jar lid	17.5
L	unscrewing jar lid	16.5	G	sweeping	16.9
H	shovelling	13.5	H	shovelling	11.9
G	sweeping	13.5	F	threading needle	9.7
F	threading needle	13.1	D	striking match	8.7
A	writing	10.6	K	toothbrush	8.5
D	striking match	10.0	E	scissors	6.8
B	throwing ball	9.4	I	dealing cards	3.3
J	hammering	9.2	C	racket	2.6
K	toothbrush	8.1	J	hammering	2.5
C	racket	8.1	B	throwing ball	1.3
E	scissors	6.2	A	writing	0.3

The 'left' responses vary between 6.2% for scissors and 17.0% for dealing playing cards and the 'either' responses between 0.3% for writing and 17.5% for unscrewing the lid of a jar. If *all* 12 actions are considered together, over half the sample would be found to have given at least one non-right response. Fleminger, Dalton and Standage (1977) used this very weak criterion of sinistrality and found less that 40% of their samples of younger adults in London to be fully dextral. In my questionnaire analyses I have not treated 'either' responses as sufficient for a non-right classification. Thus, right-handers in my descriptions are those giving no 'left' answers, left-handers are those giving no 'right' answers, and mixed-handers are those giving any combination of 'right' and 'left' (and 'eithers' may have been given by any of these groups; no questionnaire has been encountered which gave 100% 'either' responses). On these criteria, incidences in several samples were

60 – 70% right-handers, 25 – 35% mixed-handers and 3 – 5% left-handers.

The simple dichotomy of self-classification has now been replaced by a three way grouping, recognizing that about a third of the population changes hands between tasks. In the literature on handedness estimates of incidence have varied between 1 – 30%, suggesting that handedness is a 'slippery' and unreliable phenomenon. If about 30% of the population can 'float' between the dextral and sinistral categories, depending on the tasks used and the investigator's criterion, the notorious variability of incidences has been explained.

How has mixed-handedness been treated in theory and research? Many have recognized, like Brain (1945), that handedness is not absolute but a question of degree; but have gone on to point out that social pressures must have induced many sinistrals to adopt dextral habits. Thus, the mixed hander may represent a 'shifted sinistral'. This argument allows a return to the discrete dichotomous classification; it assumes that there are 'true' left-handers, but that sometimes the expression of their left-handedness is distorted. The argument offered a possible explanation of mixed-handedness in the days when many left-handers were forced, often by cruel methods, to use the right hand. It is not an acceptable explanation today when such pressures are the exception rather than the rule and when sinistral writers have been shown to prefer the *right* hand for other actions under *less* social control (Gillies, MacSweeney and Zangwill 1960).

The graded nature of preference has been partially recognized in attempts to quantify questionnaire performance using various indices, based on the proportions of 'right', 'left' and 'either' responses. The problem with all such indices and quotients is that actions such as writing and unscrewing the lid of a jar are given equal weight. In the Edinburgh Handedness Inventory (Oldfield 1971), this difficulty is compounded by asking subjects to judge how easily they could use the 'other' hand for each action. McMeekan and Lishman's (1975) reliability study found that subjects do not make these judgements consistently. Briggs and Nebes (1975) claim to have *improved* the Annett questionnaire by requiring judgements of the strength of preference for each action and by transforming it into a scorable inventory. In my view, judgements of strength of preference are more likely to be measuring characteristics like optimism and extraversion than handedness. Scores based on preference questionnaires are not very useful because in addition to the problem of the scaling of items mentioned above, the distribution obtained is J-shaped.

Another reaction to the phenomenon of mixed-handedness has been to try to discover structure among questionnaire items through factor analysis (Bryden 1977). Instead of looking for what 'goes together' through factor analysis, my approach was to ask whether objective grounds could be found for discriminating subgroups of mixed-handers through a computer run association analysis (Annett 1970a). This is a method for dividing and subdividing a sample, to give a branching classification, each division being made on the item most highly correlated with all others at that stage. The analysis yielded a very large number of patterns, each very little different from its adjacent branches. This outcome convinced me that there are no major subgroups of mixed-handers and that there are all degrees of preference between extreme right and extreme left. Handedness is not a discrete variable but a continuous one.

Measures of Relative Manual Skill

Woo and Pearson (1927) described data for grip strength collected at the instigation of Sir Francis Galton at the Health Exhibition of 1884, for 7000 males aged 6 to 81 years. The mean difference between hands was remarkably constant with age despite changes in absolute power of grip. The differences were distributed in a single normal curve, with no dip at around 0 to suggest dextral and sinistral subgroups in the population. The mean was to the right of 0 and about 65% were stronger with the right hand.

I have collected measures of the speed of each hand in moving pegs from one row to another in several samples, including two large studies of schoolchildren (Annett 1970b; Annett and Turner 1974) and two of students (Annett 1970a, 1976). The task has been found reliable (Annett, Hudson and Turner 1974). The distribution of differences between the hands is continuous, unimodal and with mean to the right of 0. It is rather peaked and with a slight negative skew, but otherwise resembles that found by Woo and Pearson. For some years I did not see how a normal distribution of differences in skill could give rise to a J-shaped distribution of preferences. The co-ordination of these two distributions is the key step that allows us to reformulate the problem of handedness and to see that the only thing that is special about human handedness is that the mean is to the right of 0 difference between the hands in skill.

THE CO-ORDINATION OF PREFERENCE AND SKILL

Annett (1970a) described 283 subjects for whom peg moving speeds and preference demonstration data were available. These included 110 mixed-handers whose patterns of preference could be classified into groups suggested by the association analysis and the groups ordered for mean differences between the hands in skill. Figure 1.1 shows the mean differences for each preference class in this Hull sample, details of the classes being given in the legend. The weakest non-right classification was that of subjects reporting left hand use only for needle threading, sweeping and shovelling; in the Hull sample this group's mean

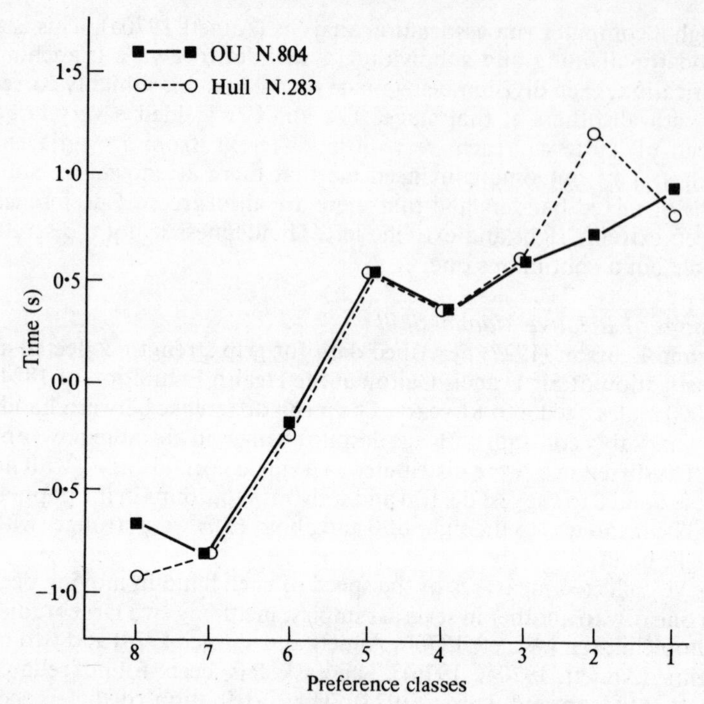

Figure 1.1 Mean left hand minus mean right hand peg moving time in subjects grouped for hand preference (after Annett 1976). The preference classes are: 1 right for all actions, 2 left for any of F, G, H* only, 3 left for L and no others except above, 4 left for I and no others except above, 5 right writing but left for any other primary action**. 6 left writing but right for any other primary action, 7 left for all primary actions but right for any others, 8 left for all actions. *Letters refer to questionnaire items as in Table 1.1. **Primary actions were A, B, C, D, J and K.

difference was more *dextral* than that of consistent right-handers. In a later sample of Open University (OU) students, also represented in the figure, class 2 again showed the weakest departure from full right-handedness, but the mean was between those of classes 1 and 3. Unscrewing the lid of a jar, class 3, was next along the continuum, then dealing playing cards, class 4. The fact that class 5 was not quite in line between 4 and 6 need not detain us here; numbers were small and the definition of classes may be improved, as discussed in Annett (1976). The important point is that for most preference classes, the Hull and OU samples gave almost identical mean differences between the hands in skill. The apparently elusive left-hander has now been pinned down; degrees of sinistrality can be identified along a highly stable continuous dimension.

Figure 1.2 represents the preference classes as areas under the normal

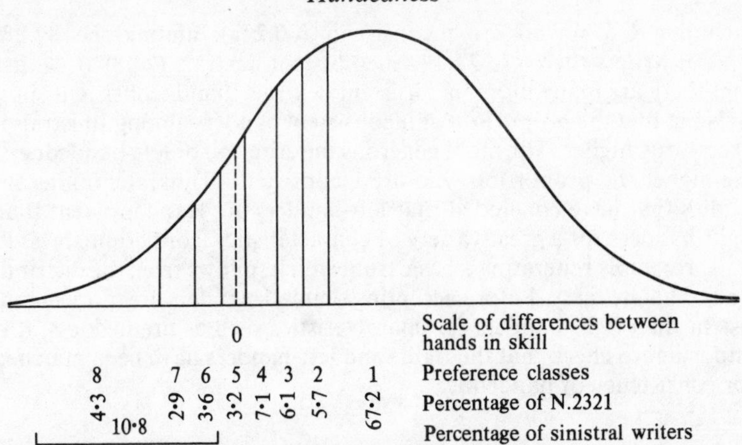

Figure 1.2 Idealized representation of the relation between hand preference classes and the normal distribution of differences between the hands in skill. 0 represents equal right and left hand skills.

curve, using incidences found in the 2321 subjects of Table 1.1 and estimating the location of no difference between the hands (0) from the OU sample. Those with mixed hand preferences straddle the point 0; it is not surprising that they use one hand for some things and the 'other' for others since they could probably have developed the skilled use of either hand given any pressure to do so. Some have definitely greater skill with the left hand (4.3%) and are consistently left-handed. The majority are far enough to the right of 0 to develop consistent right preferences (67.2%). On any plot of preferences, the consistent handers would achieve the maximum and minimum scores and subjects in classes 2 – 7 inclusive would be spread thinly over the range of the scale; hence the J-shape. Having demonstrated that the J-shaped distribution of preferences derives from a normal distribution of differences between the hands in skill we can now ignore the statistically inconvenient J and use only the very useful distribution of the normal curve.

There are two points which should be made about inconsistent handedness. First, the finding that up to one third of the population is fairly evenly balanced in skill leads to the expectation that many children would be uncertain which hand to use when first learning a new task. This is probably sufficient to account for the inconsistencies observed by Gesell and Ames (1947) and the widely held belief that all children go through an inconsistent *stage* is probably false. Secondly, the observation of Humphrey (1951) that self-classified left-handers are much less consistent in their use of the left hand than self-classified right-handers in the use of the right hand can be simply explained through inspection of Figure 1.2. There are 10.8% sinistral writers including 6.5% who are inconsistent (60.2%); among the 89.2% dextral writers there are 22.1% inconsistent dextrals (24.8%). Notice that there are many more inconsistent dextrals than inconsistent sinistrals but that the *proportion* of inconsistent handers among sinistrals is necessarily higher. The more generous the criterion of left-handedness, the higher the proportion who are inconsistent. Thus, the numerous studies that have concluded that left-handers are less consistent than right-handers for a great variety of characteristics from brainedness to skill are simply reiterating a basic truth which follows from the distribution of handedness. Before accepting that left-handers are more inconsistent than right-handers for characteristics such as brainedness, it is important to check that the right- and left-handers have been matched for consistency of handedness.

RELATIONS WITH OTHER ASYMMETRIES

There are a great many anatomical and functional asymmetries which can be considered for association with handedness. Some, like rate of inspiration through each nostril and asymmetries of the scrotum, I have *not* attempted to assess in student's laterality practical classes. Some, for which data has been assembled in one or more classes over several years, in schoolchildren and in personally visited families, include footedness, eyedness, arm folding, hand clasping, hair parting and hair whorl (at the crown of the head), lateral position of the nose, winking eye, hand used for comfort sucking in childhood, and simultaneous writing and drawing. From time to time it is suggested that if *all* possible asymmetries were thoroughly tested and examined together in some vast compilation of data, the confusions about laterality might be resolved and everything would fall neatly into place. I am sure that this is an illusion. For the majority of asymmetries examined there is no association with handedness or only a very weak correlation. At best, as for footedness, there is a high but still imperfect correlation. Eyedness is interesting because of the belief that cross laterality, contrary hand and eye preferences, might lead to difficulties in learning to read and write, and also because of some dispute in the literature about its association with handedness. About one third of right-handers are left-eyed. If enough consistent left-handers are tested about one third will be found right-eyed. Thus, hand and eye preference are associated but very imperfectly. Cross laterality is very common and unlikely to be a specific cause of reading delay.

The question of the association of handedness and cerebral speech (brainedness) can be examined through three main sources of evidence. First, studies of the speech hemisphere have been made at the Montreal Neurological Institute through the technique of injecting a quick acting but short lived sedative drug into the carotid artery on one side (Wada

1949). By testing each side on different days, the role of both hemispheres can be assessed; information which is not available by any other method. The Montreal evidence has important limitations which prevent its use in estimating incidences in the general population; the patients studied were selected on account of doubts about their brainedness, usually because of sinistral tendencies in themselves or their relatives; also, they were epileptics of long standing whose brains had been functioning abnormally for some years. The findings described by Rasmussen and Milner (1975) for 371 patients show that left-, right- and bilateral-brainedness can occur in both right- and left- plus mixed-handers (grouped together in the report). Bilateral speech is relatively rare. Right-sided and bilateral speech are more common in non-right-handers than in right-handers at very high levels of significance, for subjects both with and without evidence of early brain injury. Among left-handers without evidence of early brain injury, the majority are left-brained, like most right-handers. Thus the early assumption, still often expressed in popular literature, that left-handers 'ought to be' right-brained (and so fit the simple opposite hand to brain rule) is clearly false. Early left hemisphere damage increases the probability of bilateral or right hemisphere speech in both right- and left-handers, but the increase is greater in left-handers. After early left brain damage, 81% of right-handers and 30% of left-handers continue to talk with that side. This suggests that shifts of the speech hemisphere are not easily made, especially in right-handers.

Estimates of the incidence of right-brainedness in the population can be made only from patients with unilateral brain lesions recorded as consecutive series (so that entry to the series is independent of handedness or brainedness). Of five series identified by Zangwill (1967) in the world literature, two were shown by Annett (1975) to differ from the others in one or more main variables. Three can be combined to give a substantial number of cases, as shown in Table 1.2. The proportion of right-handers suffering loss or disorder of speech (dysphasia) was 33% and of left-handers 36%. The difference is in the direction expected if some left-handers have bilateral speech, but small enough to agree with the Montreal findings that bilaterality is not common.

The total of 533 individuals recorded as suffering dysphasia

Table 1.2 *Combined data from three studies of unilateral brain lesions: Conrad (1949), Newcombe and Ratcliff (1973) and Bingley (1958)*

Handedness		Left		Right	
Side of brain lesion		Left	Right	Left	Right
N. cases, total	1605	53	61	827	664
N. dysphasics	533	23	18	461	31
% of N. dysphasic		4.3	3.4	86.5	5.8

following unilateral brain lesion offer the best estimates available of population parameters. First, the incidence of left-handedness among the dysphasics (7.7%) is about the same as in the total patients in the three series (7.1%), suggesting that the classification of the dysphasics' handedness was not affected by the presence of this symptom. In Hécaen and Ajuriaguerra's (1964) series 11% of non-dysphasics and 29% of dysphasics were recorded as left-handed. Presumably patients and their relatives were questioned more closely in this clinic series when the symptom of speech loss was present and some with weak sinistral tendencies were called left-handed.

Right-brainedness is usually regarded as a rare phenomenon; some authors doubt its existence in right-handers and point out that it occurs in less than half of left-handers. Table 1.2 finds 41 (9.2%) of dysphasics with right unilateral lesions which implies that nearly 1 person in 11 is right-brained. Hécaen and Ajuriaguerra found a similar proportion of dysphasics with right-sided lesions (9.7%) but classified them *all* as left-handed. In the combined series in Table 1.2, 36.7% of right-brained speakers were left-handed. The discrepancy between series is almost certainly due to the generous criterion of sinistrality of Hécaen and Ajuriaguerra. The unexpected finding that the majority of right-brained speakers are right-handed will be considered further below.

The third type of evidence bearing on the relations between handedness and brainedness concerns perceptual asymmetries in normal subjects. It has been confirmed many times since Kimura's (1961) first application of the technique of dichotic listening to problems of cerebral dominance, that right-handers are more likely to report digits and other speech messages presented to the right ear than to the left ear, when the competing messages are presented simultaneously. Analogous advantages have been found for visual perception in the right visual field. There have been many searches for reversals of the usual directional bias in left-handers, almost invariably with negative results. Typically, the significant mean differences of right-handers are reduced or absent in sinistrals. Discussion of the findings usually refers to the possibility that cerebral asymmetry is reduced or absent in left-handers and that they are inconsistent, possibly, with bilateral representation of speech. The results are rarely analysed to show whether the small *mean* differences of left-handers are due to a general reduction of differences between the sides, or to individuals who are strongly lateralized but in the contrary direction. Lake and Bryden (1976) made this analysis for 72 right- and 72 left-handers. The latter were *not* more likely to have equal scores at both ears but they included a higher proportion with the atypical superiority of the left ear. Similarly, Lishman and McMeekan (1977) found that left-handers and mixed-handers did not have reduced asymmetries, but more often reversed the direction of asymmetry.

In summary, all three sets of evidence show that handedness and brainedness are significantly associated but far from perfectly. There are no simple generalizations to be made of the type, 'All left-handers . . . ' or 'No right-handers . . . '. All possible combinations of handedness and brainedness exist; the brainedness of right-handers is more often contralateral than ipsilateral to the preferred hand.

QUESTIONS OF CAUSE AND THE RIGHT SHIFT THEORY

There are two things to be explained about human handedness. First, why do people differ, and secondly, why are there more right-handers than left-handers? These two aspects of the problem concern *variability* and *bias*. Several theories of the causes of handedness treat right-handedness as a universal norm and all departures from the norm as pathological. There are two main versions of this theory depending on whether the causes of the universal dextrality are supposed to be cultural or physical. If hand usage depends on social influences and training, then left-handedness is due to pathologies of personality such as negativism; refusal to use the right hand is a mark of stubborn rebellion. Hence the severe measures taken against many left-handers of older generations in our society. If the universal right-handedness is thought to depend on some physical superiority, presumably of the left hemisphere, left-handedness is attributed to pathology of that hemisphere, arising in early life and most probably during birth. The evidence that left-handers are more likely to be born of high risk pregnancies (first or fourth and later) is weak in studies claiming positive findings (Bakan 1977) and contradicted by many negative results (Hicks, Pellegrini and Evans 1978). In my data for personally visited families where the report of the birth history could be obtained from the mother (as opposed to students reports of their own birth history in most studies), difficulties were experienced no more frequently for left-handed than for right-handed children. There is no doubt that *some* left-handedness is associated with left hemisphere pathology and that pathological left-handers form a higher proportion of all left-handers than pathological right-handers of all right-handers (see Satz 1973 for estimates). This follows from the distribution of asymmetry, for reasons similar to those discussed above for inconsistency.

The most important reason for doubting that human variability of handedness is pathological is that variability is characteristic of other species. Chimpanzees (Finch 1941), monkeys (Lehman 1978), rats (Peterson 1934) and mice (Collins 1968) are equally divided between right and left preferent animals and about half show mixed preferences. What these species do not show is bias to one side. The animal findings are just what we would expect if their preferences depended on a normal distribution of differences in skill, like that of Figure 1.2

except with a mean centred at 0. This suggests that human handedness differs from that of other mammals, including other primates, in only one respect, that the distribution is shifted in a dextral direction. Hence my conclusion that the only special feature of human handedness is the right shift.

Questions of cause can now be put in terms of the causes of the normal distribution of differences (the variability) and the causes of the right shift (the bias). Searches for genetic determinants in other species have proved negative. If the distribution of differences in other species depends on non-genetic and presumably random influences on the development of the two sides of the body, why not in man also? The right shift theory assumes that left-handedness depends on chance; right-handedness also depends on chance but the dice are loaded by some factor which makes a dextral outcome more probable than a sinistral one.

When we ask what factor biases the chances toward dextrality and is specific to man, the obvious first candidate is whatever factor induces left hemisphere speech in the majority. Speech, like the bias to the right hand is unique to man among primates. Thus, the bias of the handedness distribution could be a by-product of left hemisphere specialization. The positive but imperfect association of handedness with other variables arises because some other asymmetries are also biased to varying extents by the left hemisphere advantage, but chance is a major determinant.

To explain the occurrence of right hemisphere speech, the simplest possible hypothesis is that in some individuals the left hemisphere factor is absent and in this case both handedness and brainedness depend on chance, and chances which are independent of each other. The proportion of the population lacking the right shift factor (RS−) would be twice the proportion of those with right-brainedness, about 18.5% on the estimate above. The distributions of asymmetry of skill now assumed by the theory are represented in Figure 1.3. Roughly one fifth of the population are RS− and have a mean difference between the hands in skill of 0 and four fifths are RS+ with a mean shifted to the right of 0. The proportion manifesting left-handedness varies with the *criterion* of sinistrality, which can range over a wide range of the continuum as was shown in Figure 1.2. The proportion of left-handed writers is generally less than the proportion with hand speed differences below 0; hence we would expect less than half of those who are RS− to be sinistral writers, as found for right-brained dysphasics above.

There are other implications of the right shift theory which have been examined. Aside from those relating the theory to the dysphasia series mentioned above (and in Annett 1975), the most important concern handedness in families. If most (but not all) left-handers are RS−, and if the RS+ factor is transmitted genetically, the children of two left-handed parents should have hand speed differences distributed as for

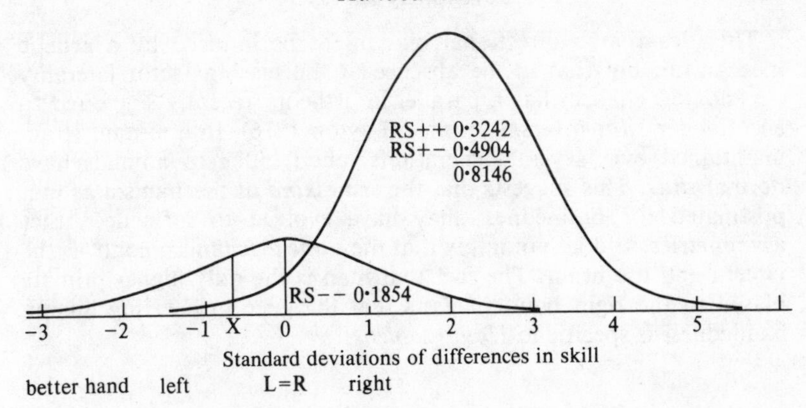

Figure 1.3 Hypothesized distribution of the RS+ (genotype *RS*++, +−) and RS− (genotype *RS*−−) subgroups of the population. The RS− mean is at 0 and the RS+ mean shifted to the right by about 2 sd s. The shift and genotype frequencies are deduced from clinical studies of dysphasia. X is a possible threshold or criterion of sinistrality in the population (after Annett 1978).

the RS− group in Figure 1.3. In 45 children of L×L parents, the variance was at least as great as in other samples, but the mean close to 0; 40% were sinistral writers, a figure close to the 37% found for right-brained dysphasics who are also assumed to be RS− (Annett 1974).

Ramaley (1913) was the first to collect data from students on the handedness of themselves and their families. In that and later studies, the chances of sinistrality clearly increase with the number of left-handed parents, but the proportions do not fit expectations for a recessive gene which determines left-handedness. I have now been able to show that the family data fits the assumptions of the right shift theory, given the additional postulate that the shift depends on a single dominant gene (Annett 1978). Instead of a recessive gene for left-handedness we must postulate a recessive gene which is *neutral* for handedness. The gene frequencies, given in Figure 1.3, are derived directly from the estimate of the population incidence of right-brainedness in Table 1.2. The numbers of left-handers born in R×R, L×R and L×L families have been successfully predicted in series varying widely in the incidences of left-handedness recorded, from 3.6 – 23.7% for parents and from 4.8 – 39.6% in children. This would not be possible unless the varying incidences depended on the stable underlying continuum identified above and on RS+ and RS− distributions along the continuum with parameters consistent with the findings for dysphasia. The handedness of monozygotic and dizygotic twins is also predictable from the model, given the single further postulate that the expression of the right shift/left hemisphere speech factor is less effective in twins than singletons.

The idea that a directional bias might be induced by a genetic mechanism, but that in the absence of the biasing factor laterality depends on chance, has a parallel in a theory recently suggested to account for *situs inversus* in mice (Layton 1976). In a mutant strain maintained over several generations, about 50% of animals have normal *situs*. This suggests that the same *kind* of mechanism as that postulated for brainedness may have evolved to influence other asymmetries. It does not imply that the *same* mechanism controls the viscera and the brain. The fact that man is the only higher primate biased to the right hand suggests that the gene influencing human handedness is specific to *Homo sapiens*.

REFERENCES

Annett, J., Annett, M., Hudson, P. T. W., and Turner, A. 1979. 'The control of movement in the preferred and non-preferred hands.' *Quart. J. exp. Psychol. 31*, 641 – 52.

Annett, M. 1970a. 'A classification of hand preference by association analysis.' *Brit. J. Psychol. 61*, 303 – 21.

Annett, M. 1970b. 'The growth of manual preference and speed.' *Brit. J. Psychol. 61*, 545 – 58.

Annett, M. 1974. 'Handedness in the children of two left-handed parents.' *Brit. J. Psychol. 65*, 129 – 31.

Annett, M. 1975. 'Hand preference and the laterality of cerebral speech.' *Cortex 11*, 305 – 28.

Annett, M. 1976. 'A coordination of hand preference and skill replicated.' *Brit. J. Psychol. 67*, 587 – 92.

Annett, M. 1978. *A single gene explanation of right and left handedness and brainedness*. Coventry: Lanchester Polytechnic.

Annett, M., Hudson, P. T. W., and Turner, A. 1974. 'The reliability of differerences between the hands in motor skill.' *Neuropsychologia 12*, 527 – 31.

Annett, M., and Turner, A. 1974. 'Laterality and the growth of intellectual abilities.' *Brit. J. Educ. Psychol. 44*, 37 – 46.

Bakan, P. 1977. 'Left-handedness and birth order revisited.' *Neuropsychologia 15*, 837 – 9.

Bingley, T. 1958. 'Mental symptoms in temporal lobe epilepsy and temperal lobe gliomas.' *Acta Psychiat. et Neurol. Scand. 33*.

Brain, W. R. 1945. 'Speech and handedness.' *Lancet 249*, 837 – 41.

Briggs, G. G., and Nebes, R.D. 1975. 'Patterns of hand preference in a student population.' *Cortex 11*, 230 – 8.

Bryden, M. P. 1977. 'Measuring handedness with questionnaires.' *Neuropsychologia 15*, 617 – 24.

Collins, R. L. 1968. 'On the inheritance of handedness: I Laterality in inbred mice.' *J. Hered. 59*, 9 – 12.

Conrad, K. 1949, cited by Zangwill 1967.

Corballis, M. C., and Morgan, M. J. 1978. 'On the biological basis of human laterality.' *The Behavioral and Brain Sciences 1*, 261 – 336.

Finch, G. 1941. 'Chimpanzee handedness.' *Science 94*, 117 – 18.

Fleminger, J. J., Dalton, R., and Standage, K. F. 1977. 'Age as a factor in the handedness of adults.' *Neuropsychologia 15*, 471 – 3.
Gardner, M. 1967. *The ambidextrous universe*. London: Allen Lane.
Gessell, A., and Ames, L. B. 1947. 'The development of handedness.' *J. Genet. Psychol. 70*, 155 – 76.
Gillies, S. M., MacSweeney, D. A., and Zangwill, O. L. 1960. 'A note on some unusual handedness patterns.' *Quart. J. exp. Psychol. 12*, 113 – 16.
Hécaen, H., and Ajuriaguerra, J. 1964. *Left-handedness*. New York: Grune and Stratton.
Hicks, R. A., Pellegrini, R. J., and Evans, E. A. 1978. 'Handedness and birth risk.' *Neuropsychologia 16*, 243 – 5.
Humphrey, M. E. 1951. 'Consistency of hand usage.' *Brit. J. Educ. Psychol. 21*, 214 – 25.
Kimura, D. 1961. 'Cerebral dominance and the perception of verbal stimuli.' *Canad. J. Psychol. 15*, 166 – 71.
Kimura, D., and Vanderwolf, C. H. 1970. 'The relation between hand preference and the performance of individual finger movements by the left and right hands.' *Brain 93*, 769 – 74.
Lake, D. A., and Bryden, M. P. 1976. 'Handedness and sex differences in hemispheric asymmetry.' *Brain and Language 3*, 266 – 82.
Layton, W. M. 1976. 'Random determination of a developmental process.' *J. Hered. 67*, 336 – 8.
Lehman, R. A. 1978. 'The handedness of rhesus monkeys: I Distribution.' *Neuropsychologia 16*, 33 – 42.
Lishman W. A., and McMeekan, E. R. L. 1977. 'Handedness in relation to direction and degree of cerebral dominance for language.' *Cortex 13*, 30 – 43.
McMeekan, E. R. L., and Lishman, W. A. 1975. 'Retest reliabilities and interrelationships of the Annett Hand Preference questionnaire and the Edinburgh Handedness inventory.' *Brit. J. Psychol. 66*, 53 – 60.
Newcombe, F., and Ratcliff, G. 1973. 'Handedness, speech lateralization and ability.' *Neuropsychologia 11*, 399 – 407.
Oldfield, R. C. 1971. 'The assessment and analysis of handedness: The Edinburgh inventory.' *Neuropsychologia 9*, 97 – 113.
Peterson, G. M. 1934. 'Mechanisms of handedness in the rat.' *Comp. Psychol. Monog. 9*, 1 – 67.
Provins, K. A. 1956. '"Handedness" and skill.' *Quart. J. exp. Psychol. 8*, 79 – 94.
Ramaley, F. 1913. 'Inheritance of left-handedness.' *The American Naturalist 47*, 730 – 8.
Rasmussen, T., and Milner, B. 1975. 'Clinical and surgical studies of cerebral speech areas in man.' In K. J. Zulch, O. Creutzfeldt and G. C. Galbraith (eds) *Cerebral localization*. Heidelberg: Springer-Verlag-Berlin.
Satz, P. 1973. 'Left-handedness and early brain insult: an explanation.' *Neuropsychologia 11*, 115 – 17.
Sheridan, M. R. 1973. 'Effects of S – R compatibility and task difficulty on unimanual movement time.' *J. Mot. Behav. 5*, 199 – 205.
Wada, J. 1949, cited by Rasmussen and Milner 1975.
Woo, T. L., and Pearson, K. 1927. 'Dextrality and sinistrality of hand and eye.' *Biometrika 19*, 165 – 99.
Zangwill, O. L. 1967. 'Speech and the minor hemisphere.' *Acta Neurol. et Psychiat. Belgica 67*, 1013 – 20.

Chapter 2

Visual Illusions

ROSS H. DAY

Although there is usually a fairly close correspondence between objects, situations and events as we perceive them and as they are recorded and measured by independent means, differences nevertheless occur. These are often large, persistent and experienced by most observers. Such differences between the perceived and the physically real are called perceptual illusions. Here we will be concerned with the main facts, theories, problems and trends emerging from recent research on visual illusions. Selected experimental studies, theories, the relationship between illusions and veridical perception, components of illusions, and some general conclusions will be discussed in that order after brief consideration of some broader issues. This review is necessarily highly selective and confined to particular problems and issues. Readers interested in longer and more detailed analyses of experimental results, theories and criticisms of both are referred to the papers by Over (1968) and Coren and Girgus (1977, 1978) and the monographs by Fisher (1968), Robinson (1972) and Gregory and Gombrich (1973). Over's paper contains a critical evaluation of the major theories, and Robinson's book is a comprehensive and detailed account of both data and theory.

GENERAL ISSUES

Why Study Illusions?

Why study illusions at all? After all, the correspondence between the perceived and the real is usually quite close and there is no evidence that the differences interfere in a significant way with our normal behaviour. There are at least two good reasons for doing so. First, perceptual illusions have not been fully or satisfactorily explained. In scientific terms that is reason enough. Failure so far to reach acceptable explanations after over a century of close experimental enquiry may be due in large part to an implicit assumption that there is a single, universal principle in terms of which all illusions can be explained. It now seems highly likely, as will become clear below, that there are a number of unrelated effects which sometimes occur together. Secondly, one class of illusions is an exception to the general rule of correspondence between perception and reality. It is conceivable, indeed likely, that by explaining these exceptions general principles associated with veridical perceptual functioning will emerge.

Types of Illusion

Contrary to an impression that is easily gained from the literature on illusions, the effects are neither restricted to vision nor confined to relatively simple geometrical patterns. Visual illusions in line figures and patterns happen to be readily demonstrable and are often large and compelling. Illusions also occur in consequence of observer postures and movements (see Howard and Templeton 1966), in modalities other than vision, notably in the tactile, haptic (tactile-kinaesthetic) modes, and between modalities, i.e. stimulation of one sensory modality may produce an illusion in another. The size-weight illusion (see Cross and Rotkin 1975) is an example of an intermodal effect. While illusions occur in the tactile and haptic modes, they are not necessarily the same as or even related to those in vision, as has been made clear by experiments on the haptic radial-tangential illusion (Wong 1977) that has a superficial resemblance to the horizontal-vertical illusion. Wong's experiments show that the radial-tangential illusion is a function of the times taken to move the arm radially and tangentially to the body.

Illusions and After-effects

Illusions can occur as a result of either simultaneous or successive stimulation by specified elements of the stimulus pattern. Conventionally, the first is referred to as an illusion and the second as a figural or spatial after-effect. Ganz (1966) has argued that these two classes are essentially the same since with successive stimulation the processes generated by the inducing elements (those which induce the illusion) outlast the period of stimulation and interact with those associated with the test elements (those in which the illusion is manifest). In these terms there is no real difference between the two. On first consideration this argument is plausible. Pollack (1967) has pointed out that there are some marked differences between illusions and spatial after-effects which indicate different processes and origins. However, the recent observation that a group of illusions involving intersecting lines (see 'Blurring and Loss of Contrast' below) are sensitive to changes in figure-ground luminance contrast, while others are immune to such changes, suggests that the former group and spatial after-effects might be closely related. After-effects are also known to be sensitive to variations in luminance contrast.

Distortions and Representations

Most research on illusions has been concerned with distortions of properties such as size, shape, movement and orientation, i.e. with *discrepancies* between the perceived and the real. However, there is another broad class of illusions that are sometimes referred to as 'illusions of reality' (Gombrich 1961). These are not distortions of the physical state of affairs but representations or imitations of it. Painted land- and seascapes, drawings, cartoons, photographs and moving pictures are instances of this class. The fidelity with which reality is represented varies widely from, for example a 3D movie which is occasionally difficult to distinguish from the actual situation, through *tompe l'oeil* paintings to sketchy likenesses and cartoons that are easily distinguishable from what they represent. Illusions of reality have attracted considerable attention in the last decade or so and their study under the heading of pictorial perception has developed into an area of active research. Considerable attention has been given to cultural differences in perceiving photographs and pictures (Deregowski, 1973). It is to be emphasized that depictions of objects and events are as much illusions as distortions of them. Gombrich (1961, 1972, 1973) and Kennedy (1974) have discussed the main problems and issues associated with these forms of illusions. A link between representations and distortions of reality is suggested below in terms of two inappropriately invoked perceptual processes – those of perceptual constancy and perceptual completion – associated with veridical perception.

EXPERIMENTAL STUDIES

The aim of parametric studies of illusions is to identify key variables and their mode of interaction and thereby to establish the primary basis of an illusion. This tradition, always strong, continues unabated in contemporary experimental studies. An outstanding example of the manner in which the key variables in an illusory pattern can be identified by concentrated research is provided by Wenderoth's (1978) experiments on the 'rod-and-frame' effect, the effect of the orientation of a frame on that of an enclosed, straight rod.

Here discussion is restricted to those findings that appear to bear on a range of perceptual illusions and that suggest interesting departures in research rather than data specific to a particular effect.

Blurring and Loss of Contrast

Look at Figure 2.1a, 2.1b and 2.1c, the Hering, Orbison and Ehrenstein illusions, with the eyes nearly closed so that the figures are blurred. Better still, make a slide of each and blur the patterns by defocusing the image on a screen. It will be observed that the illusory distortions of parallelness and squareness are either markedly reduced or totally absent. This is not so with the illusions of length and alignment in Figure 2.1d, 2.1e and 2.1f. In fact, that in Figure 2.1d, the Müller-Lyer

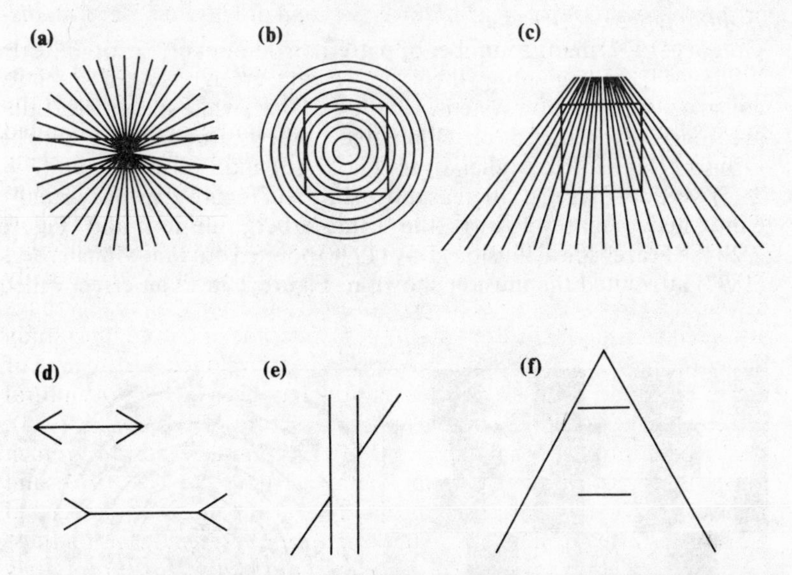

Figure 2.1 Six figure illusions: (a) Hering, (b) Orbison, (c) Ehrenstein, (d) Müller-Lyer, (e) Poggendorff, (f) Ponzo. The 'intersection' illusions in the top row are considerably reduced or eliminated by blurring the patterns or by reducing luminance contrast. Those in the bottom row are not so affected.

illusion, increases slightly. The diminution or disappearance of illusions involving criss-crossing lines – intersection effects – with blurring has recently been noted by Weale (1978). The reduction of the Hering illusion with increase in viewing distance and reduction in illumination described much earlier by Marshall and Di Lollo is probably due also to blurring occasioned by these manipulations.

Why should blur reduce intersection illusions and not others? One possibility is the elimination by blurring of high spatial frequency components that contribute to the sharpness of edges and to fine detail, as shown by Campbell and Robson (1968). There are numerous alternative possibilities. Blur has a number of effects; as well as loss of sharpness it results in reduced contrast, broadening of the lines, and darkening at the intersections. Recently, Stuart (1978) measured the marked diminution of intersection illusions with blurring and showed that it is attributable mainly to loss of contrast. This outcome is consistent with Wallace's (1975) finding that the Zöllner illusion, another intersection effect, is diminished by lowered contrast.

The observation that figural distortions in patterns consisting of intersecting and crossing lines are notably reduced with lowered contrast strongly suggests that these effects represent a particular class of illusion. It is conceivable that they are the outcome of lateral inhibitory processes (Blakemore, Carpenter and Georgeson 1970).

Isoluminance and Irradiation

Gregory (1977) made a number of patterns isoluminant, i.e. of uniform luminance, by presenting them in red and green, using a specially constructed projection system. He showed that, while some distortions are markedly reduced or eliminated, others are unaffected. The Orbison (Fig. 2.1b), Müller-Lyer (Fig. 2.1d) and Ponzo illusion (Fig. 2.1f) were not affected whereas those shown in Figure 2.2 were virtually eliminated. Figure 2.2a is the Münsterberg illusion and Figure 2.2b the Frazer spiral illusion. Day (1978) pointed out that Münsterberg (1897) attributed the illusion shown in Figure 2.2a to an effect called

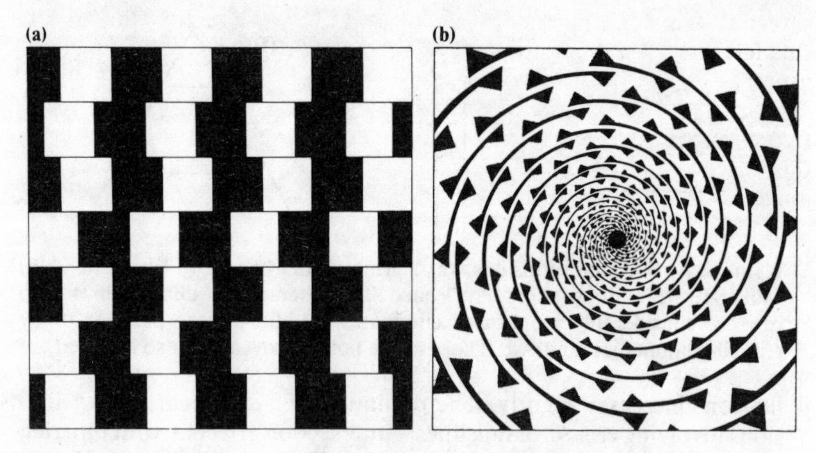

Figure 2.2 Two illusions that are eliminated when the patterns are made isoluminant, i.e. of uniform brightness: (a) Münsterberg, (b) Frazer. The Münsterberg illusion is probably due to irradiation of brightness.

'irradiation', a tendency for light regions to 'invade' dark regions. As a result of this effect the short horizontal edges in Figure 2.2a appear slightly oblique and, in consequence, the whole contour appears to tilt to produce converging and diverging edges.

The effects due to isoluminance and those due to blurring appear on the face of things to be different. The Orbison illusion (Fig. 2.1b) is considerably reduced by blurring, i.e. loss of contrast, but not by isoluminance. This suggests that while the blur-affected illusions possibly derive from lateral inhibitory processes (see 'Theories of Spatial Distortions' below) the isoluminance-affected illusions are due to irradiation between light and dark regions.

The Effects of Figure Fragmentation

What happens to an illusion if the figure is broken up, so that the various elements are spatially separated? Data from separate and unrelated experiments indicate that when such fragmentation of the figure elements occurs, either in the same plane or in depth, the illusion is reduced. Yanasigawa (see Oyama 1960), Pollack and Chaplin (1964) and Fellows (1968) showed that if the oblique lines forming arrowheads in the Müller-Lyer figure (Fig. 2.1d) are moved outward from the ends of the shaft, the illusion declines, disappears and, in the case of the figure with the inward-directed arrowheads, eventually reverses. In the case of the Poggendorff illusion (Fig. 2.1e) Tong and Weintraub (1974) showed that if the oblique lines are separated from the parallels by a gap, the illusion is much smaller. Reduction in illusions occurs also when the parts of the figure are separated in depth. Gogel and his associates (Gogel 1975; Gogel and Newton 1975; Gogel and Teitz 1976) have shown that when elements of the figure are so separated the illusion is smaller, the greatest reduction occurring when the test element is nearer.

It seems likely that some illusions depend on the integrity of the figure, i.e. on the elements forming a perceived configuration. When this perceptual organization is destroyed the illusion declines or disappears. It is possible that these illusions represent inappropriate component-object constancies (see 'Illusions and Veridical Perception' below). Fragmentation of the figure may destroy the object or configurational property necessary for the occurrence of these constancies.

The role of figural organization is clear in a different sort of experiment by Restle (1976). When the two figures in the Müller-Lyer illusion (Fig. 2.1d) are arranged so that their apexes are in perfect vertical alignment those pointing inward seem too far *in* and *vice versa*, the opposite that would be expected from the apparent distance between them. Restle suggested that, when the observer's task is to judge the vertical or horizontal alignment of the apexes, the figure is perceptually organized differently from when the task is that of judging the distance between the apexes. The reduction in the Poggendorff misalignment illusion, when a gap occurs between the obliques and the parallels (Tong and Weintraub 1974), also seems to derive from the loss of figural wholeness or integrity.

Primary and Secondary Illusions

Data from at least two sources suggest that some illusions are secondary outcomes of more basic effects. In a pattern of black and white lines there is a loss of contrast between the lines and an enhancement of contrast between lines lying end to end, effects that have been called assimilation and dissimilation of contrast (Day and Jory 1978). It has been argued that the apparent contour visible in Figure 2.3 might be due in part to the loss of contrast in the grating and the enhancement of contrast in the gaps that together form the white 'stripe' running across it. That is, the illusory contours along the edges of the band could be secondary outcomes of apparent differences in brightness between the

Figure 2.3 The illusory contours on either side of the centre strip are probably secondary outcomes of changes in brightness in the pattern. The brightness between the parallel lines is less than that of the background (assimilation) and that between the ends of the lines greater (dissimilation).

apparently darkened interspaces and apparently lightened white gaps forming the stripe (Day and Jory 1978).

Cultural Differences

Segall, Campbell and Herskovits (1966) revived a much earlier interest in cultural differences in illusions (Rivers 1905) by establishing the magnitude of the Müller-Lyer, Sander parallelogram and horizontal-vertical (H-V) illusion (two versions) for thirteen samples of non-Western, mainly African, groups and three samples of Western peoples. The non-Western groups were generally less susceptible to the Müller-Lyer and Sander illusions but more susceptible to the H-V illusions than the Western groups. The results were interpreted in terms of differences in visual inference determined by both culture and the ecology of the environment. Robinson (1972) has pointed out a number of criticisms of this conclusion and summarized some studies, including one involving Australian aboriginals, which fail to support it.

Three recent reports confirm cultural differences in one line illusion and suggest a basis for them. Leibowitz and his colleagues (Leibowitz, Brislin, Perlmutter and Hennessy 1969; Leibowitz and Pick 1972; Kilbride and Leibowitz 1975) showed that the Ponzo illusion (Fig. 2.1f) is progressively reduced as representations of depth, e.g. converging railway tracks, and textured terrain, are progressively eliminated (see Fig. 2.4). While this was so for Ugandan villagers who had earlier perceived drawings as three-dimensional, it was not so for villagers who perceived the drawings as two-dimensional (Kilbride and Leibowitz 1975). The critical factor appears to be a sensitivity to symbolic depth cues in various versions of the Ponzo figure, not merely a suppression of 'flatness' cues as earlier believed. In some respects this conclusion is not so very different from that reached earlier by Segall, Campbell and Herskovits (1966).

THEORIES

Theories of Spatial Distortions

Over (1968) in his critical evaluation of theories of figure illusions identified three main classes of theory seeking to explain spatial distortions: physiological, information-processing, and judgemental theories. Those in the first class stress the role of neural processes in the displacement and distortion of contours, the second, selective attention to different parts of the figure, and the third, cognitive misinterpretation of stimulus features. Attempts to explain line illusions in terms of physiological processes include that by Ganz (1966), which is based on lateral inhibition in sensory systems. Information-sampling theories include those involving eye-movements and the centration theory of Piaget (1961). In regard to the role of eye-movements, not only do line illusions occur when the retinal image of the pattern is mechanically stabilized as by Pritchard (1958) but when it is perfectly stabilized as an after-image (Evans and Marsden 1966). If, as the latter show, illusions of size, alignment, direction and shape occur with perfect stabilization, eye-movements cannot be regarded as a primary determinant. However, as far as is known, there has been no attempt so far to compare quantitatively the magnitude of illusions with and without eye-movement. A difference would, of course, suggest a *contribution* from eye-movement. Of the theories based on judgemental, i.e. cognitive, processes that of Gregory (1966) which rests on inferences from depth information and the operation of size constancy is the most developed and widely discussed. While this theory has been extensively criticized (Hotopf 1966; Robinson 1972), its shortcomings are probably due to a failure to recognize that there are different classes of visual constancy each of which can be inappropriately invoked to produce an illusion.

Since Over's (1968) review a variation on each of the three explanatory themes has been proposed. Blakemore, Carpenter and Georgeson (1970) have exploited recent data on inhibitory interaction between neural processes associated with contours to explain the acute angle effect, the apparent enlargement of an acute angle. Pressey (1974) has argued that there is a tendency in perception for the extreme values of an object property to approach the average value for a particular figure, a tendency called assimilation. Pressey has interpreted illusions of size, area and direction in terms of this perceptual averaging process. Finally, Day (1972) has extended the 'misapplied constancy' principle developed by Gregory (1966) to include a wider range of illusions including those due to observer movement and posture.

Theories of Pictorial Representation

We have noted that the perception of drawings and pictures as depicting reality in varying degrees is as much an illusion as apparent distortions. Gibson (1971) has distinguished two theories of picture perception: the point-projection and symbol theory. He has rejected both as inadequate and proposed a third couched in terms of the information available in the optic array. Topper (1977) has cogently criticized Gibson's categorical classification of point-projection and symbol theories and argued strongly that both projections and symbols are involved in a picture. Pictures, he states, contain at least two components – visual representations of objects and depictions of symbolic signification – in varying degrees.

ILLUSIONS AND VERIDICAL PERCEPTION

Processes of Veridical Perception

There is a long history of attempts to interpret perceptual illusions in terms of processes that normally maintain veridical perception. The argument underlying such attempts is that a process concerned primarily with representing in perception the real external state of affairs is invoked inappropriately, thus giving rise to a misrepresentation, i.e. an illusion. The processes accorded greatest attention so far are those involved in perceptual constancy, the veridical perception of size, shape, orientation, velocity, and other properties despite variations in their projection at the eye. Such attempts have met with considerable criticism (see Coren and Girgus 1977, 1978; Hotopf 1966). One reason for this is an assumption, implicit in such attempts, that *all* illusions are attributable to inappropriately invoked constancy processes. Two other and possibly more important reasons are that so far, only the processes associated with perceptual constancy have been considered and, furthermore, no recognition has been given to the strong possibility that there are different types or classes of constancy in perception.

At least two groups of processes involved in the maintenance of veridicality in perception can be identified, those that mediate perceptual constancy and those that mediate perceptual completion. While the first are well known, it is not generally recognized that there are probably three classes: those involving relationships between the object and its field as in size and brightness constancy, those involving relationships between object and observer as in uprightness and orientation constancy (Gajzago and Day 1972) and, hardly recognized at all, those involving relationships between the parts of an object and the object itself. For example, the edge of a book is perceived to be more or less the same length even though its representation at the eye varies as the book is tilted and turned.

The second group of processes, completion processes, refers to a strong tendency in visual perception for objects to appear complete even though their visual representations are spatially or temporally incomplete. Thus, an object appears to be spatially whole and complete even though its image is not, due to interruption or intervention by other objects. For example, a book is seen as complete when a pencil is laid across it occluding part of it and dividing the visual image in two. Again, when the eyes are swept from one side of a room to the other the room is perceived as a complete room even though only a small part of it is visible at any one moment.

'Inappropriate' Constancy and Completion

Numerous illusions can be reasonably attributed to the operation of the processes associated with perceptual constancy and completion in inappropriate circumstances. For example, if the stimuli which indicate distance are manipulated, then the further of two objects of the same size can be expected to appear larger, as in Figure 2.4. Illusions due to inappropriate operation of constancy processes have been dealt with in detail by Gregory (1966, 1968) and Day (1972). The main criticism to be made about these earlier arguments is not that inappropriately invoked constancy processes bring about the illusion, but that a particular illusion is often attributed to the wrong class of perceptual constancy. For example, the Müller-Lyer illusion shown in Figure 2.1d is frequently attributed solely to inappropriately invoked size constancy. It seems more likely that it is due to inappropriate object-component constancy; the shaft appears longer or shorter than its true length because it is part of a large or small object. Normally, the variable projection of an object part is perceptually constant in relation to the objects. If the object itself is changed in size, then a part of it which remains the same size appears to be of a different size.

It can be argued that the 'illusions of reality' such as landscapes, portraits, photographs and etchings are due to inappropriately invoked completion processes. Even though the information for form, solidity and depth are minimal, the perceptual system completes the flat projection to a close approximation to reality. That is, not only is interrupted form completed as in cartoons and etchings but incomplete depth involving only a few depth stimuli is also completed to a close approximation to the real state of affairs. It is conceivable too (but entirely speculative) that a figure exposed bit by bit behind a slit and which is perceived as a complete figure (Parks 1965; Rock and Sigman 1973) appears so because of a temporal completion process which is invoked inappropriately. This process is normally involved in visual perception as we scan a room or large object with a narrow cone of clear vision.

THE COMPONENTS OF ILLUSION

There is no reason to suppose that an illusion such as the Müller-Lyer (Fig. 2.1d) or the Ponzo (Fig. 2.4c) is an inappropriate invocation of a single class of perceptual constancy. The Müller-Lyer effect does not occur only when arrow-like forms are attached to the ends of the central shaft. The effect occurs with a variety of attachments such as circles, squares and co-extensive lines (Day 1972). However, the illusion tends to be greater when they are arrow-like thus giving a depth effect (Brigell, Uhlarik and Goldhorn 1977). It is possible that the illusion in the figure with attached circles or squares (the dumbell effect) is an instance of inappropriately invoked component-object constancy; the line appears longer or shorter since it is part of a larger or smaller configuration. When the attachments consist of oblique lines, a depth component is added so that the central line appears relatively near or far. That is, an inappropriately invoked field constancy is added.

A similar point can be made about the Ponzo illusion. It will be recalled that the magnitude of this effect increases as depth features are added to the figure (Leibowitz and Pick 1972; Kilbride and Leibowitz 1975), as in Figure 2.4. Apparent elongation of a line occurs also when it is simply enclosed between two others at right angles to it with no suggestion of depth, as in Figure 2.4d. This according to Fisher (1968) is a context effect. The illusion with depth features (Fig. 2.4a and 2.4b) can be reasonably attributed to the operation of size constancy as suggested by Gregory (1966). That, with a pair of enclosing parallels, is more likely to be due to a component-object constancy. A recent study by Schiffman and Thompson (1978) clearly shows that apparent depth due to converging lines (Fig. 2.4a, 2.4b and 2.4c) and context (Fig. 2.4d) both contribute to the illusion.

Among the numerous problems yet to be solved in regard to visual figure illusions is the contributions of different classes of constancy process inappropriately invoked by the figure.

SOME CONCLUSIONS

What general conclusions can reasonably be reached from this brief review of recent data and theories about visual illusions? There is one which can be drawn with some confidence. If, as has been noted, intersecting line illusions diminish with reduced contrast while others are not so affected, some (but not the same ones) are absent in isoluminant

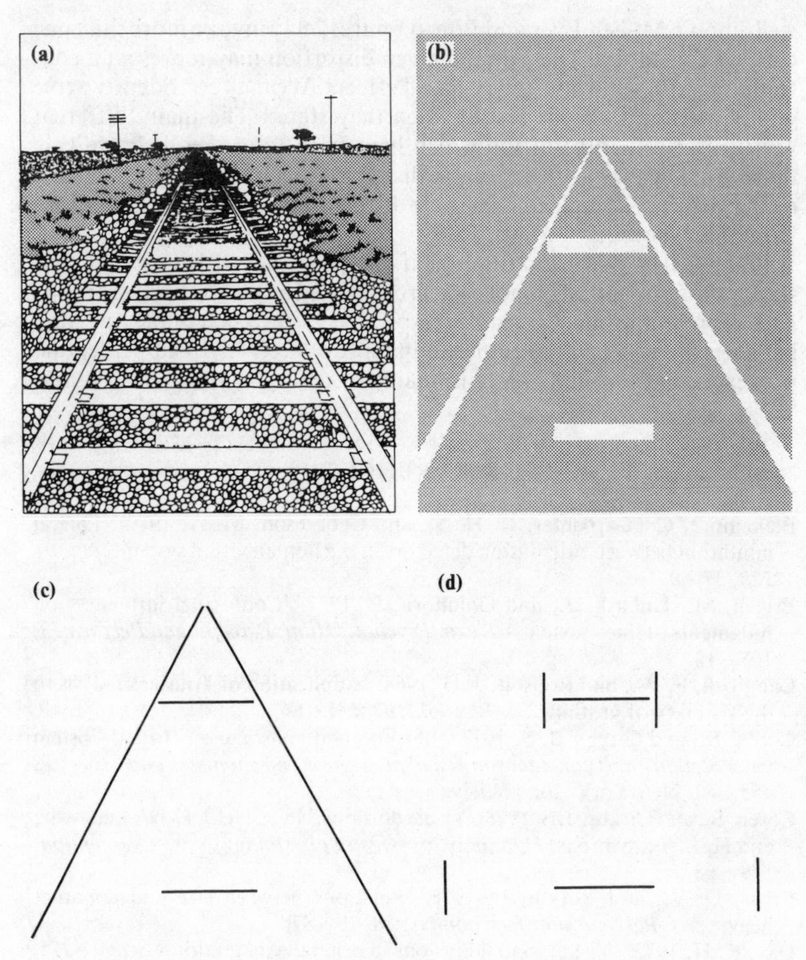

Figure 2.4 The Ponzo illusion is probably an outcome of two component effects. Perspective giving rise to 'inappropriate' constancy is present in (a), (b) and (c). A context effect alone is involved in (d).

conditions, some are secondary outcomes of a more basic effect, and still others are attributable to the inappropriate invocation of constancy and completion processes, then it must be concluded that there are separate, probably independent classes of illusion. The only common feature shared by the different classes is the difference between their appearance and the physical state of affairs.

A second conclusion is that the different classes of perceptual constancy and perceptual completion, when invoked under conditions inappropriate to their normal role in perception, give rise to characteristic illusions. However, certain figures and patterns, including the well-known Müller-Lyer and Ponzo figures, may invoke more than one class of constancy. Therefore, a given distortion may represent a confounding of several constancy-based effects. We may confidently agree with Coren and Girgus (1978) when they state, 'The many different varieties of visual distortion which have been found make it unlikely that we are dealing with any single distorting mechanism. The available evidence seems to indicate that these distortions represent contributions from many sources . . . '. (p. 550)

Finally, it is worth noting that if the processes of perceptual constancy *and* perceptual completion are accepted as a basis for distortions and representations of reality respectively, then a connecting link between the two is to be found in inappropriately invoked perceptual processes that normally serve to maintain reality in visual perception.

REFERENCES

Blakemore, C., Carpenter, R. H. S., and Georgeson, M. A. 1970. 'Lateral inhibition between orientation detectors in the human visual system.' *Nature 228*, 37 – 9.

Brigell, M., Uhlarik, J., and Goldhorn, P. 1977. 'Contextual influences on judgments of linear extent.' *J. exp. Psychol.: Hum. Percept. and Perform. 3*, 105 – 18.

Campbell, F. W., and Robson, J. G. 1968. 'Application of Fourier analysis to the visibility of gratings.' *J. Physiol. 197*, 551 – 66.

Coren, S., and Girgus, J. S. 1977. 'Illusions and constancies.' In W. Epstein (ed.) *Stability and constancy in visual perception: mechanisms and processes* 255 – 83. New York: John Wiley.

Coren, S., and Girgus, J. S. 1978. 'Visual illusions.' In R. Held, H. W. Leibowitz and H. L. Teuber (eds) *Handbook of sensory physiology*, Vol. 8 *Perception*, 549 – 68.

Cross, D. V., and Rotkin, L. 1975. 'Relations between size and apparent heaviness.' *Percept. and Psychophys. 18*, 79 – 87.

Day, R. H. 1972. 'Visual spatial illusions: a general explanation.' *Science 175*, 1335 – 40.

Day, R. H. 1978. 'A note on the Münsterberg or café wall illusion.' *Perception 7*, 123 – 4.

Day, R. H., and Dickinson, R. G. 1976. 'The components of the Poggendorff illusion.' *Brit. J. Psychol. 67*, 537 – 52.

Day, R. H., and Jory, M. K. 1978. 'Subjective contours, visual acuity and line contrast.' In J. C. Armington, J. Krauskopf and B. Wooten (eds) *Visual psychophysics: its physiological basis*. New York: Academic Press.

Deregowski, J. B. 1973. 'Illusion and culture.' In R. L. Gregory and E. H. Gombrich (eds) *Illusion in nature and art*. London: Duckworth.

Epstein, W. (ed.) 1977. *Stability and constancy in visual perception: mechanisms and processes*. New York: John Wiley.

Evans, C. R., and Marsden, R. P. 1966. 'A study of the effect of perfect retinal stabilization on some well-known visual illusions, using the after-image as a method of compensating for eye movement.' *Brit. J. Physiol. Opt. 23*, 242 – 8.

Fellows, B. J. 1968. 'The reverse Müller-Lyer illusion and "enclosure".' *Brit. J. Psychol. 59*, 369 – 72.

Fisher, G. H. 1968. *The frameworks for perceptual localization*. Newcastle upon Tyne: University of Newcastle upon Tyne.

Gajzago, C., and Day, R. H. 1972. 'Uprightness constancy with head inversion in young children and adults.' *J. exp. Child Psychol. 14*, 43 – 52.

Ganz, L. 1966. 'Is the figural after-effect an after-effect? A review of its intensity, onset, decay and transfer characteristics.' *Psychol. Bull. 66*, 151 – 65.

Gibson, J. J. 1971. 'The information available in pictures.' *Leonardo 4*, 27 – 35.

Gogel, W. C. 1975. 'Depth adjacency and the Ponzo illusion.' *Percept. and Psychophys. 17*, 125 – 32.

Gogel, W. C., and Teitz, J. D. 1976. 'Adjacency and attention as determiners of perceived motion.' *Vis. Res. 16*, 839 – 45.

Gogel, W. C., and Newton, R. E. 1975. 'Depth adjacency and the rod-and-frame illusion.' *Percept. and Psychophys. 18*, 163 – 71.

Gombrich, E. H. 1961. *Art and illusion: a study in the psychology of pictorial representation*, 2nd edn. Princeton, NJ: Princeton University Press.

Gombrich, E. H. 1972. 'The mask and the face: the perception of physiognomic likeness in life and in art.' In E. H. Gombrich, J. Hochberg and M. Black (eds) *Art, perception and reality*. Baltimore: Johns Hopkins University Press.

Gombrich, E. H. 1973. 'Illusion and art.' In R. L. Gregory and E. H. Gombrich (eds) *Illusion in nature and art*. London: Duckworth.

Gregory, R. L. 1966. *Eye and brain*. London: World University Library.

Gregory, R. L. 1968. 'Perceptual illusions and brain models.' *Proc. roy. Soc. B, 171*, 279 – 96.

Gregory, R. L. 1977. 'Vision with isoluminant colour contrasts: 1 A projection technique and observations.' *Perception 6*, 113 – 19.

Gregory, R. L., and Gombrich, E. H. (eds) 1973. *Illusion in nature and art*. London: Duckworth.

Helmholtz, H. von. 1860. *Handbuch der physiologischen optik*, part II. Leipzig: Voss.

Hotopf, W. H. M. 1966. 'The size constancy theory of visual illusions.' *Brit. J. Psychol. 57*, 307 – 18.

Howard, I. P., and Templeton, W. B. 1966. *Human spatial orientation*. New York: John Wiley.

Kennedy, J. M. 1974. *A psychology of picture perception*. San Francisco: Jossey-Bass.

Kilbride, P. L., and Leibowitz, H. 1975. 'Factors affecting the magnitude of the Ponzo perspective illusion among the Baganda.' *Percept. and Psychophys. 17*, 543 – 8.

Leibowitz, H., Brislin, R., Perlmutter, L., and Hennessy, R. 1969. 'Ponzo perspective illusion as a manifestation of space perception.' *Science 166*, 1174 – 6.

Leibowitz, H., and Pick, H. A. 1972. 'Cross-cultural and educational aspects of the Ponzo illusion.' *Percept. and Psychophys. 12*, 430 – 2.

Marshall, A. J., and Di Lollo, V. 1963. 'Hering's illusion with impoverishment of the stimulus in scotopic and photopic vision.' *Amer. J. Psychol. 76*, 644 – 52.

Münsterberg, H. 1897. 'Die verschobene Schactbrettfigur.' *Zeitschr. f. Psychol. 15*, 184 – 8.

Over, R. 1968. 'Explanations of geometric illusions.' *Psychol. Bull. 70*, 545 – 6.

Oyama, T. 1960. 'Japanese studies on the so-called geometrical-optical illusions.' *Psychologica 3*, 7 – 20.

Parks, T. E. 1965. 'Post-retinal visual storage.' *Amer. J. Psychol. 78*, 145 – 7.

Piaget, J. 1961. *Les méchanisms perceptifs*. Presses Universitaires de Gravee. Paris.

Pollack, R. H. 1967. 'Comment on "Is the figural aftereffect an aftereffect?"' *Psychol. Bull. 68*, 59 – 61.

Pollack, R. H., and Chaplin, M.-R. 1964. 'Effects of prolonged stimulation by components of the Müller-Lyer figure upon the magnitude of the illusion.' *Percept. and Mot. Skills 18*, 377 – 82.

Pressey, A. W. 1974. 'Evidence for the role of attentive fields in the perception of illusions.' *Quart. J. exp. Psychol. 26*, 464 – 71.

Pritchard, R. M. 1958. 'Visual illusions viewed as stabilized retinal images.' *Quart. J. exp. Psychol. 10*, 77 – 82.

Restle, F. 1976. 'Morinaga's paradox and figure-ground organization.' *Percept. and Psychophys. 20*, 153 – 6.

Rivers, W. H. R. 1905. 'Observations on the sense of the Todas.' *Brit. J. Psychol. 1*, 321 – 96.

Robinson, J. O. 1972. *The psychology of visual illusion*. London: Hutchinson.

Rock, I., and Sigman, E. 1973. 'Intelligence factors, in the perception of form through a moving slit.' *Perception 3*, 9 – 28.

Schiffman, H. R., and Thompson, J. G. 1978. 'The role of apparent depth and context in the perception of the Ponzo illusion.' *Perception 7*, 47 – 50.

Segall, M. H., Campbell, D. T., and Herskovits, M. J. 1966. *The influence of culture on visual perception*. Indianapolis: The Bobbs-Merrill Company.

Stuart, G. W. 1978. 'The effect of blurring on the Zöllner and related illusions.' Unpublished thesis, Monash University.

Tong, L., and Weintraub, D. J. 1974. 'Contour displacements and tracking errors: probing 'twixt Poggendorff parallels.' *Percept. and Psychophys. 15*, 258 – 68.

Topper, D. R. 1977. 'On interpreting pictorial art: reflections on J. J. Gibson's invariance hypothesis.' *Leonardo 10*, 295 – 300.

Wallace, G. K. 1975. 'The effect of contrast on the Zöllner illusion.' *Vis. Res. 15*, 963 – 6.

Weale, R. A. 1978. 'Experiments on the Zöllner and related optical illusions.' *Vis. Res. 18*, 203 – 8.

Wenderoth, P. M. 1978. 'An analysis of the rod-and-frame illusion and its variants,' in R. H. Day and G. V. Stanley (eds) *Studies in perception*. Perth, Western Australia: Univ. of West. Australia Press and Monash Uni. Publ. Committee.

Wong, T. S. 1977. 'Dynamic properties of radial and tangential movements as determinants of the haptic horizontal-vertical illusion with an L figure.' *J. exp. Psychol.: Human, Percept. and Perform. 3*, 151 – 64.

Chapter 3

Without Awareness

N. F. DIXON and S. H. A. HENLEY

> 'Conscious awareness is itself rather late in the sequence of mental processing.' (Posner and Boies 1971, p. 407)

In this chapter we shall review evidence for preconscious processing and perception without awareness drawn from eleven areas of research.

Common sense, common observation and data from psychophysical measurement suggest that awareness of incoming information is a necessary condition for response. However, the findings from many different lines of research militate against such a simplistic view of the perceptual process and imply instead that conscious experience must be regarded as the product of a system in parallel with that mediating the flow of information through the organism. Though coupled, as depicted in Figure 3.1, each system may operate independently of the other. Just as it is possible to have such subjective experiences as dreams and hallucinations in the absence of, or unaffected by, external stimulation, so also it is possible for information to enter the organism and determine behaviour without ever itself being represented in consciousness.

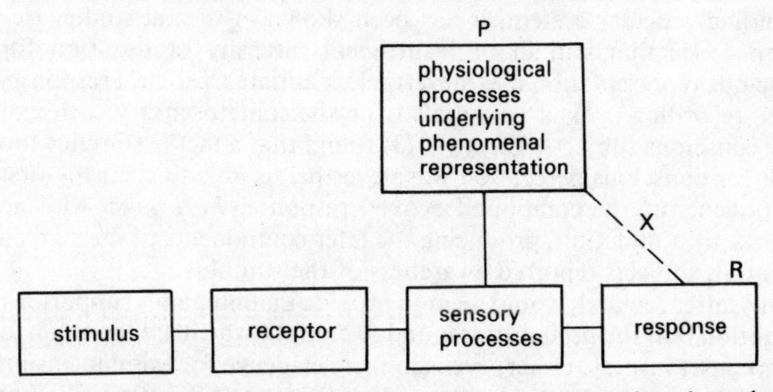

Figure 3.1 Processes which mediate the flow of information through an organism and those concerned with conscious representation of this information may be regarded as belonging, respectively, to two systems either of which may function independently of the other.

Given the very limited channel capacity of conscious experience, when compared with that for the gathering of information, it would seem highly likely that the criteria for conscious representation must be applied to incoming information at some *preconscious* stage of cerebral processing. While these criteria are primarily concerned with the *meaning* of incoming information, awareness of the latter also depends upon such 'top down' factors as attention and set, whereby the subject attempts to control perceptual inflow, and such 'bottom up' factors as the intensity and duration of the external stimulus. As to the latter it is useful to regard all stimuli as having two independent attributes: information content and energy level. While either or both of these determine entry into consciousness, there *are* energy levels below which information may be registered but not represented in consciousness.

If the above assumptions are correct, two corollaries follow: first, a preconscious semantic analysis must be applied to most if not all items of sensory information, and secondly, as a consequence of this analysis, there will be many items of incoming information which (because not meeting the criteria for conscious entry), do not achieve conscious representation.

Now the validity of this argument, depicted in Figure 3.2 as a flow diagram, hinges upon evidence for a relationship between brain, mind and behaviour rather different from that traditionally held.

Various sorts of evidence are pertinent to this viewpoint. We begin with the simplest – that for cerebral registration of subliminal stimuli.

PHYSIOLOGICAL AND RELATED STUDIES

Consistent with the finding that consciousness of an external stimulus depends upon a certain minimum level of cortical activation by the ascending reticular system, it has been shown in several studies (see Dixon 1971) that stimuli of insufficient intensity or duration for conscious representation may nevertheless initiate a cerebral response. Thus, recording evoked potentials from the somatosensory cortex of fully conscious subjects, Libet (1973) found that a tactile stimulus too weak for conscious perception was nevertheless able to elicit the first components of the compound evoked response. *Pari passu* with an increase in stimulation, producing the later components of the evoked potential, subjects reported awareness of the stimulus.

This latter research would seem to provide unambiguous support for the notion that the brain can respond to stimuli, which are too weak to enter consciousness. Other, even simpler, evidence for this conclusion have been provided by the demonstration (Riggs and Whittle 1967) that cortical responses evoked by a stabilized retinal image or by the stimuli to the non-dominant eye during binocular rivalry (Cobb *et al.* 1967) continue to occur *after* the stimulus information has faded from consciousness.

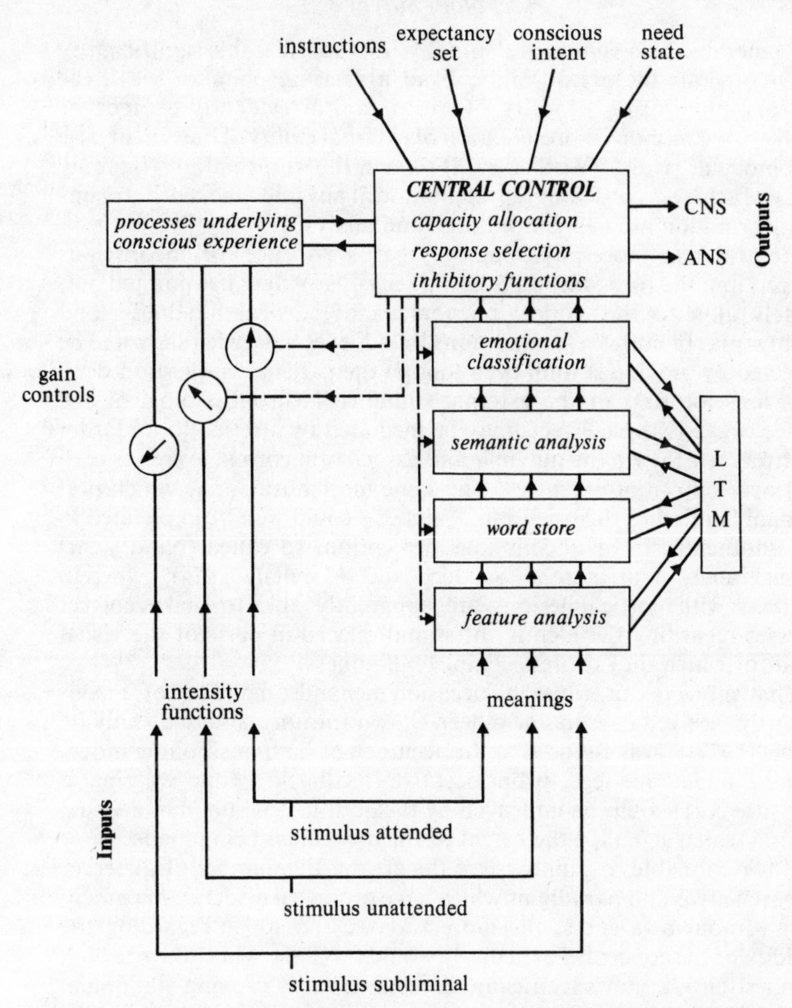

Figure 3.2 In this model the discrepancy between incident information and conscious capacity is catered for by a central control mechanism to which all inputs are referred. The central control's allocation of incoming information to conscious representation, overt behaviour or autonomic responses is governed by three factors: the meaning/emotional significance and intensity levels of external stimuli, and such 'top down' factors as set and attention. Allocation (and aborting) of information, and restrictions on spread of associations are achieved by centrifugal gain controls and inhibitory pathways (dashed lines).

In view of the relationship (Libet 1973) between conscious awareness and the *late* positive component of the evoked potential, the finding, by Harter *et al.* (1973) that only the *early* components of a visual evoked response are generated by a *suppressed* stimulus is of considerable significance.

Of obvious biological value, from a survival point of view, the sensory monitoring capacity of the organism evidently exceeds its ability for conscious representation of external reality. Thus, in the case of binocular rivalry (Walker 1978) though the information from only one eye achieves conscious representation at any one time, both streams of information are being monitored and analysed.

Returning to more physiologically based evidence for unconscious perception, the foregoing data would seem, as Walker has pointed out, closely akin to the clinical phenomena of cortical blindness, and amblyopia. In both these conditions 'blind' eyes have been shown to be affected by moving stimuli even though the patients in question deny any consciousness of the external stimulus. Neurophysiological evidence suggests these effects may be mediated by a retina to midbrain pathway which, via the pulvinar and association cortex, exercises control over opto-motor centres. The same mechanism – one which presumably underlies the orienting response – could well be implicated in yet another form of unconscious perception, so called 'blind sight' (Weiskrantz, Warrington, Sanders and Marshall 1974), wherein patients with cortical lesions are apparently able to make correct guesses regarding the identity of stimuli placed in parts of the visual field for which they profess complete blindness.

That subjects can, when the occasion demands, make use of unconsciously received cues has also been shown for normals. In a study by Greer (1977) it was found that the accuracy of limb positioning movements, under reduced proprioceptive feedback (from wearing a pressure cuff) could be improved by the addition of subliminal visual stimuli which signalled the extent of the movement being made.

It is reasonable to suppose that the greater the number of different research areas and paradigms which have produced evidence of perception without awareness, the more sure we should be regarding the validity of the concept. Particularly would this be so where the research in question was not specifically directed towards proving subliminal perception, nor carried out by a proponent of this phenomenon. The work on 'blind sight' falls into this category. So also do the following two experiments.

The first concerns an unusual case of anomalous colour vision investigated by Ruddock and Waterfield (1978). The subject in question is virtually blind for light of wavelength greater than 610 nm. However, though unable to see a 3 cycle/degree horizontal grating, when viewed through a red filter this same grating produced rivalry with a vertical green grating presented to the other eye.

Under a control condition with the vertical grating to one eye and a plain white card to the other, viewed through green and red filters respectively, the subject perceived *only* the green grating without ever experiencing binocular suppression.

These data suggest the interesting possibility that an effective stimulus may be subliminal along dimensions other than those of intensity and duration; that there is perhaps an effective range of subliminality for every parameter of sensory inflow. Results from a study by Martin, Hawryluk and Guse (1974) may be said to point in this direction. They found that cortical evoked potentials and galvanic skin responses can be determined by audio *frequencies* above the consciously audible range.

So much for a variety of findings, from diverse paradigms, which suggest that sensory mechanisms can monitor and the brain respond to external stimuli of which the mind remains unaware: what of the effects of such unconscious registration?

BEHAVIOURAL STUDIES OF SUBLIMINAL PERCEPTION

In a review of the field (Dixon 1971), covering close on one hundred studies, it was concluded that visual, auditory or tactile stimuli, at signal to noise ratios too low for representation in consciousness, may nevertheless exert effects upon conscious perception of supraliminal stimuli, upon verbal behaviour, adaptation level, dreams, memory, and the perceptual threshold itself. It was further concluded: (i) that the effects of a subliminal stimulus may differ qualitatively from that of the same stimulus above the conscious threshold, and (ii) that they tend to increase with reduced stimulus energy, and are maximized when the subject is relaxed rather than focally attentive. Finally, evidence was advanced to show that the effects of subliminal stimuli may interact with those of need states, personality traits, and unconscious psychopathology, to produce significant effects on behaviour.

Probably the single most important outcome from all this research is that it provided a new view of the relationship between brain, mind, and behaviour, which may be summarized by saying that whereas conscious experience is primarily concerned with the representation of data for the planning of subsequent actions (see Shallice 1972), the precursors of conscious experience, namely the monitoring and registration of external stimuli, the latters' structural and semantic analysis, their lexical access and priming of associations, proceeds below awareness and may never itself achieve conscious representation.

Subliminal Effects on Conscious Percepts

In recent years there has been further evidence from many areas for this viewpoint. Much of it concerns the effect of stimuli, presented below the conscious threshold, upon the perception of simultaneously presented supraliminal stimuli. In a research by Henley and Dixon (1974), subsequently replicated by Mykel and Daves (1979), it was found that imagery evoked by musical stimuli presented to the left ear was significantly determined by subliminal cue words on the other ear. In both these studies it was shown that the effect only occurred to a significant degree when the music was routed to the right hemisphere and the words to the left.

Laterality. The implication from these two researches, that processing of particular sorts of sensory information depends upon the hemisphere at which they arrive has received support from two additional studies. In the first (Dixon and Henley 1974) subjects were required to say whether a shape, described auditorily as 'round' or 'square' was the same or different from an actual shape placed simultaneously in the right or left hand. The hypothesis that reaction times for correct judgements would be fastest for the condition when the two stimuli were applied, respectively, to the right ear and left hand, and slowest when the words were presented to the left ear and the shapes to the right hand, was confirmed.

Consistent with this result was the finding by Fonagy (1977) that when nouns were presented subliminally in either the right visual field or the left visual field the responses that they evoke typify the processing characteristics of the hemisphere at which they arrive. Whereas words to the left hemisphere tended to evoke common linguistic associations, those on the right tended to evoke words referring to objects with similar spatial characteristics.

Effects on adaptation level and illusions. Other examples of the effects of unconsciously registered stimuli upon an established percept include the influence of subliminal 'anchors' upon adaptation level and the inducing of visual illusions by such stimuli as a background array of converging lines, which are exposed so briefly as to evade conscious representation. The conclusion from these experiments (see Dixon 1971) that the cerebral processes underlying visual illusions are not necessarily those providing for conscious experience – that they reflect instead the end product of some earlier stage of sensory processing – has relevance for a wide range of phenomena: such as misplaced constancy scaling, not to mention the interaction between learned cues (which are themselves not consciously registered) and the visual coding of an object's size, shape, etc. which eventuate in phenomenal regression. An implication of some interest from these phenomena is the apparent resistance of preconscious processing to modification by consciously represented knowledge or beliefs. Thus, the relative intractability of such involuntary responses as neurotic tics and psychosomatic symptoms to the conscious cognitive processes of insight and interpretation could well result from the same general principle, namely, that information processing and conscious representation may both enjoy a degree of autonomy from each other.

Semantic analysis without awareness. The determination of conscious perceptual experience by a secondary stimulus of which the subject remains unaware has also been found for verbal stimuli, thus, entailing the notion of unconscious semantic analysis and lexical access.

For example, the effect of a subliminal verbal cue (i.e. 'happy' or 'sad') upon perception of a neutral face, as previously demonstrated by Smith *et al.* (see Dixon 1971) has been confirmed by Somekh and Wilding (1973). They used a binocular paradigm with the faces presented to one eye and the words to the other. A new finding from this research was that whereas supraliminal presentations of structurally similar words influenced perception of the face, this did not occur when the same stimuli were presented below the conscious threshold – a result with interesting implications for theories of word processing. An experiment by Henley (1975) carried the issue one stage further by showing that the decision time for interpretation of a visually presented face could be significantly shortened by subliminal auditory cues. Other studies in this group include those from proponents of microgenetic theory (Kragh and Smith 1970). From Kragh's work has been developed the Defence Mechanism Test that after a fifteen year validation study, is now a standard part of the selection procedure for entry into the Swedish Airforce. The test involves reproducing the central figure in a briefly exposed TAT (Thematic Apperception Test) card.

It seems that, though totally unaware of a peripherally placed 'ugly threatening male face', this latter may seriously interfere with the subject's response. It is these interference effects, or 'defensive reactions', that have been found to have a significant prognostic value for subsequent accident proneness and psychosomatic disorders in flying personnel and also deep sea divers.

Comparable data have also come from the use of a metacontrast paradigm (MCT) in which conscious perception of a human figure is distorted by a preceding, masked, threat stimulus (see Smith and Danielsson 1979).

Whereas all these studies are concerned with the influence of unperceived stimuli upon the preconscious processing of meaningful material, those by Andersson *et al.* (1970) are devoted to subliminal influences upon such sensory phenomena as the colour of after-images and the duration of movement after-effects.

Yet other demonstrations of the fact that a secondary stimulus, presented below the threshold of consciousness, may affect responses to simultaneous stimuli above this threshold, have been given by Fisher (1976) Silverman (1976), Henley (1976) and Mackay (1973). Whereas Fisher's data concerns the effect of subliminal auditory threatening words upon a person's body image, the extensive studies by Silverman and his colleagues have concentrated upon the influence of tachistoscopically exposed words, and/or pictures, upon consciously perceived projective material.

Subliminal versus unattended stimuli. Though both are concerned with the effect of a secondary stimulus, outside of awareness, upon the perceived meaning of a supraliminal stimulus, the experiments by Henley (1976) and Mackay (1973)* mark an important difference between paradigms from different areas of research. Both studies were concerned with the disambiguating effects of cue words presented to one ear, upon response to homophones (e.g. pale/pail) in the Henley experiment, and to ambiguous sentences (e.g. 'She sat by a bank') in the Mackay study. Both studies suggested that the perceived meaning of ambiguous material may be determined by cues of which the subject remained unaware. Where the researches differed, was in the means whereby unconsciousness of the secondary stimulus was achieved. In the Henley experiment the cues were strictly subliminal, i.e. presented 5 decibels below the auditory awareness threshold. In Mackay's investigation unconsciousness was achieved, as in many other studies of dichotic listening (Lewis 1970, 1972; Corteen and Wood 1972; Corteen and Dunn 1974; Forster and Govier 1978; Treisman, Squire and Green 1974) by requiring the subject to attend to material on one ear and ignore that on the other. This difference between the two studies, which produced equivalent results, exemplifies the distinction drawn by Norman (1969) between 'bottom up' and 'top down' control of perception – a distinction, as illustrated in Figure 3.2, between stimulus and subject control of perceptual input.

The allocation of analysers. Besides attesting to the reality of unconscious semantic analysis, the foregoing experiments are among those that touch on another interesting problem; the allocation of analysers to different streams of information, when these arrive simultaneously over different channels. Whereas the experiments by Mackay (1973), Smith *et al.* (see Dixon 1971), Henley and Dixon (1974), Somekh and Wilding (1973), and Bradshaw (1974) suggest that a secondary subliminal (or unattended) stimulus determines the perceived meaning of a simultaneous supraliminal display, other researches – by Lewis (1970, 1972), Treisman *et al.* (1974) and Underwood (1976) – have shown that response times to words or pictures are *increased* rather than decreased by such secondary stimuli on another channel, as are related in meaning to the consciously perceived primary stimulus. It should be noted that while this latter group of studies involved paradigms that relied on selective *inattention* to achieve unawareness of the secondary stimuli, similar results were obtained in two, more recent and less ambiguous, experiments by Philpott and Wilding (1979), which employed strictly subliminal stimuli on the secondary channel. In this

*Data from three experiments by Newstead and Dennis (1979) suggest that Mackay's results may have depended upon the fact that his paradigm allowed attention switching between 'sentences'.

research subjects had to name colours, shapes, or words presented to one eye while words or shapes were presented below the awareness threshold to the other eye. As in the previous studies, it was found that response latencies for naming the consciously perceived items were a positive function of the relatedness in meaning of the subliminal stimuli.

Considered *in toto* these two groups of experiments appear to pose something of a paradox. Although in both cases the secondary and primary stimuli are related in meaning, responses are facilitated in one paradigm but inhibited in the other. However, as depicted in Figure 3.3, the paradox may be resolved by assuming that whereas the secondary stimulus served a purely disambiguating role at some preconscious stage of processing, in the first group of experiments; the paradigm for obtaining a *naming* response, in the second group of experiments, *invites competition for a single analyser* and it is this which slows the naming response. There is one final point of interest. While most of the

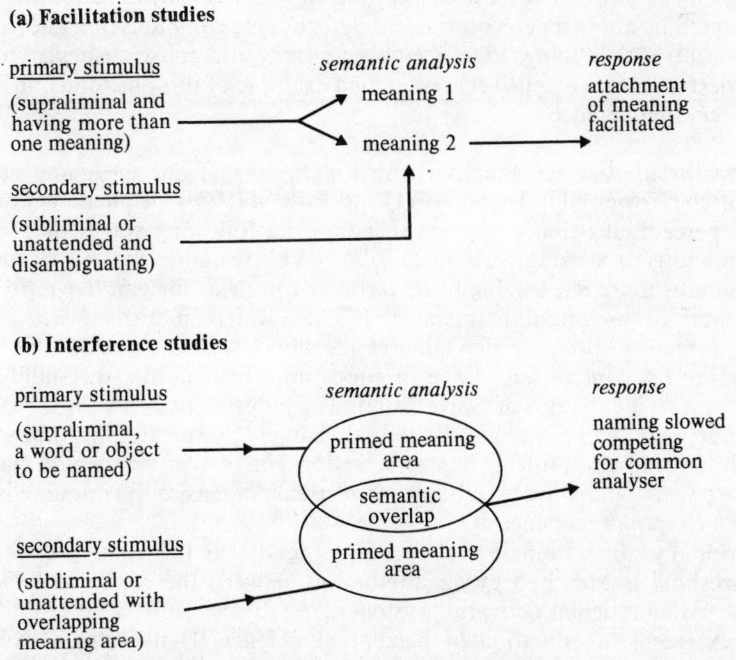

Figure 3.3 A comparison between the processes involved in two paradigms that concern interactions between stimuli above and below the conscious threshold. (a) typifies data from Smith *et al.* (1959), Somekh and Wilding (1973), Mackay (1973), Henley and Dixon (1974) and Bradshaw (1974); (b) typifies data from Lewis (1970, 1972), Treisman *et al.* (1974), Underwood (1976) and Philpott and Wilding (1979).

experiments considered in this section were concerned with the effects, in one way or another, of a stimulus outside of awareness upon something consciously perceived, the researches by Corteen and his colleagues and by Forster and Govier, imply a further talent of preconscious perceptual mechanisms – namely the capacity for simultaneous processing of two unrelated inputs without interaction or loss.

Data from these latter experiments suggest that if important information in an unattended message would disrupt the primary task (of say shadowing), its effects can be isolated and confined to the appropriate output of an autonomic response. The possible significance of this isolating mechanism for the genesis of psychosomatic disease will be considered below.

Categorization before Identification

The researches referred to so far do not exhaust the evidence for preconscious processing, and semantic analysis prior to awareness. Equally relevant are those (see review by Carr and Bacharach 1976) which suggest that there are situations in which a subject can 'know' something about a perceptual event *before* being conscious of it and, as a result of this 'knowledge' regulate its entry into consciousness. The oldest and most extensively researched example of this phenomenon is perceptual defence.

Perceptual defence. Summarizing the findings from the many researches reviewed in Dixon (1971) and Erdelyi (1974) the phenomenon of perceptual defence appears to entail the following stages of preconscious processing: structural followed by semantic analysis of the stimulus material, leading to activation of pre-existing emotive representations in long-term memory (LTM), which in turn evokes an autonomic response, which initiates a feedback (or more strictly a 'feed forward') control on the awareness and recognition thresholds. Research involving successive brightness judgements has shown that perceptual defence involves an actual change in subjective brightness, while paradigms utilizing Signal Detection Theory have confirmed that the phenomenon involves changes in d' (sensory sensitivity) rather than in β (response tendencies).

Finally, data from several sources suggest that this control of the threshold is exercised by an interaction between the cortex and the ascending reticular activating system.

A recent investigation of perceptual defence (Henley and Dixon 1976) illustrates a basic feature of this model, namely the specificity of the relationship between components of the stimulus and the internal representation with which it makes contact. Based on the theory that the conflict areas most usually encountered in schizophrenic psychopathology include problems over aggression, social stimuli, and the maternal relationship, the hypothesis was tested that schizophrenic

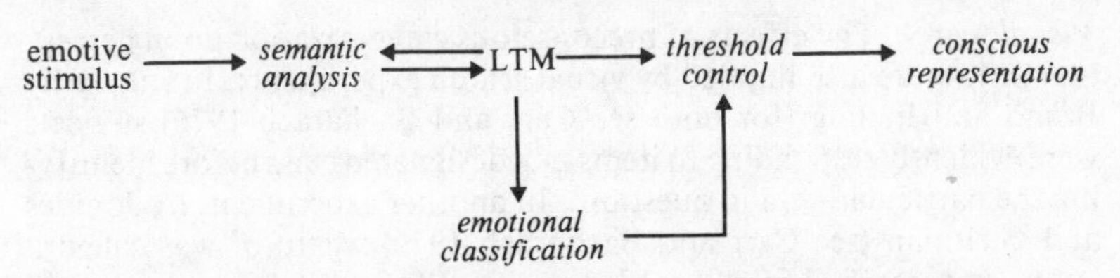

Figure 3.4 Flow diagram for threshold control.

subjects would show perceptual defençe for pictures and words referring to these emotionally charged issues. Using the method of binocular stimulation and closed loop control (see Dixon 1971), hospitalized chronic schizophrenics provided a continuous record of the sensitivity of one eye (for a spot of light on an illuminated screen) while the word 'breast' or pictures depicting, respectively, a mother scolding, whipping or feeding a child were presented, at subliminal intensities, to the other eye. Presentation of these critical stimuli were randomly interspersed with that of neutral control words and pictures. Results confirmed the prediction that only the former would elevate the sensory threshold for a neutral test patch, a finding consistent with data from other researchers (see Silverman 1976 for a summary of this work) that schizophrenic psychopathology as revealed in projective tests, is particularly sensitive to influence by subliminal stimuli depicting either aggression or gratification of a mother-related symbiotic fantasy.

This is another instance where evidence for preconscious processing and in particular for the model outlined in Figure 3.2 is not confined to the data from experiments using strictly subliminal stimuli. Using the paradigm of dichotic listening, Corteen and Wood (1972) showed that when words (city names) previously associated with electric shock were presented to the unattended ear during the shadowing of prose on the other ear, palmar sweating was evoked.

Since unshocked associates of the critical words also evoked significant galvanic skin responses (gsr's), but neutral unassociated control words did not, we can assume that the material on the unattended channel was subjected to a full semantic analysis. And since the subjects in this experiment did not report hearing words on the unattended ear nor did the critical words interfere with the shadowing task, it seems reasonable to assume that the various processing stages involved – registration, semantic analysis, and evoking of an autonomic response – occurred outside of awareness. That subjects were indeed unaware of the unattended stream of information was subsequently confirmed by Corteen and Dunn (1974). Following a failure to replicate these experiments by Wardlaw and Kroll (1976), Forster and Govier (1978) have provided further support for the original findings. Their plausible (and experimentally backed) explanation for the Wardlaw and Kroll failure to replicate, was that the latter workers did not bring about adequate conditioning in the pretest shock trials.

Visual search. The effects of preconscious categorization upon perceptual inflow are also implied by visual search experiments. In studies by Brand and Ingling (for both see Carr and Bacharach 1976) subjects were evidently responding to items of a designated class before identifying the particular item in question. In another experiment, by Jonides and Gleitman (see Carr and Bacharach 1976) when 'o' was called a letter, and searched for among letters, or called a number and searched for among numbers, search time was a linear function of set size. But if the same symbol was called a number and searched for among letters (or vice versa) set size had no effect upon search time.

Binocular rivalry. Yet another example of the fact that the organism's monitoring capacity exceeds that for conscious representation and that preconscious processing selects for awareness is provided by binocular rivalry. Despite numerous attempts to explain the phenomenon in terms of peripheral suppression, a considerable body of research, reviewed by Walker (1978), supports the theory, originally espoused by Helmholtz (see Walker 1978), that the phenomenon reflects a central selective process that occurs below awareness but *after* a preconscious analysis of the two monocular fields.

Evidence for this theory is typified by the following findings:

(1) Only changes in the suppressed monocular field affect the temporal course of rivalry. This holds true even when the change is itself subliminal (see Walker 1978).

(2) Depth perception still occurs even when one member of a stereo pair is totally suppressed, and this even when the field in question had never achieved a state of dominance (Kaufman; see Walker 1978).

(3) When two scenes, one portraying some undesirable piece of behaviour (e.g. rape or murder), and the other a neutral control picture, are presented dichoptically, and so briefly that only one of the pictures is consciously seen, policemen and institutionalized offenders saw the undesirable scene significantly more often than did normal control subjects, (Toch and Schulte, Shelley and Toch, Berg and Toch; see Walker 1978).

    In a comparable research, Moore (see Walker 1978) found that violence is perceived significantly more often by males than by females.

(4) When different faces are presented dichoptically (Galton, Engel, Ross; see Walker 1978) the consciously perceived composite face is considered more attractive by the subject than either of the component faces.

(5) Dichoptic presentations of different letter strings such as SHAR/SHAP or FCIAND/FREUMD result in conscious perception of the meaningful words SHARP and FRIEND, respectively (Rommetveit *et al.*; see Walker 1978).

All in all these various findings suggest that within the space of milliseconds a complex sequence of events – registration, comparison, selection, and construction, guided by such factors as the subject's personality, occupation, aesthetic preferences, or merely rules of language – may run its course prior to delivery into consciousness of the finished product.

THE DETERMINATION OF VERBAL BEHAVIOUR

All the researches considered so far were concerned, in one way or another, with the effect upon conscious perceptual experience of stimuli that were never themselves represented in consciousness.

No less interesting and important for the theme of preconscious processing are those instances in which a stimulus outside of awareness effects verbal behaviour *without* any mediating conscious percept. Two sorts of experiment have demonstrated this phenomenon, those where the subject is required to guess which of a finite class of stimuli is being presented below threshold on any one trial, and those where the subject, with no prior knowledge of the stimuli to be presented, is required to give free associations following each stimulus presentation. Data from the first group of experiments (see Dixon 1971; Rollman and Nachmias 1972) suggest that preconscious reception and processing of subliminal stimuli exercises a selective function on the probability matrix underlying guessing behaviour. Evidently, there is sufficient unconscious structural analysis of the incoming information to actuate primed representations. These studies do not necessitate postulating any preconscious semantic analysis of the input. Their main value is in providing further unequivocal evidence for the reality of subliminal perception. The point is perhaps most strikingly illustrated by the work of Rollman and Nachmias (1972). In the course of using signal detection methodology to examine Luce's low threshold theory these researchers presented chromatic discs at low signal to noise levels. As in any simple signal detection task their subjects responded 'present' or 'absent' on each trial. Where the research differs from previous studies was in the treatment of false negatives. Each time the subject incorrectly reported 'stimulus absent' he was asked to guess what colour the disc would have been if it had been presented.

In the event, their 'guesses' about attribution of a stimulus, which they had said wasn't there, showed a significant tendency to name the currently presented colour (a result which accords with the data from Ruddock and Waterfield (1978) described earlier). There could hardly be a less ambiguous demonstration of subliminal perception!

Whereas data from the foregoing experiments imply no more than an unconscious recognitive response, following structural analysis of the stimulus array, other studies (see Dixon 1971) suggest that subliminal verbal material may undergo a full semantic analysis prior to priming semantically associated responses. Thus, asked to say, 'the first word that comes to mind', following the receipt of a subliminal stimulus, subjects not only gave indications, such as long reaction times and gsr's, that they had registered the emotional significance of the stimulus but also produced verbal responses that were semantically related to the latter. The nature of these associated responses suggests that prior to achieving conscious representation, verbal stimulus material is not only subjected to a semantic analysis but as a consequence of this primes a network of verbal associates rather more extensive than that activated by the conscious representation of a word. About this phenomenon, which contrasts with what has been called, 'the restricting effects of awareness' (Spence and Holland; see Dixon 1971), several points may be made. First, it implies a full semantic analysis of stimuli below the conscious threshold. Secondly, since the responses that it evokes are qualitatively different from those produced by the same stimulus presented above the conscious threshold, it constitutes evidence for the fact that the perceptual processes involved were truly preconscious. Thirdly, the fact that many of the responses bore a symbolic (in the Freudian sense) relationship to the stimulus, suggests that when the signal to noise ratio is sufficiently low the stimulus sets in motion those mechanisms that underly primary process thinking. Electrophysiological and behavioural studies by Shevrin and his colleagues (see Shevrin 1975) are relevant to this issue. From paradigms which involved recording responses to subliminal presentations of a visual rebus*, there emerged three results of particular interest. First, in a comparison between like-sexed adolescent twins who differed in repressiveness, it was found that whereas the repressive subjects showed lower amplitude evoked responses, and fewer associations to the subliminal rebus, than did their non repressive twin, this relationship was reversed for supraliminal stimuli. A second finding was that reducing stimulus duration from 0.03 sec to 0.001 sec not only increased the amplitude of a visual evoked response but also the number of primary process (clang) associations to the rebus. Finally, in another research, which involved presenting the rebus stimulus before sleep, it was found that whereas conceptual associates (to 'pen' or 'knee') were given by subjects after being woken from non-REM (rapid-eye-movement) sleep, primary process clang and rebus responses tended to occur following REM sleep.

Besides its significance for our understanding of what Neisser (1963) has called 'the multiplicity of thought', the foregoing data, like those from studies of perceptual defence, lend credence to the notion of a hierarchy of preconscious processing stages as depicted in Figure 3.2. Data from Spence and Holland (see Dixon 1971), from the pattern

*A picture of two objects (e.g. a pen and a knee) the names of which combine to make a word (e.g. Penny).

masking experiments of Marcel and Patterson (1978), and from Weiskrantz's (1977) observations of the way in which apparent memory deficits in amnesic patients are largely due to the unwanted intrusion into consciousness of semantic associates, suggests that, so far as spheres of meaning are concerned, the aforementioned hierarchy not only tapers towards it's apex but also moves from primary to secondary processing of sensory inflow.

There is one final point before concluding this section. The diffuse associational activity, with evoking of symbolic concrete sensorial responses, that appears to be initiated by subliminal stimuli could well implicate the parallel primary processing mechanisms of the right hemisphere. First, Fonagy (1977) has shown that whereas a subliminal word presented to the left hemisphere tends to evoke secondary process associations (e.g. GRASS→'green') the same word presented to the right hemisphere tends to evoke responses connating objects that *look like* (i.e. symbolize) that referred to by the stimulus (e.g. GRASS→ 'hair' or 'bed of nails').

The second research, by Sackeim *et al.* (1977), has shown that susceptibility to subliminal stimuli is significantly more marked in people showing right hemisphericity and particularly is this so when such individuals are in a passive, non-alert state. Besides suggesting two good reasons why subliminal effects are not always found with all subjects, this experiment appears to show a relationship between conditions conducive to subliminal effects and those conducive to the occurrence of primary process thinking.

CLINICAL USES OF UNCONSCIOUS PERCEPTION

One of the most compelling pieces of evidence for the theory that sensory information is subjected to a semantic analysis, at a preconscious stage of processing, comes from those responses to the emotional significance of a stimulus that occur prior to or even without, such a stimulus achieving phenomenal representation. Of the researches so far considered those involving perceptual defence (Henley and Dixon 1976; see also Dixon 1971) and subception (Lazarus and McCleary; see Dixon 1971), those involving the effects of subliminal stimuli on the retrieval of emotionally significant items from long-term memory (Spence and Gordon; see Dixon 1971), those involving abnormal association reaction times and gsr's to words presented below the conscious threshold (Dixon 1971), and, finally, those involving cortical responses and symbolic dreams to emotionally important auditory stimuli presented during sleep (Oswald *et al.*, Berger; see Dixon 1971) share the fact that response processes, which are normally sensitive to the conscious appraisal of threat, may also be triggered by what amounts to a reflex physiological mechanism sensitized by past learning to the meaning of certain stimulus arrays.

In recent years the clinical implications of these data from academic laboratory experiments have found expression in a number of interesting studies. These include the evoking of anxiety in normal subjects by threatening film material presented below the conscious level (Tyrer *et al.* 1978b); the exacerbation of ego pathology in a variety of neurotic and psychotic disorders by tachistoscopic presentation of stimulus material specific to the underlying conflicts of the disorders concerned (see Silverman 1976); the effects of threatening stimuli presented below the auditory threshold upon aspects of the body image (Fisher 1976); the use of the Poetzl effect (see Dixon 1971) to explore the psychopathological bases of psychosomatic illness, and the recording of threshold change on one eye as a function of critical stimulus presentations, below the conscious threshold, to the other eye, as a means of investigating schizophrenic psychopathology (Henley and Dixon 1976). Whereas most of the aforegoing studies have been concerned with pinpointing the sorts of conflict areas specific to such abnormalities as depression, schizophrenia, homosexuality, stuttering, anorexia and psychosomatic disease, others have actually used subliminal stimuli in the successful treatment of phobias (Silverman, Frank and Dachinger 1974; Tyrer *et al.* 1978a) and obesity (Silverman, Martin, Ungaro and Mendelsohn 1978).

In the case of phobias a typical approach has been the use of subliminal presentation of the phobic object as part of the normal desensitization routine (Silverman *et al.* 1974).

For obesity, on the other hand (Silverman *et al.* 1978), the preferred method has been to reduce the underlying anxiety that gave rise to overeating. In the latter study the words, 'Mommy and I are one' that are aimed to gratify an underlying symbiotic fantasy which has been shown to reduce ego-pathology in a number of other disorders (see Silverman 1976) were flashed for 4 ms in each of many training sessions over an 8 week period. When compared with a randomly selected control group of obese women who had been flashed a neutral message, the fifteen experimental subjects showed a significant weight loss over the subsequent 12 week follow up period.

There are three points of particular interest regarding the Silverman paradigm. First, the effects found appear to depend upon the stimulus presentation being totally outside of awareness. As shown in several earlier researches (see Dixon 1971) presentations near or above the threshold were without effect. Secondly, apart from the symbiotic message which appears to reduce pathology in a number of disorders, the sorts of stimuli used by Silverman are only effective if specific to the disorder in question, e.g. only a stimulus suggesting incest effected homosexual psychopathology and was without effect on depressives and schizophrenics. The reverse held true for stimuli depicting aggression.

A third point concerns the validity and reliability of these studies. Not only have significant results been obtained in some thirty studies by

Silverman and his co-workers but their most recent foray (Silverman, Ross, Adler and Lustig 1978) in which they showed that the skill of dart throwing could be significantly improved or impaired by a subliminal message signifying, respectively, approval or disapproval of competition with father has been successfully replicated, with positive results by a pair of independent researchers.

As to why the symbiotic gratification message should be apparently such a universal panacea one has only to consider Harlow's work on infant monkeys, not to mention the extensive studies of maternal deprivation in humans, to find it not implausible that closeness to the maternal parent in childhood ranks high in importance as an early buttress against future anxieties.

In concluding this section it is perhaps worth noting that striking parallels can be drawn (Dixon 1964, 1979) between the effects found in laboratory demonstrations of subliminal perception and the characteristics of at least some psychosomatic disorders. These common characteristics include: activation of unconscious areas of conflict by stimuli, the significance of which the subject remains unaware; the relative absence of conscious affect (Nemiah and Sifneos 1970); symbolic conversion of the precipitating stimulus; and the evoking of a somatic response mediated by the autonomic nervous system.

SUMMARY

This paper has outlined data from eleven areas of research – subliminal perception, binocular rivalry, signal detection, perceptual defence, 'blind sight', stabilized images, selective attention, sleep and dreams, the Poetzl effect, visual search, and pattern masking – involving many different paradigms, which provide support for the model depicted in Figure 3.2 on page 33. They suggest:

(1) The capacity for conscious experience is the product of a system which may operate independently of that responsible for the transmission of information through an organism.
(2) The criteria for representation in consciousness that include the signal to noise ratio and meaning of incoming sensory information, must be applied at some preconscious stage of processing.
(3) Whether or not stored or incoming information achieves conscious representation may also depend upon such 'top down' factors as set and selective attention.
(4) Given the many factors that ultimately determine the content of subjective awareness it is necessary to postulate a preconscious central control mechanism which, besides regulating conscious entry, exercises a selective function on lower levels of sensory processing.
(5) The complex activities that comprise preconscious processing

include extensive monitoring of the external scene, structural and semantic analysis of sensory inflow, lexical access, emotional classification, a two way commerce with long term memory, and, in all probability, differential contributions from the two hemispheres of the brain.

REFERENCES

Andersson, A., Fries, I., and Smith, G. W. 1970. 'Change in afterimage and spiral after-effect serials due to anxiety caused by subliminal threat.' *Scan. J. Psychol. 11*, 7 – 16.

Bradshaw, L. 1974. 'Peripherally presented and unreported words may bias the perceived meaning of a centrally fixated homograph.' *J. exp. Psychol. 103*, 1200 – 2.

Carr, T. H., and Bacharach, V. R. 1976. 'Perceptual tuning and conscious attention, systems of input regulation in visual information processing.' *Cognition 4*, 281 – 302.

Cobb, W. A., Morton, H. B., and Ettlinger, G. 1967. 'Cerebral evoked potentials evoked by pattern reversal and their suppression in visual rivalry.' *Nature 216*, 1123 – 5.

Corteen, R. S., and Dunn, D. 1974. 'Shock-associated words in a nonattended message: a test for momentary awareness.' *J. exp. Psychol. 102*, 1113 – 44.

Corteen, R. S., and Wood, B. 1972. 'Autonomic responses to shock-associated words.' *J. exp. Psychol. 94*, 308 – 13.

Dixon, N. F. 1964. 'Communication without awareness: the implications of subliminal perception.' *J. Psychosom. Res. 8*, 337 – 41.

Dixon, N. F. 1971. *Subliminal perception: the nature of a controversy*. London: McGraw-Hill.

Dixon, N. F. 1979. 'Psychosomatic disorder: a special case of subliminal perception?' In M. J. Christie and P. G. Mellett (eds) *Psychosomatic approaches to medicine: 1 Behavioural Science Foundations*. London: John Wiley, in press.

Dixon, N. F., and Henley, S. H. A. 1974. 'Laterality effects in perceptual matching – a preliminary note.' *Perception 3*, 99 – 100.

Erdelyi, M. 1974. 'A new look at the New Look: perceptual defence and vigilance.' *Psychol. Rev. 81*, 1 – 25.

Fisher, S. 1976. 'Conditions affecting boundary response to messages out of awareness.' *J. Nerv. Ment. Disease 162*, 313 – 22.

Fonagy, P. 1977. 'The use of subliminal stimuli in highlighting function differences between the two hemispheres.' Paper given to December meeting of the Experimental Psychology Society at Birkbeck College, London.

Forster, P. M., and Govier, E. 1978. 'Discrimination without awareness?' *Quart. J. exp. Psychol. 30*, 282 – 95.

Greer, C. L. 1977. 'The role of muscle receptors in the control of movement.' Ph.D. Thesis, University of London.

Harter, M. R., Seiple, W. H., and Salmon, L. E. 1973. 'Binocular summation of visually evoked responses to pattern stimuli in humans.' *Vis. Res. 13*, 1433 – 46.

Henley, S. H. A. 1975. 'Cross modal effects of subliminal verbal stimuli.' *Scand. J. Psychol. 16*, 30–6.
Henley, S. H. A. 1976. 'Responses to homophones as a function of cue words on the unattended channel.' *Brit. J. Psychol. 67*, 559–67.
Henley, S. H. A., and Dixon, N. F. 1974. 'Laterality differences in the effects of incidental stimuli upon evoked imagery.' *Brit. J. Psychol. 65*, 529–36.
Henley, S. H. A., and Dixon, N. F. 1976. 'Preconscious processing in schizoprenics: an exploratory investigation.' *Brit. J. med. Psychol. 49*, 161–6.
Kragh, U. and Smith, G. J. W. 1970. *Percept. Genetic Analysis.* Lund, Sweden: Gleerups.
Lewis, J. L. 1970. 'Semantic processing of unattended messages during dichotic listening.' *J. exp. Psychol. 85*, 225–8.
Lewis, J. L. 1972. 'Semantic processing with bisensory information.' *J. exp. Psychol. 96*, 455–71.
Libet, B. 1973. 'Electrical stimulation of cortex in humans, and conscious sensory aspects.' In A. Iggo (ed.) *Handbook of sensory physiology 2.* New York: Springer.
MacKay, D. G. 1973. 'Aspects of the theory of comprehension, memory and attention.' *Quart. J. exp. Psychol. 25*, 22–40.
Marcel, A., and Patterson, K. 1978. 'Word recognition and production: reciprocity in clinical and normal studies.' In J. Requin (ed.) *Attention and performance VII.* New Jersey: Lawrence Erlbaum.
Martin, D. G., Hawryluk, G. A. and Guse, L. L. 1974. 'Experimental study of unconscious influences: ultrasound as a stimulus.' *J. Abnorm. Psychol. 83*, 589–608.
Mykel, M., and Daves, W. 1979. 'Emergence of unreported stimuli into imagery as a function of laterality of presentation.' *Brit. J. Psychol.*, 70, 253–8.
Neisser, U. 1963. 'The multiplicity of thought.' *Brit. J. Psychol. 54*, 1–14.
Nemiah, J. C., and Sifneos, P. E. 1970. 'Affect and fantasy in patients with psychosomatic disorders.' In O. W. Hill (ed.) *Modern trends in psychosomatic medicine, 11*, 26–34.
Newstead, S. E., and Dennis, I. 1979. 'Lexical and grammatical processing of unshadowed messages: a re-examination of the Mackay effect.' *Quart. J. exp. Psychol. 31*, 477–88.
Norman, D. A. 1969. *Memory and attention: an introduction to human information processing.* San Diego: John Wiley.
Philpott, A., and Wilding, J. 1979. 'Semantic interference from subliminal stimuli in a dichoptic viewing situation.' *Brit. J. Psychol.*, 70, 559–63.
Posner, M. I., and Boies, S. J. 1971. 'Components of attention.' *Psychol. Rev. 78*, 391–408.
Riggs, L. A., and Whittle, P. 1967. 'Human occipital and retinal potentials evoked by subjectively faded visual stimuli.' *Vis. Res. 7*, 441–51.
Rollman, G. B., and Nachmias, J. 1972. 'Simultaneous detection and recognition of chromatic flashes.' *Percept. and Psychophys. 12*, 308–14.
Ruddock, K. H., and Waterfield, V. A. 1978. 'Selective loss of function associated with a central visual field defect.' *Neuroscience letters 8*, 93–8.
Sackeim, H. A., Packer, I. K., and Gur, R. C. 1977. 'Hemisphericity, cognitive set and susceptibility to subliminal perception.' *J. Abnorm. Psychol. 86*, 624–30.
Shallice, T. 1972. 'Dual functions of consciousness.' *Psychol. Rev. 79*, 383–93.

Shevrin, H. 1975. 'Does the averaged evoked response encode subliminal perception? Yes: a reply to Schwartz and Rem.' *Psycho. Physiol. 12*, 395 – 8.

Silverman, L. H. 1976. 'Psychoanalytic theory: the reports of my death are greatly exaggerated.' *Amer. Psychol. 31*, 621 – 37.

Silverman, L. H., Frank, S. G., and Dachinger, P. 1974. 'A psychoanalytic reinterpretation of the effectiveness of systematic desensitization: experimental data bearing on the role of merging fantasies.' *J. Abnorm. Psychol. 83*, 313 – 18.

Silverman, L. H., Martin, A., Ungaro, R., and Mendelsohn, E. 1978. 'The effect of subliminal stimulation of symbiotic fantasies on behaviour modification treatment of obesity.' *J. Consult. Clin. Psychol. 46*, 432 – 41.

Silverman, L. H., Ross, D. L., Adler, J. M., and Lustig, D. A. 1978. 'Simple research paradigm for demonstrating psychodynamic activation: effects of Oedipal stimuli on dart-throwing accuracy in college males.' *J. Abnorm. Psychol. 87*, 341 – 57.

Smith, G. J. W., and Danielsson, A. 1979. 'Anxiety and defensive strategies in childhood and adolescence.' *Psychol. Iss., Vol. 12, Monog. 3*. New York: Int. Univ. Press.

Somekh, D., and Wilding, J. M. 1973. 'Perception without awareness in a dichoptic viewing situation.' *Brit. J. Psychol. 64*, 339 – 49.

Treisman, A., Squire, R., and Green, J. 1974. 'Semantic processing in dichotic listening? A replication.' *Mem. and Cog. 2*, 641 – 6.

Tyrer, P., Lee, I., and Horn, P. 1978a. 'Treatment of agoraphobia by subliminal and supraliminal exposure to phobic cine film.' *Lancet*. Feb. 18th, 358 – 60.

Tyrer, P., Lewis, P., and Lee, I. 1978b. 'Effects of subliminal and supraliminal stress on symptoms of anxiety.' *J. Nerv. Ment. Dis. 166*, 611 – 22.

Underwood, G. 1976. 'Semantic interference from unattended printed words.' *Brit. J. Psychol. 67*, 327 – 38.

Walker, P. 1978. 'Binocular rivalry: central or peripheral selective processes?' *Psychol. Bull. 85*, 376 – 89.

Wardlaw, K. A., and Kroll, N. E. A. 1976. 'Autonomic responses to shock-associated words in a non attended message: a failure to replicate.' *J. exp. Psychol: Hum. Percept. and Perform. 2*, 357 – 60.

Weiskrantz, L. 1977. 'Trying to bridge some neurophysiological gaps between monkey and man.' *Brit. J. Psychol. 68*, 431 – 45.

Weiskrantz, L., Warrington, E. K., Sanders, M. D., and Marshall, J. 1974. 'Visual capacity in the hemianopic field following a restricted occipital ablation.' *Brain 97*, 709 – 28.

Chapter 4

Memory Disorder

DAVID GAFFAN

A weakening of memory is one of the most commonly noticed signs of mental deterioration. With diseases that cause diffuse brain damage, or simply with age, the power of memory may suffer a decline that is obvious in everyday experience and is accompanied by equally obvious impairments in reasoning and motor control.

However, this chapter is concerned with a very much rarer condition, organic amnesia, which is caused by localized brain damage. Amnesic patients suffer from so severe a memory impairment that they must generally live in hospital, or under very close supervision. 'Typically they are unable to tell you where they are, what year it is, who is the Prime Minister, what they had for breakfast or to supply any of the vast number of details of daily existence that a normal person takes for granted.' (Baddeley 1975). But their impairment is much more specific than a general mental deterioration. Powers of reasoning and of verbal intelligence, as measured by standard clinical tests, may be entirely unaffected in pure cases of amnesia; and even certain specific types of memory test may be performed at normal levels. The amnesic syndrome is relevant to our understanding of the brain processes underlying normal memory in a way that memory impairment as part of general mental deterioration is not.

Two questions are discussed below. First, what aspects of normal memory are impaired in amnesia, and what aspects are left intact? Secondly, what is the brain damage that causes amnesia? These questions are discussed first in relation to amnesic patients, and then in relation to experimental animals in which the effects of localized brain damage on memory have also been investigated.

THE IMPAIRMENT OF HUMAN AMNESICS

As might be expected, amnesics perform much worse than matched control subjects in many formal memory tests. For example, in free recall, where a subject is asked to give the words from a previously presented list, amnesics are impaired even when the list is presented five or ten times (Warrington and Weiskrantz 1968). Severe deficits are also seen in more natural free recall such as recall of a short story (Talland 1965). The other normal method of testing memory is by a recognition memory test, where the subject is asked at the retention test to pick out the items that were presented in the acquisition list, the 'targets', from newly introduced 'distractor' items. The items used may be words, faces, or pictures, and amnesics perform poorly with all types of material (Warrington 1974). Given the severity of the defects in free recall and recognition, most experimentalists have concentrated not on the large area of memory tasks that reveal a profound amnesic impairment but on the smaller area of memory tasks where amnesics perform well, sometimes as well as controls. In order to delimit the impairment it is necessary to discover what amnesics can remember as well as what they cannot.

Motor Skills

Examples of motor skills which can be taught in a laboratory and show gradual improvement with practice are mirror-drawing, rotary pursuit, bimanual tracking, and high-speed tapping. It has been shown that a severely amnesic patient could acquire all these skills and retained the improvement from one session to the next, although verbally denying any acquaintance with the apparatus used (Milner 1962; Corkin 1968). An amnesic pianist has been described who was able to learn a new tune and play it from memory next day after being given the first few bars (Starr and Phillips 1970).

Very Old Memories

It is sometimes claimed that very old memories are left intact in amnesia. Loss of memory for events before the onset of the disease is known as retrograde amnesia; the term contrasts with anterograde amnesia, the inability to remember events after the onset of the disease. Whereas it is possible to study anterograde amnesia under controlled conditions, with acquisition and retention tests arranged according to the needs of an experimental design, the acquisition conditions for retrograde amnesia are lost in the pre-morbid past. If a patient recalls an event from his childhood, one possibility is that very old memories are preserved in this patient; a second is that the memory is false, since it is often impossible to check the veracity of personal recollections; a third is that the memory is true but has been preserved not by old age but by exceptional strength acquired through frequent rehearsal. The best experimental evidence comes from a study by Sanders and Warrington (1971). They compiled a questionnaire of public events covering the whole of the adult life-time of a group of 5 amnesic subjects, and compared the accuracy of their answers with that of 100 control subjects' answers. The latter scored above chance throughout the period covered, while the amnesics never scored above chance.

Although it is not clear how much of the memory of public events is laid down at the time of their occurrence and how much by rehearsal afterwards, this study does not support the notion that early memories are in general preserved in amnesia. None the less, personal facts about early life, for example one's place of birth, may be highly overlearned and for that reason preserved in amnesia; and early learned skills are not lost, which is not surprising since motor skills are not affected by anterograde amnesia either (see above).

The conclusions of Sanders and Warrington (1971) have been questioned by Marslen-Wilson and Teuber (1975) on the basis of results obtained from one amnesic patient with a similar questionnaire technique. This patient gave some correct answers to forced-choice questions. It is difficult to know whether or not this result arose by chance, since only a small number of questions were given to only one patient.

Cued Recall

Consider a task in which subjects are asked to respond within a short time-limit to instructions like, 'Give me an English word whose first three letters are ALC'. Many will not find such a word within the time limit; some may say 'Alcohol', some 'Alcove', and a few will give some other response.

Cued recall is illustrated by the fact that subjects will behave quite differently if they have recently read a list of words including, say, 'Alcove'. They will then give this word almost unanimously in response to the instruction above.

Notice that cued recall refers to a measurement of memory, namely the effect of an acquisition list containing 'Alcove' on a subsequent retention test, which as it happens consists of a guessing game. The strength of cued recall does not reflect the subject's ability to guess, but the subject's ability to benefit from prior experience. As in any other memory task, the difficulty of recall can be increased by increasing the retention interval between acquisition and test; the number of errors, that is, failures to give the word from the acquisition list, will then increase.

Amnesics have been shown to perform either as well as control subjects, or very nearly as well, in a variety of cued recall tasks. This is not simply because the task is easy, since in many cases the control subjects have made a substantial proportion of errors. The cues used have been not only the first three letters, as just described, but also semantic cues and rhyming cues (see Weiskrantz and Warrington 1975, for a review of this work).

The importance of these findings is best explained by returning to the tasks that do demonstrate an amnesic impairment. In a recognition memory task or a free recall task the amnesic reads a list of words at acquisition and subsequently retention is at very low levels in both tasks. The simplest explanation seems to lie in the commonsense notion that reading a word, like any other event, leaves a trace of itself in the subject's memory; that the trace can subsequently be used for various different kinds of memory task; and that the patient with a bad memory does not have the trace. However, exactly the same events take place at acquisition in a cued recall task, namely, the subject reads a list of words; but when memory is measured in this way, no amnesic deficit is found. The simple explanation just mentioned must be modified in one of two ways:

(1) One might suppose that the amnesic subject does have the trace of the word 'Alcove', but that accessing or making use of that trace in free recall requires a retrieval process which is disrupted in amnesia; whereas the presentation of a cue accesses the trace directly, obviating any retrieval difficulties. The problem here is how to explain the impairment in recognition memory. It seems that presentation of the word 'Alcove' itself in a retention test must also provide direct access to the trace, if presentation of 'ALC' does; yet the amnesic subject is unable to recognize as recently presented a word he is able to recall in response to a cue.
(2) More plausibly, one might abandon the supposition that memory of an event is represented by a unitary trace of that event. Perhaps reading a word produces a change in two or more different memory stores in the brain, not all of which are disturbed in amnesia. This suggestion implies that when a subject recognizes a previously presented word in a recognition memory test, he is not using the same trace as when he gives that word in response to a cue.

Digit Span

Digit span is defined as the number of digits, in the numerical sense, that a subject can repeat immediately without error after one demonstration. For example, a subject with a digit span of five will be able to repeat the sequences 43897 or 58612 but will sometimes make a mistake with longer sequences such as 174893. The sequence is spoken once by the tester and the subject must repeat it as soon as the tester stops.

All amnesics have a normal digit span. Drachman and Arbit (1966) presented digit strings of varying length to amnesic and control subjects; if an error was made after a string had been presented once, that same string was presented again until it was repeated with no errors, the number of presentations required defining the 'trials to criterion' for that string. The string length that was learned in just one trial, that is to say the digit span, was the same for amnesic as for control subjects. But as the length was increased above span, the amnesics required many more trials to reach criterion than the control subjects did. Drachman and Arbit concluded that amnesic patients' short-term memory for digits was intact, while their long-term memory for the same material was impaired.

An apparently similar experiment, but with important differences, was reported by Baddeley and Warrington (1970). They presented the same eight-digit list ten times, requiring immediate recall on each occasion; but the presentations were separated by tests of other eight-digit lists which were each newly constituted. The purpose of this procedure is to study unintentional learning, since subjects are not told, and typically do not apprehend, that any lists are being repeated. A gradual improvement in recall of the critical list was observed in Baddeley and Warrington's experiment, and the amnesics' performance was indistinguishable from the control subjects'. This result indicates, contrary to Drachman and Arbit's conclusion, that in some circumstances long-term memory for digit strings can be unimpaired in amnesia. Probably the crucial difference between the two experiments is the knowledge that a list is going to be tested again, which would promote complex learning strategies as opposed to simple facilitation by repetition.

Distraction in Short-Term Memory

Baddeley and Warrington (1970) conducted the following experiment on short-term verbal forgetting. The subject was presented briefly with three words to remember, and was then immediately plunged into a distracting task to prevent rehearsal. After different amounts of time on different trials (each using a new set of words), the distracting task stopped and the subject was asked to recall the three words. The probability of recall declined systematically with increasing time on the distracting task; but at all intervals up to the longest tested, which was 60 s, the amnesics' recall was as good as the control subjects'.

Baddeley and Warrington argued from this result that short-term memory, as opposed to long-term memory, was intact in amnesics. One problem with this formulation is that amnesics' performance was unimpaired even at 60 s by which time the performance of both groups had fallen to an apparently stable level of recall. One might suppose that if a sharp distinction is to be drawn between short- and long-term memory, performance at long delays should reflect a long-term memory component as well as a much reduced short-term component. If so then the hypothesis that amnesics are impaired in long-term but not in short-term memory might be taken to predict that an amnesic impairment would gradually appear as the retention interval lengthened. Although the theoretical issues raised by the distinction between short- and long-term memory are complex and controversial (see Deutsch and Deutsch 1975), it is at least clear that Baddeley and Warrington's group of amnesics were totally unimpaired in this task.

A different result has been reported by Butters and Cermak (1975). Using essentially the same task but with a different group of amnesics, they found that after 18 s of distraction recall was significantly better in control subjects than in a group of amnesics. However, one individual amnesic performed just as well as controls; Butters and Cermak suggested that this patient alone of their subjects resembled Baddeley and Warrington's amnesics.

Two views might be taken of this discrepancy. First, it might be suggested that Baddeley and Warrington's amnesics were pure amnesics whereas Butters and Cermak's amnesics were also somewhat demented in general. Secondly, it might be suggested that Butters and Cermak's amnesics were typical amnesics, whereas Baddeley and Warrington's amnesics had an unusually high ability (for amnesics) to maintain memory in the face of distraction. In either case it seems that this short-term memory task is one that is not necessarily disrupted in amnesia.

SUMMARY

What is the fundamental defect which gives rise to the memory impairment of amnesics? Very many different proposals have been made, and some have been so closely argued that it is impossible to do justice to them in a brief overview. The interested reader is referred to reviews by Baddeley (1975), Butters and Cermak (1975), and Weiskrantz and Warrington (1975).

At a less ambitious theoretical level, there are some similarities discernible among the tasks that do not show an amnesic impairment. Consider first the recall tasks at which amnesics fail most spectacularly: free recall of lists of words, short stories, and day-to-day events. These are all very complex memory performances, in the following sense.

First, the processes of retrieval at the retention test make use of serial thought, passing through several stages to arrive at the answer, and this is reflected in relatively long response latencies. If you are asked unexpectedly what you ate for supper last night, it may take you a little while to answer, during which time you will perhaps find it necessary to think about certain subsidiary questions such as what you were doing yesterday afternoon, where you spent the evening, and so on. More formally, studies of free recall of lists of words have recently emphasized the complexity of the retrieval process (for review see Wickelgren 1977, pp. 396 ff). It is necessary in such recall to suppress words that have already been recalled, to apply to the list various criteria of organization (the temporal order of the words, their relations of meaning, and so on), and to switch strategies of recall during pauses of output when one strategy has dried up. Free recall seems to be a fine example of sequential thought, using many different aspects of memory capacity at different stages; as such it is perhaps all the more theoretically uninformative as a task which reveals a memory impairment, since an overall deficit might be the result of a deficit in any of the sub-processes involved.

Secondly, free recall is also complicated in the processes taking place at the time of acquisition. The subject is allowed time to think of the relations between items or events, and to build up the complex memory structures needed later for retrieval.

By contrast, the tasks at which amnesics are not impaired are much simpler. In a motor skill such as rotary pursuit or fast tapping, the performance required leaves little time for complex encoding or retrieval strategies. In cued recall, the cue rapidly elicits a single item. In a digit span test the items are presented rapidly and the question is not whether the subject can subsequently elaborate them into a structure for later recall, but whether they can be immediately repeated. In the short-term distraction task, the subject is plunged into distraction without being given time for complex encoding. In all these cases the correct response at the retention test is retrieved quickly, if at all.

Aspects of these differences in complexity between tasks at which amnesics are and are not impaired have been invoked by several theorists. Warrington and Weiskrantz (1975) have suggested that the amnesic impairment is seen when a retrieval process must select one from many alternatives, and is much reduced when the candidates for retrieval are few. Talland (1965) suggested also that amnesics' fundamental impairment was in complex retrieval strategies. Butters and Cermak (1975) argue that at the time when a memory is acquired amnesics tend to employ less complex encoding. Similarly Wickelgren (1977, pp. 325 ff) argues that amnesics treat items one by one adequately but are incapable of encoding them into a higher-order organization by forming 'new chunk nodes'. Gaffan (1976) suggests that the fundamental deficit of amnesics is in recognition memory, and that complex recall makes use of recognition memory in a way that simple associative tasks do not. This list of theories is not complete.

NEUROPATHOLOGY IN AMNESIA

What evidence is available suggests that amnesia is caused by bilateral destruction of either: (i) medial temporal structures including the hippocampus (Scoville and Milner 1957); or (ii) the mammillary nuclei (Brion 1968); or (iii) the fornix, which is a pathway connecting (i) with (ii) (Hassler and Riechert 1957; Brion, Pragier, Guérin and Teitgen 1969; Heilman and Sypert 1977). The evidence for this generalization, although generally accepted, is by no means conclusive (Horel 1978). For example, Gardia-Bengochea *et al.* (1954) briefly reported that they had severed the fornix in a group of severely epileptic patients and observed no neurological or mental effects. However, such negative evidence should be treated cautiously. In the first place, no post-mortem evidence was available to confirm that the fornix had indeed been sectioned bilaterally. In the second place, it is not impossible that the memory of the patients was impaired but that they were so seriously ill that the impairment was not noticed. Lest this seem unlikely, it should be pointed out that Scoville (Scoville and Milner 1957) made bilateral medial temporal lobe ablations in a group of 30 patients of whom 25, in whom the hippocampus had been ablated, were later found to be amnesic; but they were so ill that the amnesia was not noticed at first.

However, it should not be supposed that all patients diagnosed as amnesic suffer from exactly the same symptoms and from effectively equivalent brain damage. Some disagreements in the literature have been pointed out above (under 'Very Old Memories' and 'Distraction in Short-Term Memory'). One clinician's typical amnesic may be also suffering from general dementia by the standards of another clinician, and the latter's pure amnesic may be atypically unimpaired in some respects by the standards of the former. Lhermitte and Signoret (1972) pointed out, moreover, that groups of patients all diagnosed as amnesic, but with different aetiologies, showed qualitatively different patterns of impairment in a range of memory tests. Whatever the clinical usefulness of the concept of the amnesic syndrome, one needs to know in detail what mental impairments follow from what brain damage; and this is difficult to establish from the clinical literature, since post-mortem neuropathological evidence is very rarely available. For these and other reasons it is necessary to supplement the information about human amnesics with data gathered from behavioural tests of animals with brain damage produced experimentally.

MEMORY IMPAIRMENT IN MONKEYS

Orbach, Milner and Rasmussen (1960) trained two groups of monkeys in a variety of learning tasks. One group was a control group and the other had medial temporal lobe lesions similar to those which had produced amnesia in patients (Scoville and Milner 1957). One task was designed, according to Orbach *et al.*, to mimic the essential features of the tasks that demonstrate a substantial impairment in human amnesics. On each trial the monkey had to choose between two objects, a faucet knob and a 35 mm film cassette. The faucet knob always covered a peanut, the cassette never. Between trials of this task a distracting task was presented. The result was that the brain-damaged monkeys learned as fast as the controls. This experiment and others like it have sometimes been taken to indicate that lesions of the hippocampal system in animals do not produce an equivalent of the amnesic syndrome (Kimble 1968; Horel 1978).

However, in view of the preceding discussion of human amnesia, it is not clear that simple associative tasks of that kind are closely similar to the recall tasks at which amnesics are grossly impaired. Applying the analogy drawn by Orbach *et al.* in the opposite direction, Gaffan (1972) trained a human amnesic on a learning task with a choice between two objects, one of which was rewarded. The task was learned in 19 trials, and a second task of the same type was learned in two trials.

One human memory task that is easily adapted for use with animals is the recognition memory test. A monkey will readily learn to perform according to the rule, 'when given a choice between two objects, choose the one that has been already presented once'. Once that rule has been learned it is possible to give acquisition lists of objects and to test memory for those objects by pairing them with new objects; the ability to choose consistently the old objects over the new objects indicates that the old objects have been remembered. This task is known as delayed matching to sample.

There are other tasks that are also analogous to recognition memory tests. Perhaps the closest analogy is recognition memory for pictures, where a monkey can be taught to press a panel when a familiar picture – one that has been presented before – is seen, but not to press in response to a new picture appearing for the first time.

The effect of bilateral fornix transection has been tested in several different versions of such recognition memory tasks. In all of them the fornix-transected monkeys showed an impairment (Gaffan 1974, 1977a, 1977b; Gaffan and Weiskrantz, in preparation). For example, in picture recognition the intact monkeys were able to recognize a picture as having been presented before even in the hardest version of the task, when up to 18 pictures were presented in between the first and second presentations of a test picture; but after fornix transection they failed in a much easier version, with only 2.7 intervening pictures on average.

By contrast, the fornix-transected monkeys were not impaired in a different test that required associative memory rather than recognition memory (Gaffan, 1974). In the associative task the monkeys were required to recall at each retention test whether the presented object, which was in all cases one that had been already presented once, had been rewarded or not at its first presentation. Thus, if a fornix-transected monkey is presented with an acquisition list of objects, some rewarded and some not, his memory for that list is normal if it is subsequently tested by requiring him to discriminate the objects that were rewarded from those that were not, but is impaired if it is tested by requiring him to discriminate the objects that were presented from a new set that were not (Gaffan and Weiskrantz, in preparation). This dissociation is further evidence for the suggestion made above in the discussion of cued recall in human amnesics: that instead of thinking of the memory of an event as a single trace of that event, we should think of an event producing several different traces in specialized memory stores, not all of which are necessarily impaired when memory is disordered.

REFERENCES

Baddeley, A. D. 1975. 'Theories of amnesia.' In A. Kennedy and A. Wilkes (eds) *Studies in long term memory*. London: John Wiley.

Baddeley, A. D., and Warrington, E. K. 1970. 'Amnesia and the distinction between long- and short-term memory.' *J. verb. Learn. verb. Behav. 9*, 176 – 89.

Brion, S. 1968. 'Aspects anatomo-pathologiques des amnésies.' *Int. J. Neurol. 7*, 31 – 43.

Brion, S., Pragier, G., Guérin, R., and Mme Teitgen 1969. 'Syndrome de Korsakoff par ramollissement bilatéral du fornix.' *Revue Neurologique 120*, 255 – 62.

Butters, N., and Cermak, L. 1975. 'Some analyses of amnesic syndromes in brain-damaged patients.' In R. L. Isaacson and K. H. Pribram (eds) *The Hippocampus II*. New York and London: Plenum Press.

Corkin, S. 1968. 'Acquisition of motor skill after bilateral medial temporal-lobe excision.' *Neuropsychologia 6*, 255 – 65.

Deutsch, D. and Deutsch, J. A. (eds) 1975. *Short-term memory*. New York: Academic Press.

Drachman, D. A., and Arbit, J. 1966. 'Memory and the hippocampal complex.' *Arch. Neurol. 15*, 52 – 61.

Gaffan, D. 1972. 'Loss of recognition memory in rats with lesions of the fornix.' *Neuropsychologia 10*, 327 – 41.

Gaffan, D. 1974. 'Recognition impaired and association intact in the memory of monkeys after transection of the fornix.' *J. comp. physiol. Psychol. 86*, 1100 – 9.

Gaffan, D. 1976. 'Recognition memory in animals.' In J. Brown (ed.) *Recognition and recall*. London: John Wiley.

Gaffan, D. 1977a. 'Monkeys' recognition memory for complex pictures and the effect of fornix transection.' *Quart. J. exp. Psychol. 29*, 505 – 14.

Gaffan, D. 1977b. 'Recognition memory after short retention intervals in fornix-transected monkeys.' *Quart. J. exp. Psychol. 29*, 577 – 88.

Gaffan, D., and Weiskrantz, L. (in press). 'Recency effects and lesion effects in delayed non-matching to randomly baited samples by monkeys.' *Brain Research*.

Garcia-Bengochea, F., Delattore, D., Esquivel, O., Vieta, K., and Claudio, F. 1954. 'The section of the fornix in the treatment of certain epilepsies.' *Trans. Amer. Neurol. Assoc. 79*, 176 – 8.

Hassler, R., and Riechert, T. 1957. 'Über einen Fall von doppelseitiger Fornicotomie bei sogenannter temporaler Epilepsie.' *Acta Neurochirurgica 5*, 330 – 40.

Heilman, K. M., and Sypert, G. W. 1977. 'Korsakoff's syndrome resulting from bilateral fornix lesions.' *Neurology 27*, 490 – 3.

Horel, J. A. 1978. 'The neuroanatomy of amnesia: a critique of the hippocampal memory hypothesis.' *Brain 101*, 403 – 45.

Kimble, D. P. 1968. 'Hippocampus and internal inhibition.' *Psychol. Bull. 70*, 285 – 95.

Lhermitte, F., and Signoret, J.-L. 1972. 'Analyse neuropsychologique et différentiation des syndromes amnésiques.' *Revue Neurologique 126*, 161 – 78.

Marslen-Wilson, W. D., and Teuber, H. -L. 1975. 'Memory for remote events in anterograde amnesia: recognition of public figures from news photographs.' *Neuropsychologia 13*, 353 – 64.
Milner, B. 1962. 'Les troubles de la mémoire accompagnant des lésions hippocampiques bilatérales.' In *Physiologie de l'Hippocampe*. Paris: Centre National de la Recherche Scientifique.
Orbach, J., Milner, B., and Rasmussen, T. 1960. 'Learning and retention in monkeys after amygdala-hippocampus resection.' *Arch. Neurol. 3*, 230 – 51.
Sanders, H. I., and Warrington, E. K. 1971. 'Memory for remote events in amnesic patients.' *Brain 94*, 661 – 8.
Scoville, W. B., and Milner, B. 1957. 'Loss of recent memory after bilateral hippocampal lesion.' *J. Neurol. Neurosurg. Psychiat. 20*, 11 – 21.
Starr, A., and Phillips, L. 1970. 'Verbal and motor memory in the amnestic syndrome.' *Neuropsychologia 8*, 75 – 88.
Talland, G. A. 1965. *Deranged memory: a psychonomic study of the amnesic syndrome*. New York: Academic Press.
Warrington, E. K. 1974. 'Deficient recognition memory in organic amnesia.' *Cortex 10*, 289 – 91.
Warrington, E. K., and Weiskrantz, L. 1968. 'A study of learning and retention in amnesic patients.' *Neuropsychologia 6*, 283 – 91.
Weiskrantz, L., and Warrington, E. K. 1975. 'The problem of the amnesic syndrome in man and animals.' In R. L. Isaacson and K. H. Pribram (eds) *The Hippocampus II*. New York and London: Plenum Press.
Wickelgren, W. A. 1977. *Learning and memory*. New Jersey: Prentice-Hall.

Chapter 5

Acquired Disorders of Language

JOHN C. MARSHALL

Acquired disorders of language are so diverse in both character and severity that little other than their underlying pathology – damage to the brain – may seem to link them together. It will be helpful to have in mind the range of disorders one is likely to meet and is attempting to understand. We therefore begin with ten examples of aphasic language:

(1) A man is asked the question, 'Who is running the store now?' He replies, 'I don't know. Yes, the bick, uh, yes I would say that the mick daysis nosis or chpickters. Course, I have also missed on the carfter teck. Do you know what that is? I've, uh, token to ingish. They have been toast sosilly. They'd have been put to myafa and made palis and, uh, myadakal senda you. That is me alordisdus. That makes anacronous senda' (Buckingham and Kertesz 1976).

(2) A Russian man is describing a movie that he has recently seen. He says (in translation), '... Po-li-ceman ... ah! ... I know! ... cashier ... money ... ah! ... cigarettes ... I know ... this guy ... beer ... moustache ... ah ... money ... Mikalai ... ah ... suit ... diver ... ah ... a mask ... a light ... ah ... up ... came ... the girl ... ' (Luria 1970).

(3) A complex, representational picture (a reproduction of a Breughel) is placed in front of a man who is then asked to describe it. He does so in the following terms, 'That's the ... you know, the ... very much like they got on the ... on something very much. I don't say that it's the proper one but it's like er er ... I can't say it but I can just ... yes, that could be it, could be a bit like that, yes. No, I wasn't thinking of that one, not at that time. I wasn't, no' (Marshall 1977).

(4) A man is asked to put his little finger in his left ear. He promptly puts his thumb in his mouth (Pieron 1927).

(5) A Frenchman is blindfolded and given a box of matches to hold and manipulate. He is asked to say what he is holding, and replies,

'Des cigarettes'. With his eyes open he names the object correctly (Beauvois, Saillant, Meininger and Lhermitte 1978).

(6) A German man is asked to write to dictation the word 'Onkel' (meaning 'uncle'). He writes *Grossvater* (grandfather). Asked to write 'schon' ('already'), he writes *niemals* (never). Given 'gestern' ('yesterday'), *morgen* (morning) is his response (Peuser 1978).

(7) A man speaks fluently and correctly. He writes well, both spontaneously and to dictation; he can also copy writing quite accurately. When asked, after a brief interval, to read back what he has himself written, he is quite unable to do so (Holmes 1950).

(8) A woman has virtually no spontaneous speech or comprehension of language. She has a pronounced echolalia; that is, she frequently repeats back what was said to her. Some examples follow (Whitaker 1976):

Examiner: 'Can you told me your name?'
Patient: 'Can you tell me your name?'

Examiner: 'She take singing lessons.'
Patient: 'She takes singing lessons.'

Examiner: 'Have you dinner?'
Patient: 'Have you had dinner?'

(9) The following conversation takes place (Symonds 1953):

Examiner: 'What was your work?'
Patient: 'I was an expert in the building trade.'
Examiner: 'What is trade?'
Patient: 'Trade? What's trade? What is that word? I don't know.'

(10) A man is asked to read aloud the isolated word ABROAD that has been placed in front of him. Fairly promptly he responds, 'overseas.' Asked to indicate how sure he is that his response was correct, he says, 'Hundred per cent' (Marshall and Newcombe 1966).

The people whose behaviour is described above have very little in common with one another, apart from the fact that each has, as an adult, sustained cerebral damage. Prior to the onset of organic brain disease or trauma, their relevant neurological development and status was within normal limits; their pre-morbid language development and mature skill was, at very least, consistent with their either normal or, in some cases, high general intellectual and educational level.

APPROACHES

The acquired aphasias that these patients manifest are of considerable interest and concern to a wide variety of people.

The Patient

First and foremost among the interested parties is the patient him- (or her-) self. Many, but not all, aphasic patients are quite aware of their disabilities, as aware as you or I are of our limited command over a foreign language that we know but dimly. Elvin and Oldfield (1951) describe a young man with a deep penetrating injury to the left temporal area who, 'on becoming aware of his surroundings . . . thought that he must be in a foreign country as speech had no meaning.'

In many patients, intelligence and volition are relatively well preserved. As Zangwill (1969) writes, ' . . . There is no clear relation between severity of language disorder and severity of intellectual loss.' It is, thus, hardly surprising that shock and frustration should initially dominate the patient's emotions. A number of people who have made an excellent recovery from severe aphasia have later written books or papers on their struggles to regain normal functioning. These self-descriptions often show a keener (and certainly a different) insight into aphasic problems than many more academic works. A book by Scott Moss (1972), revealingly entitled *Recovery with aphasia*, is highly recommended. Another valuable book, by David Knox (1971), recounts the very partial recovery of his wife, showing how, even with limited production and comprehension, the sufferer can learn to cope well with matters of everyday living and an active social life. In *Stroke*, Dahlberg, a doctor, and Jaffe, a neurolinguist, have collaborated to tell both the personal and the 'professional' story of Dahlberg's recovery from a cerebro-vascular accident (Dahlberg and Jaffe 1977).

The question of the patient's awareness of his condition is obviously relevant to planning for rehabilitation. For reasons that are not well understood, 'jargon' aphasics (some spontaneous speech from such a patient was presented in Example 1) are particularly prone to lack insight into their disability. Rochford (1974) has reported on a man whose object-naming to visual confrontation included the following responses:

Pencil → 'A bit kund – a name I use for me perk er persian.'
Angel → 'What do we call her, a girl from an opium set.'
Castle → 'Trunden ben.'

When the patient was asked if he had any difficulty finding words, he replied, 'No, none at all. I come out of my speak-making to everything like that, quite, quite, comfortably, thank you.'

The above reaction may be compared with the response of a patient with Broca's aphasia (Example 2 was from another case of this type) who has been asked why he is in hospital and what has happened to him. 'Arm no good . . . speech . . . can't say . . . talk, you see (. . .). Head fall, Jesus Christ, me no good, str, str . . . oh Jesus . . . stroke' (Gardner 1974). His speech is greatly disturbed but thought and affect are obviously appropriate to the appalling situation in which he finds himself.

The Neurologist and Neurosurgeon

The patient will come (with some rapidity, one hopes) to the attention of a neurologist and, perhaps, a neurosurgeon. The neurologist will be concerned with diagnosing the nature and extent of the damage, and with deciding what can be done to stabilize and improve the patient's condition. Some of the more common causes of damage include cerebrovascular accident ('stroke'), closed head injuries (as sustained, for example, in car accidents), penetrating missile injuries and brain tumour or abscess. The last four of these conditions will frequently require neurosurgical intervention; vascular disease may also demand such treatment.

The neurologist's concern with such variables as the nature, size, depth, and *location* of the injury leads to the discovery that in the vast majority of cases it is a left-hemisphere injury that provokes language disorder. The most striking counterexample to this claim is to be found in the left-handed, some 30% of whom may show aphasia after right-hemisphere injury. The comparable figure for right-handers is probably no more than 1%. It is also the case that the particular patterns of linguistic loss and retention that left-handed subjects display after brain damage is often unclassifiable in terms of the traditional aphasia taxonomies (Gloning 1977). In right-handers with left-hemisphere damage there is a strong tendency for fluent (Wernicke's) aphasias to be correlated with posterior (Bogen and Bogen 1976) and non-fluent (Broca's) with anterior damage (Mohr 1976). No simple dichotomy emerges in left-handed subjects (Benson 1967). It is also possible that in both left-handers and in right-handers with close relatives who are left-handed, the severity of aphasia is milder and the prognosis better than in the purely right-handed population (Luria 1970). All of this suggests that in a substantial proportion of left-handers the neural substrate for language is less focalized within a hemisphere and tends towards a more bilateral representation between hemispheres. McGlone (1977) has recently presented some very interesting evidence that the above conclusion may also be true of women, although Kertesz and McCabe (1977) did not find sex differences in recovery rates from aphasia. Newcombe and Ratcliff (1978) review, thoughtfully, the vexed question of putative biological determinants of sex-differences in higher cognitive functioning.

Of all controversies that have generated more heat than light, the issue of the 'localization of language' must stand supreme. I have, in the preceding paragraphs, already begged a number of important theoretical questions about the neural substrate for language skills. What are the 'facts'? It is not in dispute that (most) patients with relatively focal damage can be placed within a (fairly) well-defined set of diagnostic categories (Kertesz and Phipps 1977) on the basis of their pattern of performance with respect to fluency in spontaneous speech, their comprehension, repetition, and naming ability, and the information content of their speech (Goodglass and Kaplan 1972). Neither is it in dispute that there is a (fairly) good correlation between the type of aphasia (the symptom-complex) that the patient displays and the primary locus of the damage (Naeser and Hayward 1978). Similar conclusions apply to some at least of the so-called 'pure' language disorders. There is little doubt but that a fairly small, discrete lesion, appropriately placed, can lead to a gross impairment of one particular language skill with striking preservation of many other linguistic and cognitive abilities (Geschwind 1974). The condition known as 'alexia without agraphia' described in Example 7 is a good illustration of such a phenomenon. Another example would be a pure agraphia that cannot be interpreted in terms of a relatively peripheral motoric deficit (Rosati and Bastiani 1979). That subjects who have suffered massive and widespread cerebral damage (due, for example, to occlusion of the middle cerebral artery) show impairments of all linguistic skills is not, of course, in conflict with the above claims (Schuell 1974). The association of widespread damage with widespread disability is consistent with just about *any* claim concerning the structural organization of the brain.

The issue then is not whether 'localization of symptoms' (to borrow Hughlings Jackson's term) is possible. It often is. Rather the point is whether or not one can infer in any straightforward way from localization of symptoms to localization of functions. Does the existence of symptom-complexes and specific impairments imply that the brain is, 'a collection of more or less independent apparatus connected to one another by cables' (Lenneberg 1973)? Does loss of a particular ability after injury to a particular locus imply that the ability 'resides' in that locus?

Consider the phenomenon of word-finding difficulties – an illustration of the disorder has been given in Example 3. Word-finding deficits of many different types can be produced by a wide variety of focal and diffuse forms of brain damage (Geschwind 1967). However, severe anomia to confrontation naming which is not restricted to a single modality and includes word-finding difficulties in spontaneous speech with relatively well-preserved comprehension and repetition of speech is often associated with injuries in the region of the angular gyrus. Anatomically, this sounds reasonable as the angular gyrus is often regarded – on the basis of its position and pattern of connectivity to other areas – as an 'association area of association areas'. But does the correlation of local damage and behavioural impairment show that, 'nouns live in the angular gyrus'? Or is it rather that effective retrieval strategies are perturbed by such damage? Or that conceptual or semantic input to the 'mental dictionary' is blocked? In other words, the mere association of deficit and damage does not carry its own, unique interpretation with it. An excellent discussion of some of the problems involved in 'functional localization' can be found in Von Eckardt Klein (1978). The manifest conceptual difficulties of interpreting impaired behaviour in terms of localization of functions can easily tempt one into assuming that the localization of *symptoms* is unproblematic. Such an impression will rapidly be dispelled by reading Oppenheimer and Newcombe (1978) and Naeser and Hayward (1979).

The Speech Therapist

Many victims of aphasia recover a reasonable degree of communicative competence; many do not. I have already mentioned some possible correlates of prognosis (handedness and perhaps sex); others include the age of the patient, his general health, and, of course, the aetiology and extent of the injury itself. It is even possible that the magnitude of the gross anatomical asymmetries that are found for certain 'language areas' of the cortex may be correlated with the likelihood of good recovery (Geschwind, Galaburda and LeMay 1979). There are now a number of useful papers that provide some indication of the likely course of spontaneous recovery from aphasia (see Prins, Snow and Wagenaar 1978; Lomas and Kertesz 1978; Newcombe, Hiorns, Marshall and Adams 1975, and the references therein). Some trends do seem to be reproducible from one study to another: the greatest improvement takes place in the first six months post-onset, traumatic cases recover better than vascular cases, remission of other aspects of the symptom-complex often leaves the patient with residual anomic deficits in spontaneous speech. Beyond these generalizations, however, the picture that emerges is frankly one of total confusion. There is, for example, no real agreement in the literature on the seemingly simple question of whether the prognosis for expressive skills is better or worse than that for comprehension. The sheer range of individual variation, the number of parameters involved and the nature of their interaction has so far precluded the emergence of any further meaningful and reliable generalizations. There are no (published) studies of individual patients that provide enough detailed and sophisticated information for one to see any real patterns of functional recovery and reorganization. But reliable information about the time course and structure of remission would be of crucial theoretical importance and should also constrain rehabilitation possibilities and therapeutic interventions. A volume edited by Johns (1978) provides a good up-to-date account of the clinical management of a variety of language and speech disorders.

Evidence for the efficacy of most current speech therapeutic regimes is, to put it at its best, equivocal. In so far as controlled studies with groups of reasonable size are possible, either ethically, practically, or scientifically, there is very little data which indicates that treated patients differ from untreated in either speed of recovery or relative degree and scope of residual impairment (Sarno, Silverman and Sands 1970). In those instances where intensive therapy does seem to have had a beneficial effect (see Lebrun and Hoops 1976), the reasons for the improvement are far from clear. It is difficult to disentangle the effects of 'general stimulation' and 'psychological support' from those of a more technical nature, having to do with the actual content of therapy. And indeed there are incredibly few studies that even bother to specify, however vaguely, the form and content of therapy. There are a small number of relevant experimental studies, but these typically commit the opposite sin of failing to specify the extent of generalization from specifically 'trained' items to communicative competence outside the training situation.

It is, however, worth mentioning a couple of particularly interesting reports. Sparks and Holland (1976) have described a technique – Melodic Intonation Therapy – that seems to hold considerable promise in the remediation of severe expressive deficits in patients with fair comprehension. And Beyn and Shokhor-Trotskaya (1966) have shown how certain agrammatical deficits may be prevented by appropriate manipulation of the verbal environment in the immediate post-onset period. The student who wishes to enter this literature should begin by reading Darley (1972) and the volume edited by Lebrun and Hoops (1976). Hatfield and Zangwill (1975) have shown, most encouragingly, that a very adequate level of occupational resettlement is sometimes possible despite strong clinical and psychometric counter-indications. Further encouragement is provided by the very careful study of Basso, Capitani and Vignolo (1979) which does show significant gains consequent upon therapy. None the less, the only fairly safe generalizations so far are that therapy should be started as soon as possible and that it should be intensive. Some idea of what the notion 'intensive' really means can be gained by reading Farrell's book *Pat and Roald* (1969). In 1965 Patricia Neal suffered three massive brain hemorrhages; in 1968 she resumed her career as an actress.

The Linguist

It might seem too obvious to mention that linguists could both have a theoretical interest in disorders of language and could contribute to an accurate analysis of the patient's problems. Yet with the notable exception of the work of Roman Jakobson (1941), it is only within the last decade that linguists have given serious attention to the topic.

The point of a linguistic description can be best conveyed by a simple example: Imagine that you notice that a patient produces utterances like, 'He cook dinner', where his (premorbid) dialect would lead you to expect, 'He cooks dinner'. Why should this be? You guess that the patient is having articulatory or phonetic difficulties with the sound /s/. But he has no problem with saying, 'She lost her purse', where the last noun also ends in /s/. The next guess, then, might be that the deficit lies in the domain of inflectional morphology. How will the patient cope with, 'We have five cats', where 'cats' also ends in /s/ but is marking number agreement on a noun, not person agreement on a verb? What will happen with, 'The cat's in the kitchen' where the /s/ is now the contracted form of the verb 'is'? And with, 'The cat's dinner is in the kitchen' where /s/ is marking possessive case?

The point is that any language element can be described on a large number of different levels; in order to discover which level(s) is (are) impaired one must vary aspects of the structure while attempting to keep other components constant. Useful discussions of this issue, with examples drawn from a variety of patients (and languages), can be found in Myerson and Goodglass (1972), Marshall (1977) and Kean (1978). Kean's analysis of Broca's aphasia is the most explicit attempt so far to interpret a traditional symptom-complex in terms of an independently motivated level of grammatical representation (Kean 1980); this demonstration that the representations provided by phonological constituent structure appropriately partition the preserved and 'lost' elements in Broca's aphasia should prompt further re-analyses of other major syndromes.

The 'bedrock' of linguistic studies of the aphasias is to be found in articulatory and acoustic phonetics, and in phonemic and subphonemic analysis, disciplines that on a descriptive level at least are fairly firm. For any aphasic patient whose spontaneous speech contains phonological paraphasias, or whose comprehension betrays a disorder of phonetic 'hearing' one will want an inventory of the particular sounds that cause the most difficulty. A full error-analysis (in terms of both phonemes and distinctive features) and a 'confusion-matrix' of substitutions will often begin to reveal particular patterns of deviation in, for example, features of place, manner, nasality, and voicing. Blumstein (1973) provides a useful introduction to the analysis of aphasic speech at the level of segmental phonology; evidence is presented that suggests a hierarchical dissolution of feature contrasts with strong asymmetries in the direction of substitution errors between closely related sounds. Schnitzer (1972) is an interesting attempt to apply some of the technical apparatus of generative phonology (for example, the notion of ordered derivational rules) to the mispronounciations of an individual patient. Buckingham, Avakian-Whitaker and Whitaker (1978) have analysed some striking examples of alliteration and assonance in jargon aphasia; they argue that such gross perseverative phenomena are inconsistent with the standard account of the syndrome in which phonological paraphasias arise *after* a target word has been internally generated.

Can we see regularities in the breakdown of semantic structure also?

Consider the man in Example 4: Would he confuse body parts in spontaneous speech as he does in comprehension? Would other semantic fields show a similar pattern of within-class substitution? Dennis (1976) has reported on a 17 year-old girl who, subsequent to left temporal lobectomy for relief of long standing seizures, showed a far greater impairment in both the naming and comprehension of body parts than for the parts of other objects (for example trees, bicycles, or houses). The girl's comprehension errors include: 'wrist'→*elbow*, 'wrist'→ *shoulder*, and 'wrist'→*upper arm*, where → is to be read as 'points to'. Yamadori and Albert (1973) have discussed a related case, a man of 54 with a degree in engineering who had been involved in an automobile accident. This man's naming deficits were equally severe across all the categories tested, but his comprehension was particularly impaired for body parts and 'room objects'. He had more difficulty in pointing out walls, doors, windows, lights, chairs and tables than he did with 'external' objects such as a church, an automobile, a hydrant, and a street. And this despite the fact that he could repeat and spell the words for which he showed 'word-meaning deafness'. (Example 9 was from another case of this putative syndrome.) Conversely, McKenna and Warrington (1978) have reported on a severely anomic patient in whom the ability to deal with the category 'names of countries' was remarkably well-preserved.

The Clinical Psychologist

If it is to the linguist that we turn for a fine-grained analysis of the language disorder itself, it is the clinical psychologist, in collaboration with the neurologist, who, by virtue of training and experience, is best placed to give us an overall picture of the patient's impaired and preserved behavioural capacities.

The patient with frontal injuries will frequently have motoric deficits, sometimes extending to a gross hemiplegia; occipital injuries will often result in visual field deficits and other more subtle alterations of visual functioning; temporal damage may result in hearing loss (cortical deafness), parietal damage in sensory loss. When we suspect a 'pure' modality-specific aphasia (alexia without agraphia, 'word-deafness', tactile anomia and so forth), the first question to be answered is whether or not the perceptual (or pre-perceptual) impairment is sufficient to explain the condition without invoking the idea of a more central but still modality-specific *language* disorder. If we suspect a colour-*naming* deficit, can we rule out, by non-verbal tests of colour discrimination, an underlying defect of colour perception? Although the very existence of 'pure' aphasias is still disputed, there do seem to be cases that are difficult to explain without such 'disconnectionist' notions (see the discussion in Geschwind 1974). One should note, however, that 'pure' does *not* mean that the patient shows absolutely no other impairment than, say, an inability to name objects presented in one modality; rather, the idea should be interpreted to mean that whatever other deficits the patient does show are not sufficient (or necessary?) to explain the symptom in question. But we are now forced to admit that observation and theory are inextricably intertwined; the data take their place within an account of the *mechanism* that we believe is implicated in the particular performance in question.

Similar remarks apply to the interpretation of major symptom-complexes. The patient with Broca's aphasia, where the symptoms include agrammatism, will frequently have slow, laborious and misarticulated speech. Can the agrammatism – the tendency to leave out function words and inflectional endings – be understood as a simple consequence of the patient trying to minimize his 'dysarthric' difficulties by leaving out inessentials from his speech? Current evidence, including data about comprehension in Broca's aphasia, suggests that the above approach will not provide a sufficient explanation for the patient's expressive difficulties (Goodenough, Zurif and Weintraub 1977; Saffran, Schwartz and Marin 1980). An analogous situation obtains when we consider disorders of auditory comprehension. Many subjects with left hemisphere damage are, '. . . impaired in their ability to respond correctly to rapidly changing acoustic stimuli' irrespective of the verbal or non-verbal nature of the signal (Tallal and Newcombe 1978). A proportion, perhaps even a considerable proportion, of the fluent aphasic's disorder of language comprehension, and expression also (if auditory feedback is crucially implicated in the control of speech; Boller and Marcie 1978), may be tied to an inability to process rapid formant transitions. It is, however, highly unlikely that the *entire* range of deficits can be uniquely explained in these terms (Boller, Kim and Mack 1977). Why should 'simple' oral naming be impaired in Wernicke's aphasia, why should spontaneous speech be so empty of content and replete with circumlocutions (Hier and Mohr 1977)? The conclusion of a study by Coughlan and Warrington (1978) seems to have considerable generality. 'Deficits in word-comprehension and word-retrieval in the left hemisphere group could not be attributed to impairments in auditory-perceptual or articulatory processes and were considered to possibly reflect impairments in semantic memory and semantic retrieval.'

Standard psychometric testing will often provide a useful profile of the patient before special purpose investigations are undertaken; the most striking feature that emerges on, say, the Wechsler Adult Intelligence Scale, is, of course, that subsequent to focal injury the degree of impairment may differ greatly on various subtests both within and between the 'verbal' and 'performance' scales (Newcombe 1969). The clinical psychologist will be more aware than most of the range of individual variation in the population at large, both prior and subsequent to brain injury, and thus less likely than some other scholars to imagine that 18-year-old university students are an appropriate control group for a 69 year-old lady of limited education (Fox 1931).

There are now a number of aphasia test batteries that have been subjected to some kind of standardization and validation; the most interesting is probably Goodglass and Kaplan (1972). It should always be remembered, however, that what comes out of test batteries is highly dependent upon what went into their construction. I have already mentioned that the symptom-complexes postulated by nineteenth-century clinicians seem to hold up rather well when patients are evaluated by the 'objective' tests and 'minimum variance clustering algorithms' (Kertesz and Phipps 1977) so characteristic of our own age. This indeed demonstrates that the clinicians' impressions bear some relationship to 'reality'; it does not demonstrate that the particular patterns they saw (and we see) are the most theoretically-revealing patterns.

The Experimental Psychologist

Experimental psychologists have, in the past, shown little inclination to study the aphasias, often contenting themselves with mouthing the traditional platitudes about, 'what can you learn about a complex piece of machinery by hitting it with a hammer' (Marin, Saffran and Schwartz 1976). The answer, now that experimental psychologists are taking an interest, seems to be, 'quite a lot'.

To illustrate: many psychologists postulate the existence of some kind of short-term memory store, which, with other mechanisms, is involved in different types of span and superspan tasks from which its capacity can be estimated. The code in which information is held in this store is usually believed to be phonological. (I use this latter term in part to avoid here arguments about acoustic versus articulatory coding.) A question then arises as to the functional significance of this store; it is unlikely to be a special purpose device that evolved in order to facilitate keeping a telephone number in mind en route from phone book to receiver. A sensible speculation might therefore be that the normal role of the store is in response programming in spontaneous speech; it is in Morton's (1979) terms a limited capacity 'response buffer'. Some of the 'slips of the tongue' produced by both normal speakers and by brain-injured subjects might reflect 'overcrowding' and retrieval problems associated with the operation of this store (Ellis 1979).

Alternatively, the store might be part of the speech comprehension system; it could hold the signal in a partially analysed form until sufficient information has accumulated to permit a correct syntactic and semantic analysis of the utterance. Yet alternatively, the store might be implicated in both speech production and speech comprehension. And, finally, there may be two quite distinct stores, one for production, one for comprehension.

Some deficit, gross or mild, of repetition (as assessed by, say, digit or word span) is characteristic of most, if not all, aphasic subjects (Heilman, Scholes and Watson 1976), but there are, of course, a variety of reasons why this could be so. As Warrington and Shallice (1969) point out, adequate repetition is dependent, at very least, upon adequate, 'acoustic perception and motor speech capacity'. However, nineteenth- and early-twentieth-century neurologists conjectured the existence of a *specific* repetition deficit that they called 'conduction' or 'central' aphasia (Green and Howes 1977). In this condition, the impairment of repetition was held to be disproportionately severe relative to the quality of spontaneous speech and auditory comprehension. If such a condition does exist, the plausibility of certain models of normal functioning might be somewhat diminished.

Shallice and Butterworth (1977) have reported at length upon a subject (JB) who had undergone surgical removal of a meningioma from the region of the left angular gyrus. This woman's digit span performance was more than two standard deviations below the norm; yet careful analysis of a considerable number of parameters of her spontaneous speech showed that it was well within normal limits. No primary deficit of acoustic perception was evident. However, while the patient's comprehension of speech was adequate for normal conversational purposes, she did make frequent, '. . . mistakes in understanding relatively short sentences which contained much non-redundant information . . . , sentences which were syntactically complex or which could not easily be disambiguated' (Shallice and Butterworth 1977; see also Shallice and Warrington 1977). The conclusion then, for this patient, is that the impaired short-term memory (STM) store that is responsible for the span deficit is an input store involved with the comprehension, not the speech output, system.

This conclusion is consistent with that reached by Saffran and Marin (1975). Their patient had only very mild expressive difficulties in the context of gross impairment in span and many qualitative departures from normal performance on a variety of tasks containing an STM component. Although comprehension was quite adequate for most purposes, the nature of the patient's errors in immediate sentence repetition demonstrate with startling clarity the role that an input store must play in the comprehension of sentences of any degree of complexity. Some examples follow:

'The boy the dog chased went home'→
'The boy chased the dog home.'

'The soldier was watched by the man in the car'→
'The soldier watched the man in the car.'

'The houses on our street were damaged by the rain.'→
'The houses on our street were damaged by the storm.'

'The board of directors decided that retiring workers should be encouraged'→

'A board director was told that the aged employees should be given permission to retire.'

'The soldiers knew that pleasing women can be fun'→
'The soldiers knew that going with charming women can be fun.'

Normal sentence comprehension is undoubtedly 'on-line' in the sense that syntactic and semantic analysis takes place both predictively and after very short segments of the signal have been received (Marslen-Wilson and Welsh 1978). But this very fact seems to necessitate the existence of a 'back-up' or 'holding' device that keeps information in a non-semantic form. It seems that this is an efficient way to rectify false predictions and to allow subsequent context to disambiguate input that is susceptible to multiple syntactic and semantic analysis. Any purely 'heuristic' mode of processing will have an alarmingly high error rate (Caramazza and Zurif 1976).

We seem, then, to have falsified, on neuropsychological grounds, the hypothesis that a single store can act as both an input and an output buffer. And we have brought strong evidence to suggest that, in some cases of conduction aphasia, it is the input store that is damaged. This evidence, however, does not in itself cast doubt upon the theoretical validity of Morton's response buffer, for there are patients with 'conduction aphasia' who do show a high-level defect of spontaneous speech; their utterances contain frequent semantic and phonological paraphasias (Shallice and Warrington 1977). The inescapable conclusion seems to be that 'conduction aphasia' is not a unitary symptom-complex, but rather comprises at least two syndromes: in one the output store is compromised, in the other the input store. It is fully consistent with this interpretation that the clustering algorithm of Kertesz and Phipps (1977) produced a bimodal distribution of patients whose repetition ability was severely impaired: one group had high fluency and low comprehension scores, the other low fluency and higher comprehension. (An alternative interpretation of the theoretical status of short-term memory in the light of evidence from brain-damage can be found in Glanzer and Clark 1979.)

For expository purposes, I have divided the preceding commentary into 'specialities'. Yet it is as well to remember that the point of the enterprise is not to 'be' a neurologist, a psychologist, or whatever; the goal is to understand and, if possible, help the patient. The approaches mentioned should mutually extend and support each other, although it must be admitted that this is a tricky balancing act at the best of times.

I began our discussion with some remarks about the attitude and feelings of the patient himself. Since we are all potential victims, it is not totally out-of-place to conclude by considering the topic in a wider context.

The Body Politic

In this brief review, I have concentrated, as academics are both prone and 'supposed' to do, on 'scientific' studies of the aphasias. It will not, however, have escaped the reader's attention that there are a large number of socio-economic, administrative and, ultimately, political issues involved in understanding, caring for, and attempting to rehabilitate the aphasic patient.

In any society with limited resources (that is, *every* society) decisions must be taken about where money and effort are likely to produce maximum benefit. To what extent is spreading time thinly over a large number of patients a rational deployment of the therapist's labour? Would time devoted to teaching the patient's family to be therapists be time well spent? Can we train therapists so that they can properly evaluate the effects of their work? Can psycholinguists be persuaded to consider the possible practical applications of 'pure' research?

Increasing numbers of stroke and traffic accident victims lead inevitably to increasing numbers of people with greatly reduced communicative efficiency. How best can we limit the disastrous effects upon the individual and upon society at large (Sarno 1976)?

REFERENCES

Basso, A., Capitani, E., and Vignolo, L. A. 1979. 'Influence of rehabilitation on language skills in aphasic patients: a controlled study.' *Arch. Neurol. 36*, 190–6.

Beauvois, M. F., Saillant, B., Meininger, V., and Lhermitte, F. 1978. 'Bilateral tactile aphasia: a tacto-verbal dysfunction.' *Brain 101*, 381–401.

Benson, D. F. 1967. 'Fluency in aphasia: correlation with radioactive scan localization.' *Cortex 3*, 373–94.

Beyn, E. S., and Shokhor-Trotskaya, M. K. 1966. 'The preventative method in aphasia.' *Cortex 2*, 96–108.

Blumstein, S. 1973. *A phonological investigation of aphasic speech*. The Hague: Mouton.

Bogen, J. E., and Bogen, G. M. 1976. 'Wernicke's region – where is it?' *Annals of the New York Academy of Sciences 280*, 834–43.

Boller, F., Kim, Y., and Mack, J. L. 1977. 'Auditory comprehension in aphasia.' In H. and H. A. Whitaker (eds) *Studies in neurolinguistics 3*. New York: Academic Press.

Boller, F., and Marcie, P. 1978. 'Possible role of abnormal auditory feedback in conduction aphasia.' *Neuropsychologia 16*, 521–4.

Buckingham, H. W., and Kertesz, A. 1976. *Neologistic jargon aphasia*. Amsterdam: Swets and Zeitlinger.

Buckingham, H. W., Avakian-Whitaker, H., and Whitaker, H. A. 1978. Alliteration and assonance in neologistic jargon aphasia.' *Cortex 14*, 365–80.

Caramazza, A., and Zurif, E. B. 1976. 'Dissociation of algorithmic and heuristic processes in language comprehension: evidence from aphasia.' *Brain and Language 3*, 572–82.

Coughlan, A. K., and Warrington, E. K. 1978. 'Word-comprehension and word-retrieval in patients with localized cerebral lesions.' *Brain 101*, 163–85.

Dahlberg, C. C., and Jaffe, J. 1977. *Stroke: a doctor's personal story of his recovery*. New York: W. W. Norton.

Darley, F. L. 1972. 'The efficacy of language rehabilitation in aphasia.' *J. Speech and Hearing Research 37*, 3 – 21.

Dennis, M. 1976. 'Dissociated naming and locating of body parts after left anterior temporal lobe resection: an experimental case study.' *Brain and Language 3*, 147 – 63.

Ellis, A. W. 1979. 'Speech production and short-term memory.' In J. Morton and J. C. Marshall (eds) *Psycholinguistics series 2*. London: Elek.

Elvin, M. B., and Oldfield, R. C. 1951. 'Disabilities and progress in a dysphasic university student.' *J. Neurol. Neurosurg. and Psychiat. 14*, 118 – 28.

Farrell, B. 1969. *Pat and Roald*. New York: Random House.

Fox, C. 1931. 'Tests of aphasia.' *Brit. J. Psychol. 21*, 242 – 55.

Gardner, H. 1974. *The shattered mind*. New York: Random House.

Geschwind, N. 1967. 'The varieties of naming errors.' *Cortex 3*, 97 – 112.

Geschwind, N. 1974. *Selected papers on language and the brain*. Dordrecht: D. Reidel.

Geschwind, N., Galaburda, A., and LeMay, M. 1979. 'Morphological and physiological substrates of language and cognitive development.' In R. Katzman (ed.) *Congenital and acquired cognitive disorders*. New York: Raven Press.

Glanzer, M., and Clark, E. O. 1979. 'Cerebral mechanisms of information storage: the problem of memory.' In M. S. Gazzaniga (ed.) *Handbook of behavioral neurobiology 2*. New York: Plenum Press.

Gloning, K. 1977. 'Handedness and aphasia.' *Neuropsychologia 15*, 355 – 8.

Goodenough, C., Zurif, E. B., and Weintraub, S. 1977. 'Aphasics' attention to grammatical morphemes.' *Language and Speech 20*, 11 – 19.

Goodglass, H., and Kaplan, E. 1972. *The assessment of aphasia and related disorders*. Philadelphia: Lea and Febiger.

Green, E., and Howes, D. H. 1977. 'The nature of conduction aphasia: a study of anatomic and clinical features and of underlying mechanisms.' In H. and H. A. Whitaker (eds) *Studies in neurolinguistics 3*. New York: Academic Press.

Hatfield, F. M., and Zangwill, O. L. 1975. 'Occupational resettlement in aphasia.' *Scand. J. Rehab. Med. 7*, 57 – 60.

Heilman, K. M., Scholes, R., and Watson, R. T. 1976. 'Defects of immediate memory in Broca's and Conduction aphasia.' *Brain and Language 3*, 201 – 8.

Hier, D. B., and Mohr, J. P. 1977. 'Incongruous oral and written naming. Evidence for a subdivision of the syndrome of Wernicke's aphasia.' *Brain and Language 4*, 115 – 26.

Holmes, G. 1950. 'Pure word blindness.' *Folia Psychiat. Neurol. Neerl. 43*, 279 – 88.

Jakobson, R. 1941. *Kindersprache, Aphasie und allgemeine Lautgesetze*. Uppsala; Universitets Arsskrift.

Johns, D. F. (ed.) 1978. *Clinical management of neurogenic communicative disorders*. Boston: Little, Brown and Company.

Kean, M.-L. 1978. The linguistic interpretation of aphasic syndromes. In E. Walker (ed.) *Explorations in the biology of language*. Montgomery, Vermont: Bradford Books.

Kean, M.-L. 1980. 'Grammatical representations and the description of processing.' In D. Caplan (ed.) *Biological studies of mental processes.* Cambridge, Mass.: MIT.

Kertesz, A., and McCabe, P. 1977. 'Recovery patterns and prognosis in aphasia.' *Brain 100*, 1 – 18.

Kertesz, A., and Phipps, J. B. 1977. 'Numerical taxonomy of aphasia.' *Brain and Language 4*, 1 – 10.

Knox, D. R. 1971. *Portrait of aphasia*. Detroit: Wayne State University Press.

Lebrun, Y., and Hoops, R. (eds) 1976. *Recovery in aphasics*. Amsterdam: Swets and Zeitlinger.

Lenneberg, E. H. 1973. 'The neurology of language.' *Daedalus 102*, 115 – 33.

Lomas, J., and Kertesz, A. 1978. 'Patterns of spontaneous recovery in aphasic groups: a study of adult stroke patients.' *Brain and Language 5*, 388 – 401.

Luria, A. R. 1970. *Traumatic aphasia*. The Hague: Mouton.

McGlone, J. 1977. 'Sex differences in the cerebral organization of verbal functions in patients with unilateral brain lesions.' *Brain 100*, 775 – 93.

McKenna, P., and Warrington, E. K. 1978. 'Category-specific naming preservation: a single case study.' *J. Neurol. Neurosurg. and Psychiat. 41*, 571 – 4.

Marin, O. S. M., Saffran, E. M., and Schwartz, M. F. 1976. 'Dissociations of language in aphasia: implications for normal function.' *Annals of the New York Academy of Sciences 280*, 868 – 84.

Marshall, J. C. 1977. 'Disorders in the expression of language.' In J. Morton and J. C. Marshall (eds) *Psycholinguistics series 1*. London: Elek.

Marshall, J. C., and Newcombe, F. 1966. 'Syntactic and semantic errors in paralexia.' *Neuropsychologia 4*, 169 – 76.

Marslen-Wilson, W. D., and Welsh, A. 1978. 'Processing interactions and lexical access during word recognition in continuous speech.' *Cog. Psychol. 10*, 29 – 63.

Mohr, J. P. 1976. 'Broca's area and Broca's aphasia.' In H. and H. A. Whitaker (eds) *Studies in neurolinguistics 1*, New York: Academic Press.

Morton, J. 1979. 'Word recognition.' In J. Morton and J. C. Marshall (eds) *Psycholinguistics series 2*. London: Elek.

Myerson, R., and Goodglass, H. 1972. 'Transformational grammars of three agrammatic patients.' *Language and Speech 15*, 40 – 50.

Naeser, M. A., and Hayward, R. W. 1978. 'Lesion localization in aphasia with cranial computed tomography and the Boston diagnostic aphasia exam.' *Neurology 28*, 545 – 51.

Naeser, M. A., and Hayward, R. W. 1979. 'The resolving stroke and aphasia.' *Arch. Neurol. 36*, 233 – 5.

Newcombe, F. 1969. *Missile wounds of the brain*. Oxford: Oxford University Press.

Newcombe, F., and Ratcliff, G. 1978. 'The female brain: a neuropsychological viewpoint.' In S. Ardener (ed.) *Defining females: the nature of women in society*. London: Croom Helm.

Newcombe, F., Hiorns, R. W., Marshall, J. C., and Adams, C. B. T. 1975. 'Acquired dyslexia: patterns of deficit and recovery.' In R. Porter and D. W. Fitzsimons (eds) *Outcome of severe damage to the central nervous system*. Amsterdam: Elsevier.

Oppenheimer, D. R., and Newcombe, F. 1978. 'Clinical and anatomic findings in a case of auditory agnosia.' *Arch. Neurol. 35*, 712 – 19.

Peuser, G. 1978. *Aphasie*. München: Wilhelm Fink.
Piéron, H. 1927. *Thought and the brain*. London: Kegan Paul.
Prins, R. S., Snow, C. E., and Wagenaar, E. 1978. 'Recovery from aphasia: spontaneous speech versus language comprehension.' *Brain and Language 6*, 192–211.
Rochford, G. 1974. 'Are jargon dysphasics dysphasic?' *Brit. J. Dis. Commun. 9*, 35–44.
Rosati, G., and Bastiani, P. de 1979. 'Pure agraphia: a discrete form of aphasia.' *J. Neurol. Neurosurg. and Psychiat. 42*, 266–9.
Saffran, E. M., and Marin, O. S. M. 1975. 'Immediate memory for word lists and sentences in a patient with deficient auditory short-term memory.' *Brain and Language 2*, 420–33.
Saffran, E. M., Schwartz, M. F., and Marin, O. S. M. 1980. 'Evidence from aphasia: isolating the components of a production model.' In B. Butterworth (ed.) *Language production*. New York: Academic Press.
Sarno, M. T. 1976. 'The status of research in recovery from aphasia.' In Y. Lebrun and R. Hoops (eds) *Recovery in aphasics*. Amsterdam: Swets and Zeitlinger.
Sarno, M. T., Silverman, M. G., and Sands, E. S. 1970. 'Speech therapy and language recovery in severe aphasia.' *J. Speech and Hearing Research 13*, 607–23.
Schnitzer, M. L. 1972. *Generative phonology: evidence from aphasia*. Pennsylvania State University: Administrative Committee on Research.
Schuell, H. 1974. *Aphasia theory and therapy*. London: MacMillan.
Scott Moss, C. 1972. *Recovery with aphasia*. Urbana: University of Illinois Press.
Shallice, T., and Butterworth, B. 1977. 'Short-term memory impairment and spontaneous speech.' *Neuropsychologia 15*, 729–35.
Shallice, T., and Warrington, E. K. 1977. 'Auditory-verbal short-term memory impairment and conduction aphasia.' *Brain and Language 4*, 479–91.
Sparks, R. W., and Holland, A. L. 1976. 'Method: melodic intonation therapy for aphasia.' *J. Speech and Hearing Disorders 41*, 287–97.
Symonds, C. 1953. 'Aphasia.' *J. Neurol. Neurosurg. and Psychiat. 16*, 1–6.
Tallal, P., and Newcombe, F. 1978. 'Impairment of auditory perception and language comprehension in dysphasia.' *Brain and Language 5*, 13–24.
Von Eckardt Klein, B. 1978. 'Inferring functional localization from neurological evidence.' In E. Walker (ed.) *Explorations in the biology of language*. Montgomery, Vermont: Bradford Books.
Warrington, E. K., and Shallice, T. 1969. 'The selective impairment of auditory-verbal short-term memory.' *Brain 92*, 885–96.
Whitaker, H. 1976. 'A case of the isolation of the language function.' In H. and H. A. Whitaker (eds) *Studies in neurolinguistics 2*. New York: Academic Press.
Yamadori, A., and Albert, M. L. 1973. 'Word category aphasia.' *Cortex 9*, 112–25.
Zangwill, O. L. 1969. 'Intellectual status in aphasia.' In P. J. Vinken and G. W. Bruyn (eds) *Disorders of speech, perception, and symbolic behaviour*. Amsterdam: North-Holland.

Chapter 6

Early Communication and the Beginnings of Language Development

JOHN McSHANE

Talking is a linguistic, cognitive, and social activity; we plan and produce understandable speech and we plan and produce it for the purpose of communicating with other people. Our speech has both form and function. Children learning to talk are faced with the problem of mastering the complex structure of language while at the same time using their as yet imperfect system to communicate with the world around them. In this article, I will first consider, in broad outline, the form of children's language, then the function of children's language. Both will lead to a central pivot: the development of naming and the subsequent development of grammatical structure beginning about the middle of the second year. Throughout, the emphasis will be on language production and the speech environment of the child learning language. I will have nothing to say about language comprehension (see Goldin-Meadow, Seligman and Gelman 1976; Huttenlocher 1974; Shatz 1978).

FORM

Language form can be studied at many levels. Let us start with the sounds a child makes. How do these sounds develop so that children end up speaking the language of their culture, which will use only some of the many sound-distinctions that are possible? A distinction is often made between the early-appearing sounds of crying and vegetative activity, and later behaviours of cooing and babbling (Lenneberg 1967). The sounds an infant makes during the earliest weeks of life are due to reflex activities of the vocal musculature (Bosma 1975). A study by Wolff (1969) presents a detailed account of the development of crying in the first six months of life. By the sixth month consonant-like sounds will have become common due to increasing control over vocal musculature and the period from 6 months until the first words are spoken at about 1 year old is often called the 'babbling phase'. It has been claimed (Jakobson 1968) that the babbling of infants is random, that sounds are produced indiscriminately and that it is only when the first words are produced that the infant begins to make systematic use of particular sounds. Recently Jakobson's claim has been disputed by Oller, Wieman, Doyle and Ross (1976), whose evidence suggests that babbled sounds manifest many of the same basic phonetic preferences found later in childhood pronunciation of adult words. Complete mastery of the phonological system of adult language takes many years. Recent work on children over the age of 1 year has been much concerned with the extent to which the phonological system is determined by the development of higher-order linguistic processes (see Braine 1974; Smith 1973). The study of the child's phonological system has now become an area of considerable research interest and future developments will no doubt be rapid. As the technicalities of phonology are not the main concern of this article, phonological development will not be further pursued.

By about the age of 1 year a child may begin to produce recognizable words. We can now begin to study the development of a new level of form. One of the most obvious things to do is to keep a record of the words a child learns. We can then answer such questions as how quickly are words learnt and what sorts of words are learnt? Nelson (1973) has recently provided some answers to these questions. The mean age by which children will have learnt 10 words is 15.1 months and they will have learnt 50 words by 19.6 months. However, words are not added gradually to the child's vocabulary. Nelson found that there was a period of slow acquisition with only a few words per month being added followed by a period of rapid acquisition when many new words were learnt as shown in Figure 6.1. The pattern was typical for the majority of children.

What sorts of words are learnt by children? The most common sort are what Nelson called *nominals*, words that refer to things, which accounted for 65% of the children's first 50 words. When these words were examined in more detail, Nelson found that the children were learning certain types of nominals, mostly the names of food and drink, animals, clothes and toys. The children were learning the names of the things that were salient in their everyday activities and most of the words learnt referred to manipulable or movable objects. That is a simple summary; and behind it lie more complicated issues. A child learning to talk has to learn not only the words that refer to people, objects, and events but also, and more basically, that words *can be used* to refer to people, objects, and events. A child has to master the conceptual task of learning what reference is as well as eventually learning

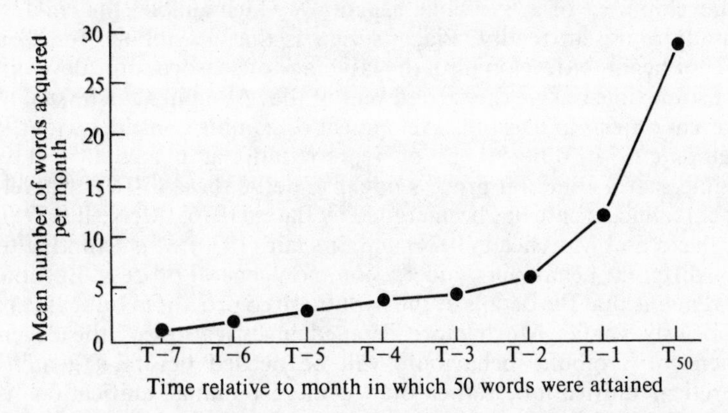

Figure 6.1 Backward learning curve (mean number of words added per month for T_{50}-*n* where *n* = number of months prior to 50 words) showing rate of acquisition of first 50 words. (After Nelson 1973. Reprinted by permission.)

the correct range of referents for a given word (e.g. learning that 'dog' refers to dogs but not cats or cows). In this article I will discuss the first of these issues but the issue of how the domain of referential words is established must be excluded for reasons of space. Discussions may be found in Bowerman (1978), Braunwald (1978), Clark (1973), Gruendel (1977), McShane (1979) and Nelson, Rescorla, Gruendel and Benedict (1978).

As a first attempt at explaining the development of reference we might consider the practice of ostensive definition: objects are pointed out to the child and named; after repeated examples the child learns the name of the object. Things are not so simple however. If this was the process a slow steady accumulation of names might be expected but we have just seen that this is not the case. Consistent with the group data of Figure 6.1 are the reports of many diary studies that there is a sudden increase in naming around the middle of the second year (see Halliday 1975; Leopold 1939 – 49). There are other deficiencies in the simple model of ostensive definition, the chief of which is the following. While ostensive definition might work in practice with a child already in possession of the concept of naming, it is incapable of explaining the origin of the concept itself as there is no explanation of why an ostensive definition should be taken as constituting a name by a child ignorant of the concept of naming.

How might the origin of the concept of naming be explained? One possibility is that Piaget's theory of cognitive development might help to provide an explanation. Piaget (1951) argues that the development of naming is made possible by a more general psychological development:

the development of a 'symbolic function', which enables the child to mentally represent reality. Piaget's view is that a symbolic function does not begin to develop until the last stage of sensorimotor development some time during the second year of life. As names can be said to represent objects and as the development of naming coincides with the development of other types of representational behaviours, it is possible that a common process might underlie these different developments. Such a case has been argued by Bates (1976), McNeill (1975), Morehead and Morehead (1974) and Sinclair (1970). It is tempting to unify different behaviours under a common general process. But, the fact remains that the details of the hypothesized process in this case are notoriously vague. Much more detailed investigation of the development of symbolic behaviours will be needed before a genuine theoretical unification, rather than a mere nominal unification, is achieved.

There are other models designed to explain how a child learns the concept of naming. Nelson (1974, 1977) has proposed that the child's initial concepts are not concepts of objects *per se* but of objects and their functional relations. It is the actions or functions of objects that initially draws the child's attention to these objects and so the child's initial concept is a *gestalt* of the object and its functional relations. Concepts gradually undergo internal reorganization so that eventually a child conceptualizes objects, attributes and actions separately. At any point during the initial development of a concept a child might learn a name for that concept but the word will not be the name of an object until the concept of the object is differentiated from the object's functional relations. Nelson argues that this development – the conceptual separation of objects and their functional relations – is responsible for the development of structured speech in that separate words are attached to objects, attributes, actions and so on, and these words are combined to express the relationships the child perceives in the environment.

Some time between the ages of 18 months and 2 years a child will begin to produce utterances that combine words together. We can now begin to discuss yet another level of form: grammatical structure. The grammatical structure of the child's early word combinations has been intensively studied in recent years. Most of the work on language structure is due to the influence of Chomsky (for an introduction to Chomsky's work see Lyons 1977). As well as producing an influential theory of language structure known as *transformational grammar*, Chomsky also exerted a large influence on psychologists with his criticism of the attempts of Skinner's *Verbal Behavior* in particular and learning theory in general to explain language development (Chomsky 1959). Chomsky's writings have set the tone for much of the last two decades of research in language development and much of this research has been concerned with the development of structure in children's language. I will postpone the discussion of language structure in order to trace our steps up to this from the point of view of function.

FUNCTION

Functional accounts of language place more emphasis on the nature of the communication than on the structure of the utterance. The communication system between mother and child begins to be established very early in the first year of life, so it would be interesting to see in what ways language can be regarded as a development of this communication system.

Until quite recently very little was known about mother – infant communication, but research in the last few years has demonstrated that there is a great deal of communication and that much of it is due to the fact that the mother actively attempts to induct her infant into a system of communication. Snow (1977), for example, has studied mother – infant conversations from the age of 3 months. At 3 months there was no real conversation in the sense of a reciprocal exchange of utterances but the mothers treated the interactions with their infants *as if* they were having a conversation. Almost any behaviour, including cooing and burping, was treated as the infant's turn in the conversation. As the infants grew older the mothers' demands on what constituted an acceptable turn increased. At 7 months (during the babbling phase) a babbled utterance was the minimum requirement but, when the infants began to learn words, babbled utterances ceased to be acceptable and a word was now demanded by the mother as a response to her own utterance. Snow's study demonstrates that mothers treat their infants as potentially communicative from the earliest months. Infant utterances that are acceptable to the mother as a response to her own utterances are treated as a turn in the conversation and unacceptable responses are rejected as turns. These early interactions between mother and infant are often regarded as laying the basis of conversational participation by the infant. Stern (1977) provides a useful introduction to the research on early mother – infant interaction and the articles in Schaffer (1977) offer more detailed accounts of particular issues. A critical review of this literature can be found in McShane (1980).

Such research begins to reveal the patterning of communicative interaction. Other studies have looked more closely at the actual communicative behaviour of the infant. Perhaps the most convenient strategy to adopt here is to pick some important types of communication and study their development. I will concentrate on two: requests and statements, partly because there is a considerable literature that relates to the development of these speech-acts and partly because they are essential prerequisites of language (Bennett 1976).

Requests

Bates, Camaioni and Volterra (1975) report that the first examples of intentional requests occur from the end of the first year onwards. To explain why requests begin to occur at this time we have to consider the more general context of the infant's cognitive development. According to Piaget's theory (see Flavell 1977) the infant's development in the first two years of life is characterized by the successively more complex organization of actions. During the first year different schemes of organization are not integrated with each other. In particular, behaviour towards persons and behaviour towards objects are not co-ordinated (Sugarman-Bell 1978). Thus, a child may interact with objects and interact with people but will not combine objects and people in the same sequence of interaction. The integration of people and objects within the same sequence of interaction begins to occur towards the end of the first year or the beginning of the second year and is correlated with the emergence of Stage V sensorimotor behaviours (Bates, Benigni, Bretherton, Camaioni and Volterra 1977; Sugarman-Bell 1978). The infant now begins to use people as an aid to obtain objects. A child who cannot obtain what he or she requires will at this stage turn to an adult and insistently ask for help. The child's utterance may not exhibit the form of language in that he or she may not utter a word but the utterance exhibits one function of language in that it is a vocalization uttered with the intention of obtaining aid. Functionally the child's utterance is a request. Soon the child may learn (or be taught) a small number of conventional sounds for requesting – words such as 'more' are common early words. In fact, some of the early object-words a child learns (i.e. words that would name objects in the adult language) may be learnt as a means of requesting and initially these words may never be used for any other function. This can even be true of such familiar early words as 'Mama' (McShane 1980).

Statements

In this section I will concentrate on statements that name or describe some object, action, or event and ignore more complicated types of statements about abstract concepts (which young children do not make). The child's earliest statements consist of naming objects or animate beings. The search for the preverbal antecedents of statements is much more complicated than for requests. One reason is the nature of a statement. While it is easy enough to see how someone could make a request without knowing the appropriate words, it is much more difficult to see how someone could name something without using a conventional word (or at least a word that has been established as inter-subjectively conventional, as happens when a child uses an idiosyncratic name for an object). Can there be any preverbal developments that smooth the way for statements? In recent years it has been argued that joint attention between mother and infant during the first year of life is developmentally related to the emergence of naming (Bates *et al.* 1975; Bruner 1975a,b). In addition there have been a number of recent studies that have explored some situations in which names are commonly used. One such situation is looking at picture-books and it is a common mother – child activity in our culture. There are many highly predictable things about looking at picture-books: the same activities are engaged in and the same objects are named repeatedly. In effect, mother and child establish a ritual, but one that changes subtly with time. Studies by Murphy (1978) and Ninio and Bruner (1978) have explored the behaviour of mothers and children while looking at books together. Ninio and Bruner found that 76% of all observed naming by the mother occurred in picture-book sequences. The mothers' speech contained four key utterance-types: a call for attention from the child ('look'); a query to the child ('what's that?'); a name ('it's a dog'); and feedback to a response from the child ('yes'). Some, or all, of these utterances were invariably used by the mother but her expectation of the child's response to these utterances changed. At first, minimal participation such as a babbled utterance was accepted as a response but once the child had learnt a few names the mother challenged a babbled utterance with, 'what's that?'. Murphy reported similar results. When the behaviour of mothers to 14- and 20-month-old children was compared Murphy found that the mother of a 14-month-old child was likely to name the picture for the child whereas the mother of a 20-month-old child was likely to ask the child, 'what is it?'. The mothers obviously had different expectations of the children's abilities. In such situations the child will learn the names of objects, if for no other reason than the fact that the names are repeatedly paired with the objects. It is not necessary that the child know anything about the concept of naming to learn the names; the names may just be utterances appropriate to a particular slot in a ritual. McShane (1979, 1980) has hypothesized that, having learnt the words, the child can come to realize, by a process of insight, that the sounds used in the ritual have a conceptual relationship to objects independently of their role in the ritual: they name the objects. Why insight? It is a psychological process of common experience and the basic achievement of any insight is a relatively sudden realization of some structural order between elements previously not seen. In the case of naming, the insight is the discovery of the conceptual relationship implicit in the behaviour already engaged in. This process has its antecedents in the nature of a ritual activity involving naming. Its consequences are a sudden increase in vocabulary previously commented on; if things have names why not find out those names? And if objects have names, why not attributes, actions and so on, and why not combine these names? In fact these are just the developments that occur. There is a sudden increase in naming (at least for most children) and the development of structured speech shortly follows.

FORM, FUNCTION AND STRUCTURE

Language development has now been discussed from the point of view of form and of function. We have reached the same point in each case: the emergence of structured speech. To some extent the different emphases are complementary. Object-word relations are conceptualized inside and outside ritual activities and both processes of conceptualization are no doubt important and complementary. However, there are differences of emphasis in discussing the form of a child's words and the function of a child's words. Approaches, based on form, chart the way a child learns words on the assumption, implicit or explicit, that the child is constructing a vocabulary of words. Approaches, based on function, chart the development of communicative utterances on the assumption that the child is learning to communicate and in the process of doing so may learn to use words within his existing communicative repertoire. It is only in recent years that theoretical models have begun to be constructed that allow the study of language development in functional terms. Accounts that place varying emphasis on language function can be found in Bates (1976), Bruner (1975a,b), Dore (1975), Halliday (1975) and McShane (1980).

When children begin to combine words together their word combinations express a small range of meanings and this range seems to be common to all languages so far studied (Brown 1973b; Slobin 1973). Children combine words according to certain principles or rules and these principles seem to be universal. Under Chomsky's influence, especially his postulations concerning language development (1965, 1968), it was thought that there were innate universal rules of grammar for combining words. However, there is another possibility: that the common word combinations of children reflect a common underlying process of conceptualizing the world. This view implies that language and thought are closely linked processes and that the organization of language reflects the organization of thought. The view has been dubbed 'the cognition hypothesis' (Cromer 1974).

Brown (1973a) remarks that a fairly short list of semantic relations will account for about 75% of early two-word utterances. His list includes:

Nominative	'That cow'	(that is a cow)
Recurrence	'More cow'	(there's another cow)
Nonexistence	'Cow gone'	(the cow is gone)
Possessive	'Daddy coat'	(that is Daddy's coat)
Locative	'Book there'	(the book is there)
Attributive	'Big horse'	(that's a big horse)
Agent-Action	'Daddy hit'	(Daddy hit something)
Action-Object	'Hit ball'	(somebody hit the ball)
Agent-Object	'Daddy ball'	(Daddy did something to the ball)

The child's utterances reflect those aspects of the environment that are salient and important to him: objects disappearing and reappearing, who owns an object or where it is located, and the various relations between agents, actions and objects. Is there any reason why these relations should be more salient than any other set we might construct? It so happens that the relations expressed in two-word speech are a pretty close match to the type of cognitive achievements that characterize the end of sensorimotor intelligence. The child, having discovered the relationship between words and objects, and approaching the end of sensorimotor intelligence, begins to seek to express his conceptualization of the events around him in language. This conceptualization is, according to Piaget's theory, common to all children and it is for this reason that the same semantic relations are expressed in a wide variety of languages by children beginning to combine words together. The examples given in the list of semantic relations above are all examples of one type of language use: making statements. If we look more generally at a child's speech, then we find that structured utterances are also being used in many other speech-acts and that the same structure may be evident across a variety of speech-acts; for example utterances such as, 'more cow' and, 'hit ball' could be descriptions, requests, or questions depending on the context in which they were uttered. Thus, the 'same utterance' can mean different things in different contexts.

Two developments that occur shortly after the initial emergence of structured speech are of particular interest: the use of language to inform, and questions. Once a child has achieved some mastery of structured speech the beginnings of the informative use of language can be seen. The use of language to inform is one of its primary functions in adult speech but in all the speech of children we have discussed up till now language has been restricted to the here-and-now, to the visible and immediate objects and events of the child's environment. The use of language to refer outside the here-and-now is one of the last functions of language to develop (Halliday 1975; McShane 1980). Its first beginnings are often seen in the prompted recall of events that have taken place ('What did you do?', 'Who did you see?') and this reflects a familiar point: the adjustment of parental speech in line with the child's developing abilities. The second development of interest is that questions now begin to emerge, although the complete mastery of the syntax of questions takes a considerable time (Labov and Labov 1978; Tyack and Ingram 1977; Smith 1933). With the emergence of questions children become able to exert some selective control over the type of information conveyed to them: they can request information if they want it. Language now contains some seeds for its own growth: language can be a means of learning language.

SPEECH TO CHILDREN

So far I have considered speech by children. It is obvious that the speech children hear must, in some sense, be the source of their language. In the heyday of transformational grammar, it was assumed that speech to children was ungrammatical, disfluent, full of false starts and hesitations and that children must therefore learn language with very little help from the environment. This assumption fuelled the further assumption that language was not learnt but was an innate ability that unfolded with age. Unfortunately for this argument the characterization of speech to children was completely wrong. Empirical research soon revealed that speech to children differs in many ways from speech to adults (see Vorster 1975; and the articles in Snow and Ferguson 1977). Speech to children, or Baby Talk (BT), is characterized by short grammatical sentences; reference to the here-and-now; few past tenses, relative clauses, or other syntactically complex constructions; repetition of key words and phrases; an exaggerated pitch and very clear pronunciation; relatively many questions and imperatives by comparison with adult speech and relatively few pronouns (except for 'we'). It is now well established that children learning language are exposed to a rather special type of input. Having established this the question now occupying the attention of researchers is whether BT actually helps language development and if so how?

It might be thought that by simplifying their speech, mothers are offering model sentences for their children to learn. Newport, Gleitman, and Gleitman (1977) have subjected this view to a critical appraisal and found it wanting. The syntactic simplifications of BT are not those we would expect if its sole purpose was to teach. They propose that the simplifications of BT that do occur are motivated by the demands of interaction, such as the need to direct the child's behaviour, and the constraints on what can be said to young children with the expectation of being understood. In support of this claim is the apparent ubiquity of BT. Even 4-year-old children adjust their speech when talking to 2-year-olds (Shatz and Gelman 1973) and it seems more reasonable to assume that this adjustment is motivated by the needs of communication rather than the desire to teach. Further, the fact that mothers hold conversations with even very young infants (Snow 1977), whom they can have no realistic expectation of teaching, suggests that BT is not primarily a teaching strategy.

Although the general characteristics of BT cannot be explained on the assumption that it is solely an attempt to teach specific things, it does not follow that BT is a bad way of teaching. The learning of specific aspects of the language code may occur in relatively particular episodes, such as learning names while looking at picture-books. Until we have more detailed studies of mother – child interaction we will not be able to pass a final verdict on the pedagogic value of BT.

SUMMARY

Language is a system of communication by means of a conventional code. In this article I have discussed some aspects of communication and some aspects of the code. Neither the linguistic code nor the system of communication can be understood in isolation from each other. Certain types of communication have their origin in preverbal developments; the case of requesting was documented. Mastery of the linguistic code is most evident from the middle of the second year onwards when there is often a dramatic increase in naming followed by the development of structured speech. Finally, the speech that children hear and its implications for language development were considered.

REFERENCES

Bates, E. 1976. *Language and context*. London: Academic Press.

Bates, E., Benigni, L., Bretherton, I., Camaioni, L., and Volterra, V. 1977. 'From gesture to the first word: on cognitive and social prerequisites.' In M. Lewis and L. A. Rosenblum (eds) *Interaction, conversation and the development of language*. New York: John Wiley.

Bates, E., Camaioni, L., and Volterra, V. 1975. 'The acquisition of performatives prior to speech.' *Merrill-Palmer Quarterly 21*, 205 – 26.

Bennett, J. 1976. *Linguistic behaviour*. Cambridge: Cambridge University Press.

Bosma, J. F. 1975. 'Anatomic and physiologic development of the speech apparatus.' In D. B. Tower (ed.) *Human communication and its disorders III*. New York: Raven Press.

Bowerman, M. 1978. 'The acquisition of word meaning: an investigation into some current conflicts.' In N. Waterson and C. Snow (eds) *The development of communication*. London: John Wiley.

Braine, M. D. S. 1974. 'On what might constitute learnable phonology.' *Language 50*, 270 – 99.

Braunwald, S. R. 1978. 'Context, word and meaning: towards a communicational analysis of lexical acquisition.' In A. Lock (ed.) *Action, gesture and symbol*. London: Academic Press.

Brown, R. 1973a. 'Development of the first language in the human species.' *Amer. Psychologist 28*, 97 – 106.

Brown, R. 1973b. *A first language*. Cambridge, Mass.: Harvard University Press.

Bruner, J. 1975a. 'From communication to language.' *Cognition 3*, 255 – 87.

Bruner, J. 1975b. 'The ontogenesis of speech acts.' *J. Child Lang. 2*, 1 – 19.

Chomsky, N. 1959. 'Review of "Verbal Behavior" by B. F. Skinner.' *Language 35*, 26 – 58.

Chomsky, N. 1965. *Aspects of the theory of syntax*. Cambridge, Mass.: MIT.

Chomsky, N. 1968. *Language and mind*. New York: Harcourt, Brace and World.

Clark, E. V. 1973. 'What's in a word? On the child's acquisition of semantics in his first language.' In T. E. Moore (ed.) *Cognitive development and the acquisition of language*. New York: Academic Press.

Cromer, R. 1974. 'The development of language and cognition.' In B. M. Foss (ed.) *New perspectives in child development*. Harmondsworth: Penguin.

Dore, J. 1975. 'Holophrases, speech acts and language universals.' *J. Child Lang. 2*, 21 – 40.

Flavell, J. 1977. *Cognitive development*. Englewood-Cliffs, N.J.: Prentice Hall.

Goldin-Meadow, S., Seligman, M., and Gelman, R. 1976. 'Language in the two-year old.' *Cognition 4*, 189 – 202.

Gruendel, J. M. 1977. 'Referential extension in early language development.' *Child Develop. 48*, 1567 – 76.

Halliday, M. A. K. 1975. *Learning how to mean*. London: Edward Arnold.

Huttenlocher, J. 1974. 'The origins of language comprehension.' In R. L. Solso (ed.) *Theories in cognitive psychology*. Potomac, Md: Erlbaum.

Jakobson, R. 1968. *Child language, aphasia and phonological universals* (trans. A. R. Keiler). The Hague: Mouton (originally published 1941).

Labov, W., and Labov, T. 1978. 'Learning the syntax of questions.' In R. Campbell and P. Smith (eds) *Recent advances in the psychology of language*, (4b). London: Plenum Press.

Lenneberg, E. 1967. *The biological foundations of language*. New York: John Wiley.

Leopold, W. 1939 – 49. *Speech development of a bilingual child*. 4 vols. Evanston, Ill.: Northwestern University Press.

Lyons, J. 1977. *Chomsky*, 2nd edn. London: Fontana.

McNeill, D. 1975. 'Semiotic extension.' In R. L. Solso (ed.) *Information processing and cognition: the Loyola Symposium*. Hillsdale, N.J.: Erlbaum.

McShane, J. 1979. 'The development of naming.' *Linguistics 17*, 879 – 905.

McShane, J. 1980. *Learning to talk*. Cambridge: Cambridge University Press.

Morehead, D., and Morehead, A. 1974. 'From signal to sign.' In R. Schiefelbusch and L. Lloyd (eds) *Language perspectives: acquisition, retardation and intervention*. London: Macmillan.

Murphy, C. M. 1978. 'Pointing in the context of a shared activity.' *Child Develop. 49*, 371 – 80.

Nelson, K. 1973. 'Structure and strategy in learning to talk.' *Monog. Soc. Res. Child Develop. 38*, (1 – 2, serial no. 149).

Nelson, K. 1974. 'Concept, word, and sentence.' *Psychol. Rev. 81*, 267 – 85.

Nelson, K. 1977. 'The conceptual basis of naming.' In J. Macnamara (ed.) *Language, learning and thought*. London: Academic Press.

Nelson, K., Rescorla, L., Gruendel, J., and Benedict, H. 1978. 'Early lexicons: what do they mean?' *Child Develop. 49*, 960 – 8.

Newport, E. L., Gleitman, H., and Gleitman, L. R. 1977. 'Mother I'd rather do it myself: some effects and non-effects of maternal speech style.' In C. E. Snow and C. A. Ferguson (eds) *Talking to children*. Cambridge: Cambridge University Press.

Ninio, A., and Bruner, J. 1978. 'The achievement and antecedents of labelling.' *J. Child Lang. 5*, 1 – 15.

Oller, D. K., Wieman, L. A., Doyle, W. J., and Ross, I. C. 1976. 'Infant babbling and speech.' *J. Child Lang. 3*, 1 – 11.

Piaget, J. 1951. *Play, dreams and imitation in childhood* (trans. C. Gattegno and F. M. Hodgson). London: Routledge and Kegan Paul (originally published 1945).

Schaffer, H. (ed.) 1977. *Studies in mother – infant interaction*. London: Academic Press.

Shatz, M. 1978. 'On the development of communicative understandings.' *Cog. Psychol. 10*, 271 – 301.

Shatz, M., and Gelman, R. 1973. 'The development of communication skills: modifications in the speech of young children as a function of the listener.' *Monog. Soc. Res. Child Develop. 38*, (5, serial no. 152).

Sinclair, H. 1970. 'The transition from sensory-motor behaviour to symbolic activity.' *Interchange 1*, 119 – 26.

Skinner, B. F. 1957. *Verbal behavior*. New York: Appleton-Century-Crofts.

Slobin, D. I. 1973. 'Cognitive prerequisites for the development of grammar.' In C. A. Ferguson and D. I. Slobin (eds) *Studies of child language development*. New York: Holt, Rinehart and Winston.

Smith, M. 1933. 'The influence of age, sex and situation on the frequency, form and function of questions asked by preschool children.' *Child Develop. 4*, 201 – 13.

Smith, N. 1973. *The acquisition of phonology: a case study*. Cambridge: Cambridge University Press.

Snow, C. E. 1977. 'The development of conversation between mothers and babies.' *J. Child Lang. 4*, 1 – 22.

Snow, C. E., and Ferguson, C. A. (eds.) 1977. *Talking to children*. Cambridge: Cambridge University Press.

Stern, D. 1977. *The first relationship: infant and mother*. London: Fontana.

Sugarman-Bell, S. 1978. 'Some organizational aspects of pre-verbal communication.' In I. Markova (ed.) *The social context of language*. New York: John Wiley.

Tyack, D., and Ingram, D. 1977. 'Children's production and comprehension of questions.' *J. Child Lang. 4*, 211 – 24.

Vorster, J. 1975. 'Mommy linguist: the case for motherese.' *Lingua 37*, 281 – 312.

Wolff, P. H. 1969. 'The natural history of crying and other vocalizations in early infancy.' In B. M. Foss (ed.) *Determinants of infant behaviour IV*. London: Methuen.

Chapter 7

Encephalization and Neural Mechanisms of Learning

I. STEELE RUSSELL

ENCEPHALIZATION AND LEARNING MECHANISMS

The vertebrate forebrain is traditionally assumed to conform to a fundamental pattern where its subdivisions are believed to be identifiable in all brains to differing degrees. The major exception to this rule is the neocortex with its thalamocortical projection systems regarded by Elliot-Smith (1910) to be a uniquely mammalian development in evolution. Later the notion of 'encephalization' of function was used by Marquis (1935) to refer to the tendency during phylogeny to reallocate control of complex functions such as sensory perception, motor control and learning from the midbrain to the forebrain. As the brain increases in size and complexity in the phylogenic series from fish to humans, functions that were originally controlled by lower structures are progressively subsumed under higher control. Thus, according to Marquis (1935) frogs without their cortex are more or less unaffected in their behaviour, and 'decorticate' birds are still able to fly from perch to perch. In marked contrast following decortication the rat, cat, and dog show increasing signs of motor disturbance. The decorticate monkey is the most severely impaired in that it is totally unable to walk. A similar trend is also claimed for vision. Following decerebration there is no apparent impairment of vision in fish, and only marginal change in birds. The decorticate rat is impaired with pattern vision, but can still discriminate brightness, position, and distance of objects when tested with the Lashley jumping stand. The cat, dog, and monkey retain only brightness discriminations, and man becomes entirely blind. Finally, Marquis also claimed that there was a comparable phyletic trend for the effect of cortical lesions on learning and memory.

Several points need to be made concerning this view of encephalization of function which still continues to be enormously influential despite the absence of any modern systematic evidence in its favour. To begin with it should be noted that it has only had heuristic plausibility for mammalian development. The notion that the reptilian and avian brain can be viewed as earlier and incomplete versions of a mammalian brain is both absurd and misleading. Although it is true that the reptile and avian forebrain is lacking in neocortex (i.e. a structure organized as a horizontal multilaminar sheet containing pyramidal cells), this does not preclude homologous development of other structures. When the physiology and the interconnections to the thalamus are considered, it is clear that both the hyperstriatum in birds and the dorsal striatum in reptiles are comparable to mammalian neocortex (Webster 1973). Thus, a decorticate mammal can in no way be considered to have 'regressed' to an avian or reptilian level of organization (Bitterman 1965; Oakley 1979).

Traditionally, views concerning the evolution of the vertebrate visual system have emphasized the superior colliculus as the highest visual centre in fish, reptiles and birds; whereas the striate cortex is assigned that role in mammals. This notion of a tectal-cortical shift of function was termed the 'corticalization' of vision by Elliot-Smith (1910) and was predicted on three main observations. These are: (i) in submammalian vertebrates the principal target of the optic nerve is the tectum, whereas for mammals it mainly projects to the thalamus; (ii) in lower vertebrates lesions of the optic tectum produce greater visual deficits than do forebrain lesions. The opposite is the case for mammals; (iii) finally, there is a clear trend for vision to increase its dependency on the cortex as opposed to the tectum as one goes from simple to complex mammals.

However, recent evidence has cast serious doubt on this idea of a progressive tectal-cortical shift in visual function. In particular, the findings from tectal ablations in mammals and forebrain lesions in fish and birds are irreconcilable with this view. The early reports that damage to the tectum of mammals produced impairments in eye orientation but not in vision have not been confirmed. Recent findings have clearly shown that severe visual deficits result from lesions of the superior colliculus in hamster, cat and tree shrew (Sprague and Meikle 1965; Schneider 1969; Casagrande *et al.* 1972). Conversely, forebrain lesions in fish and birds have been found to produce impairments similar to those found after striate cortex lesions in mammals. For example, both sharks and birds are defective in pattern vision after forebrain lesions (Graeber *et al.* 1972; Hodos and Karten 1970).

Furthermore, recent anatomical findings have shown that major differences exist in the organization of the visual projection system throughout the animal phyla. These differences are sufficiently radical as to invalidate the notion of any encephalization continuity. In all vertebrates the central visual projections are mainly contralateral, although the amount of ipsilateral connections varies considerably. In most lower vertebrates such as fish, reptiles and birds there is virtually a complete absence of any ipsilateral projections. Within mammals, however, there is a dramatic increase in number of fibres that are uncrossed in the optic chiasm from 5% in rat (Levere 1978) to 50% in primates including humans. The correspondence between the extent of overlap of the two visual fields and the amount of uncrossed fibres is well known (Walls 1939), and has led to the idea that the equal division of projections in the chiasm is the substrate of stereoscopic vision and depth perception.

Despite the fact that there are no animals with laterally placed eyes that have bilateral visual projections, there are many animals with frontally placed eyes (owls and hawks) that have a totally crossed fibre system in the chiasm. These exceptions contradicted the notions that frontal eye placement results in bilateral projections and that stereopsis requires bilateral retinal projections. Unlike primates, birds have a radically different arrangement for the neural analysis of retinal disparities. The projections from the lateral geniculate to the visual area (wulst) in birds is bilateral as opposed to the solely ipsilateral geniculostriate radiations in mammals (Karten and Nanta 1968; Fox *et al.* 1976). The visual projections can be even more bizarre in certain fish. For example sharks also have a crossed geniculotelencephalic projection which is contralateral and unlike the bilateral avian system. This thalamic crossover furthermore completely negates the contralateral projection in the chiasm (Ebbeson and Schroeder 1971). Both the significance and function of this double crossover in such fish is unclear.

Faced with these major discrepancies in the organization of the visual system between major phyla, support for the concept of encephalization has been sought within the mammalian order (Marquis 1935; Weiskrantz 1961). The differential effects of striate cortex lesions on vision have been examined in rat, cat and monkey to consider whether or not the striate cortex assumes greater importance with the increase in mammalian brain size. However, as Hodos and Campbell (1969) have pointed out, making such comparisons across these animals is not meaningful as they do not constitute a phylogenetic series. For example, there are such major differences between the geniculostriate system of primates and carnivores that the two groups are not comparable. The cat with its three layered geniculate nucleus has projections to both striate and prestriate cortex (Glickstein *et al.* 1967). The primate visual system with its six layered geniculate nucleus has only projections to striate cortex; hence removal of striate cortex in cat could not be expected to have the same effects as in primates (see Figure 7.1).

From these considerations it is clear that valid observations of the possible changing role of the cortex in vision would best be made within a primate series. The original reports of the effect of striate cortex

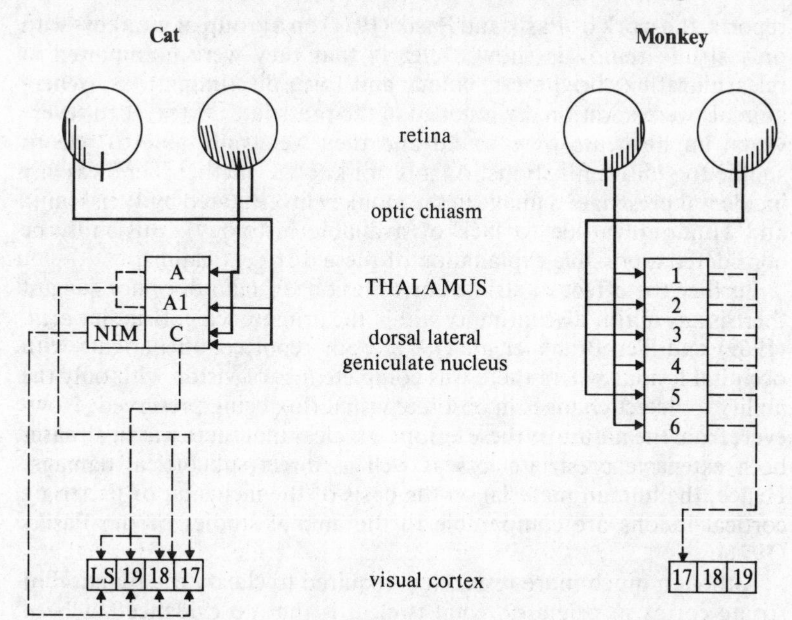

Figure 7.1 Schematic diagram of the retinal projection in cat and monkey. Note the differences in number of thalamic layers, as well as the presence of multiple pathways from the thalamus to cortex in cat but not monkey.

removal in the prosimian tree shrew found no impairment in the retention of either brightness or pattern discrimination tasks (Snyder and Diamond 1968). It was only when prestriate lesions were added to the striate removal that the animals showed deficits in relearning. Since then subsequent work has to some extent qualified the view that loss of the striate cortex is asymptomatic in tree shrew. Ward and Masterson (1970) reported acuity impairments following striate lesions, although this was not confirmed by Ware *et al.* (1972). Similarly, deficits were found only when the patterns were either enclosed by an annulus or presented with distracting background colour stimuli.

A large literature exists on the effects of striate lesions in rhesus monkey (Weiskrantz and Cowey 1970), but is much smaller when only the effects of complete lesions are considered. The main findings are still controversial. For example, individual monkeys with almost complete striate removals have been reported to have a residual visual capacity with a complete loss of detail vision in terms of contour acuity. They appear to respond to movement and are also able to localize objects in space; they can be trained to distinguish differences in amount of contours but are not able to discriminate horizontal from vertical (Weiskrantz 1963; Humphrey and Weiskrantz 1967; Humphrey 1970; Weiskrantz and Cowey 1971). In contrast to these reports, the work of Pasik and Pasik (1971) on a group of monkeys with only striate removals showed clearly that they were unimpaired in relearning flux, brightness, colour and form discriminations. Where animals were additionally lesioned in the prestriate cortex, then severe visual impairments were found and they were only able to relearn simple flux discriminations. As it is not known whether there was any incidental prestriate damage in the monkey investigated by Weiskrantz and Humphrey (due to lack of available histology), this must be considered a possible explanation of these different claims.

Further the effect of striate cortex lesions in man does not suggest there is any major discontinuity within the primate scale. Brindley *et al.* (1969) and Ter Braak *et al.* (1971) both reported on patients with occipital lesions where there was complete loss of vision with only the ability to detect changes in absolute visual flux being preserved. However, from the nature of these lesions it is clear that there was in all cases both extensive prestriate loss as well as direct subcortical damage. Hence, the human material on the basis of the inclusion of prestriate cortical lesions are comparable to the animal studies of the Pasiks (1971).

Although much more research is required to clarify the function of striate cortex in primates, what is clear is that no evidence has been found to support the theory of corticalization of vision. Similarly, the early claims that motor functions are progressively encephalized throughout phylogeny have also received no support from contemporary work (see Passingham and Ettlinger 1974). Nowadays the notion that a function retains its identity while changing its cerebral machinery as it advances up a hypothetical evolutionary ladder is no longer taken seriously. Instead, it is believed that complex functions such as visual perception are processed differently in various species. For example, form vision in the rat tends to entail local flux and orientation analysis in preference to more detailed feature extraction such as form and pattern information. In primates, the latter would have priority and would also be combined with information of colour and stereoscopic disparity. Thus, a simple visual discrimination task would be analysed by different brains in very different ways, using thereby very different neural circuits or computational routines. Given the close interdependency between sensory systems or perceptual mechanisms and learning and memory, it is clear that the principle of encephalization would be equally inappropriate for these functions as it is for the others. Thus, the notion that learning becomes increasingly dependent on cerebral cortex during phylogeny is entirely contradicted by contemporary findings in neurobiology. Indeed historically it has derived its main credibility from theoretical views of encephalization (Elliot-Smith 1910; Marquis 1935). With the demise of this theory such views about learning survive only due to intellectual inertia (Russell 1979).

LEVELS OF NEURAL FUNCTION AND LEARNING

Hughlings Jackson (1898) explained the integration of behaviour in terms of a hierarchy of various levels of overlapping control by the brain. In considering the evolution of integrative motor action he believed that a higher level of control was superimposed on lower control systems in a manner strikingly similar to the way in which the operating system of a computer program co-ordinates its various subroutines. For example, simple reflex integration is provided by the spinal cord mechanisms of reciprocal and crossed inhibitory reactions. The orchestration of these isolated segmental reactions into coherent motor activity, such as postural and locomotor movements, requires higher control from brainstem diencephalic and rhombencephalic centres. Here the upper motor control functions as an operating system to both collate and sequence these spinal subroutines, which retain their individual 'local' control programme autonomy. Further cortical influences constitute a still broader category of control over both sensory and motor functions, where telencephalic mechanisms mediate purposive activity typical of the intact animal. The important point of this Jacksonian view of brain organization is not the specific details of his formulation. Rather it is the general conceptual framework of the brain as a series of multiple control areas that are hierarchically co-ordinated together. This provides a sharply different alternative to the principle of encephalization. Further it is the main source of many current views of the brain as a system comprising of both multiple topographic representations of sensory information and multiple control levels. Recent research on the visual system has not only increased the multiplicity of such representations but has shown that they are both vertically and horizontally organized. Thus, the classic model of serial information processing by the sensory and association areas has become totally inadequate.

Lateral Dissociation of Levels of Organization

Experiments with split-brain animals provide considerable support to this notion of an inverted pyramid of control systems in the brain. Following section of the cerebral commissures it is possible to create two separate cortical hemispheres that are capable of independent perceptual functioning and are able to learn different or opposed behaviours. This apparent dissociation of higher functions of perception and memory by commissurotomy is most easily explicable by assuming cortical control mechanisms. Corroborative evidence for this is also provided by research using the functional split-brain. This preparation, although similar to the surgical split-brain in its outcome is in many ways different (Russell 1971). Both have in common the property of confining learning or memory traces to one hemisphere, yet this is achieved in quite different ways. The surgical split-brain lateralizes information by routing the sensory inputs to one hemisphere and denying access to them by the other hemisphere. It is in this sense that the effects of removal of cortex on different types of behaviour can be uniquely explored in the functional split-brain where there are none of the usual worries that are caused by total decortication. Lateralization of learning or memory can be inferred from retention by the hemisphere that was functional during training and the lack of retention by the hemisphere that was decorticate during learning. Hence, lateralization implies that the memory storage is cortical in nature. Failure to lateralize memory has the opposite implication. If the decorticate hemisphere retains the memory as well as the normal hemisphere, it is evident that the storage or the retrieval of the information was subcortical.

Research over the last few years clearly points to the fact that different types of learning have strikingly different neurological 'signatures'. Indeed a considerable body of work (Russell 1971), points to the fact that different forms of learning are processed at different neurological levels. For example, many studies of Pavlovian conditioning using a wide variety of differing procedures have consistently reported failure to lateralize the information storage to the normal hemisphere in the functional split-brain (Bures *et al.* 1964; Ross and Russell 1967; Schneider 1967; Russell *et al.* 1969). This is in agreement with similar findings for Pavlovian learning in the surgical split-brain cat (Meikle *et al.* 1962). Furthermore, the fact that many of these experiments showed there was no difference in the acquisition of associative learning by normal and hemidecorticate (i.e. single hemisphere) animals strengthens the argument that the cortex has no involvement in the processing of this type of learning. It is only when instrumental learning is considered that lateralization of information to the hemisphere with the functional cortex is found. This finding has been repeatedly confirmed, using a wide variety of tasks involving both food reward and shock motivation (Bures and Buresova 1960; Russell and Ochs 1961; Travis and Sparks 1963; Ross and Russell 1964; Schneider 1966; Kohn 1967).

While the majority of work with surgical split-brain animals has used food reward to lateralize memory to one hemisphere, there is evidence that the same results can be obtained with shock motivation both for cat and rat (Meikle *et al.* 1962; Russell and Safferstone 1973). Sechzer (1964) has claimed that motivational factors can be a determinant of information lateralization in the split-brain cat. She reported visual pattern discrimination lateralization when food reward was used; however, when shock motivation was employed there was complete transfer of learning. Interesting as these results are, their significance is far from clear. First, close examination of the data reveals a pronounced order effect, which is the factor responsible for memory lateralization rather than motivational variables. Secondly, the failure to section the anterior commissure as well as the corpus callosum has been criticized (Gazzaniga 1970; Russell 1971). The importance of this commissure for interhemispheric communication has been most clearly demonstrated by the work of Doty and Negrao (1973). Using food reward for correct choices and shock for errors, they showed that monkeys lateralized a memory trace only when both the corpus callosum and the anterior commissure were cut. If the anterior commissure was intact, the memory transferred. However, it is doubtful that the anterior commissure in cat plays the role it does in primates where the pulvinar-extrastriate visual system has evolved much more extensively (Allman 1977; Wilson 1978).

However, the importance of these experiments for the present review is to draw attention to a crucial difference between the findings of the functional and split-brain procedures. A failure to lateralize memory in the surgical split-brain animal does not necessarily mean that this function is mediated by subcortical integrating mechanisms. It is more likely to demonstrate merely an incomplete disconnection of communication between the two cortical hemispheres. In contrast, a failure to lateralize a memory trace to the normal hemisphere in the functional split-brain of necessity implies subcortical processing of information storage or retrieval because the other hemisphere was decorticate during learning.

Vertical Dissociation of Levels of Organization

A direct test of the notion that different levels of integration of complex functions exist in the brain is provided by the studies of residual function in animals whose nervous system has been simplified. The most obvious way therefore to study the role of the mammalian cerebral cortex in behaviour is to examine the residual abilities of animals following removal of neocortex. Since the classic and epoch making observations of Goltz (1892) on his *Hund ohne Grosshirn*, the general behaviour of chronically decorticated animals has been extensively investigated. In the beginning, the major emphasis of this work was to describe the residual motor reflex capacity of the animal after extirpation of cortex. Such experiments were undertaken on cats (Dusser de Barenne 1920; Ten Cate 1934), on dogs (Rothman 1923; Lebedinskaia and Rosenthal 1935) and monkeys (Karplus and Kreidl 1914).

Following Goltz's (1892) original observations of auditory reactions and localization in the decorticate dog, Zeliony (1929) attempted to establish auditory conditioning in a chronic decorticate dog without any success. As a result of this work, Pavlov (1927) was led to believe that learning was an intrinsic function of neocortex. Subsequent research found that decorticate dogs were not only capable of differential conditioning; but they were able to learn as rapidly as normal animals (Poltyrev and Zeliony 1929). Although similar findings of successful decorticate conditioning were reported by Lebedinskaia and

Rosenthal (1935), they attributed this success to cortical sparing. Shortly afterwards a series of American papers demonstrated differential conditioning between a bell and a tone in decorticate dogs (Culler and Mettler 1934; Mettler *et al.* 1935; Girden *et al.* 1936). Although the rate of learning was comparable to normal animals, the leg flexion response that was conditioned was diffuse and non-specific in the decorticate animal. Thus, although the cortex was regarded as essential for accurate and efficient responses, it was not involved in the learning *per se*. In contrast, other studies where instrumental learning was involved found the role of the cortex to be critical. Lashley (1929) observed that rats deprived of varying amounts of cortex showed impairments on a wide variety of tasks in direct proportion to the lesion size. Similarly, Bromiley (1948) was only able to obtain avoidance learning in his decorticate dog after prolonged training and under a very limited range of conditions. In particular a major difficulty to learning was attributed to such 'cortical release' factors as hyperactivity and hyperemotionality (Cannon and Britton 1927; Bromiley 1948). Due to these side-effects of decortication the animal could not tolerate restraint and also over-reacted to the shock stimulation. It was only when brief training sessions were used and when care was taken to stop training at the first signs of agitation that Bromiley could get any avoidance learning. Later work by Hernandez-Peon and Brust-Carmona (1961) and Pinto-Hamuy *et al.* (1963) have generally confirmed these earlier findings. In an extensive review of this literature (Russell 1966) it was concluded that different types of learning are processed at different levels in the neuraxis. The cortex was regarded as essential for instrumental learning, and independent of Pavlovian conditioning mechanisms.

These early studies of the effect of decortication on learning have a number of major problems. Not only were they frequently episodic in nature, but they are also flawed by serious methodological problems. Typically, observations were made on single animals and few, if any, procedural details are reported. More seriously none of these studies employed any pseudoconditioning or sensitization controls. Thus non-specific changes, rather than learning, could have been reported. Isolated experiments have been reported on a wide range of unrelated animals. To compare the effect of decortication on different types of learning in the same animal is in itself problematic, but to make such comparisons across species is meaningless. Finally, both the surgical and anatomical methods have for the most part been of an unsatisfactory kind. The methods of removal of cortical tissue were both crude and imprecise, and in the absence of antibiotics extensive brain infection was common. Many studies lack histological verification of cortical removal, and the remainder are either unsatisfactory or reveal extensive damage to both limbic and striatal structures. Thus, the effects of a reasonably pure decortication on behaviour remain unanswered by this literature.

It was with these considerations in mind that we undertook to re-examine the matter with modern behavioural techniques applied over a systematically designed and coherent series of studies in the rabbit and rat. This work benefited considerably from our development of an improved method of decortication using pial removal to devascularize the cortex. This, for the first time, permits the complete removal of cortex without either limbic or striatal damage (see Figure 7.2). A large number of decorticated animals were prepared by this means and tested in a closely related and comparable series of learning procedures.

In undertaking a systematic investigation of cortical mechanisms of Pavlovian conditioning the rabbit nictitating membrane response (NMR) was selected as a model preparation. The NMR is the movement of the third eyelid (a membrane between the upper and lower lids

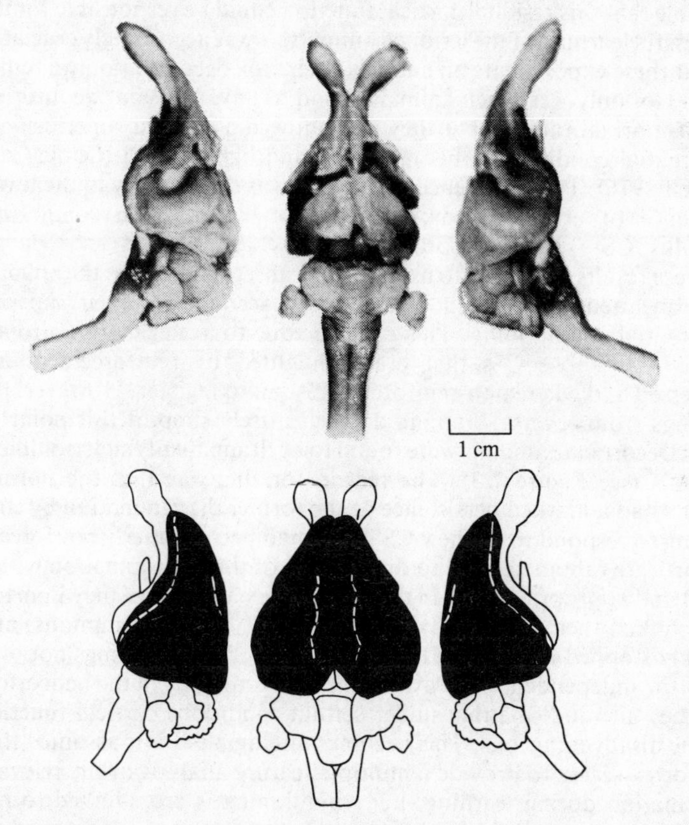

Figure 7.2 Lateral and dorsal views of a chronically decorticated rabbit brain. Decortication was achieved by removal of the pia and devascularization of the cortical surface which results in a complete degeneration of the neocortex. As can be seen, this does not produce any direct limbic or striatal damage.

found in cat and rabbit) produced by cutaneous stimulation of the abducens nerve. The principal advantages of this procedure are: (i) unlike salivary conditioning in the dog there is no problem of spontaneous or alpha responses before training, (ii) it is stable behaviourally and not susceptible to either sensitization or pseudoconditioning, (iii) it is a pure form of associative learning as it is resistant to mediation by instrumental learning.

A comparison of decorticate and normal rabbits showed that there were no differences in Pavlovian learning (Oakley and Russell 1972). Furthermore, differential conditioning to either a tone or a light, showed this was true learning and not due to such non-specific effects as sensitization or hyper-reactive responding (Oakley and Russell 1974). As these animals had some degree of cortical sparing (7 – 35%), it is possible that this residual cortical function could be responsible for the successful learning of the lesioned animals. It was accordingly crucial to repeat these experiments on animals where the decortication was complete. Not only were such animals found to have the same acquisition rate as normal rabbits, but they also showed a marked superiority in differential conditioning between tone and light stimuli (Oakley and Russell 1976). This difference in learning was due entirely to the lower incidence of errors (a lack of responses to negative conditional stimulus, CS–) by the decorticates.

These results suggested to us that in the absence of cortex the animals have an attentional deficit, which could account for their superior differential conditioning. This could be due to a 'neglect' syndrome, where only those CSs that are highlighted by reinforcement are processed and where non-reinforced CSs fail to register. However, the findings from reversal training do not entirely support this point of view. Decorticate animals were found to be dramatically superior to the normals (see Figure 7.3). The reason for this was that the normal rabbits had a marked persistence of the former discrimination by continuing to respond to the new CS– that had been formerly reinforced. Decorticate rabbits reacted to the reversal of the discrimination with a rapid and appropriate shift in their response pattern, i.e. they immediately linked their responses to the new CS+ (positive stimulus) and quickly stopped responding to the new CS–. These findings not only show the independence of Pavlovian conditioning from the neocortex, but they also indicate that under certain conditions cortical function can be disadvantageous. This becomes intelligible if it is assumed that the cortex serves to provide a multiple feature analysis of the relevant information during learning, i.e. conditioning is cross-linked to not only the onset stimulus characteristics but also to duration and offset aspects. In contrast, the animal without cortex would have a very limited feature encoding capability and, thus, register a single aspect of the stimuli. This would then explain what otherwise would appear to be a superiority of the decorticate in a reversal learning task.

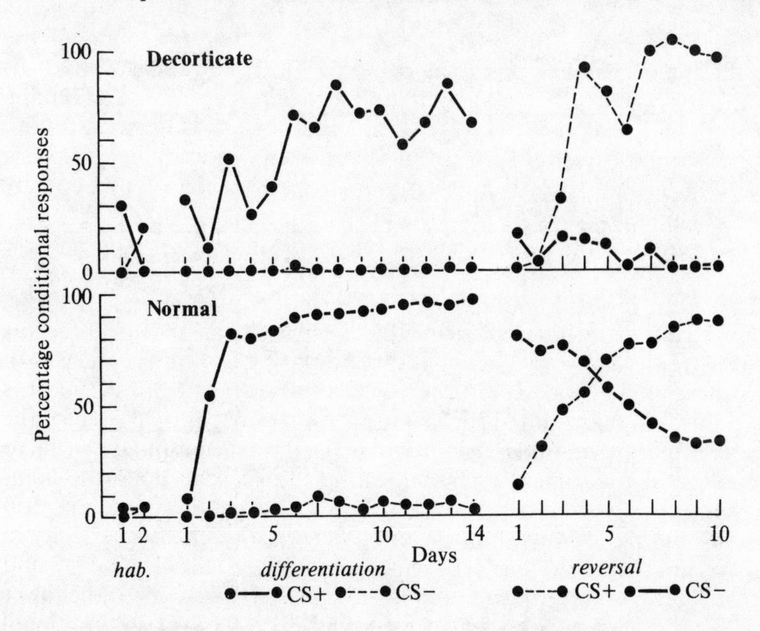

Figure 7.3 Pavlovian differentiation and reversal conditioning in normal and totally decorticate rabbits.

From these findings there can be no doubt that Pavlovian learning can occur in the complete absence of the cortex. Further, the ease with which this can occur in the decorticate, strongly suggests that under normal circumstances the cerebral cortex is probably a sleeping partner. The alternative possibility is that although the intact brain *normally uses* the cortex for associative learning, this function is readdressed to subcortical mechanisms when the cortex is damaged. To examine this possibility normal animals were first trained to make a Pavlovian differentiation, and were then completely decorticated. Perfect retention of the discrimination was found when they were subsequently tested under extinction conditions and without any re-training. These results, given in Figure 7.4, argue strongly that both the storage and retrieval of associative learning is mediated by subcortical mechanisms, even when the information is processed in the normal intact brain.

Instrumental learning differs from Pavlovian conditioning in that the brain evaluates a causal relationship between its behavioural actions and their environmental consequences. As Lashley (1951) pointed out the information processing in instrumental learning is essentially about serial order in behaviour, where initially it is characterized by an extremely detailed specification of the relations between events. With continued experience, however, the 'control programme' becomes less detailed about response sequences and more concerned with objectives

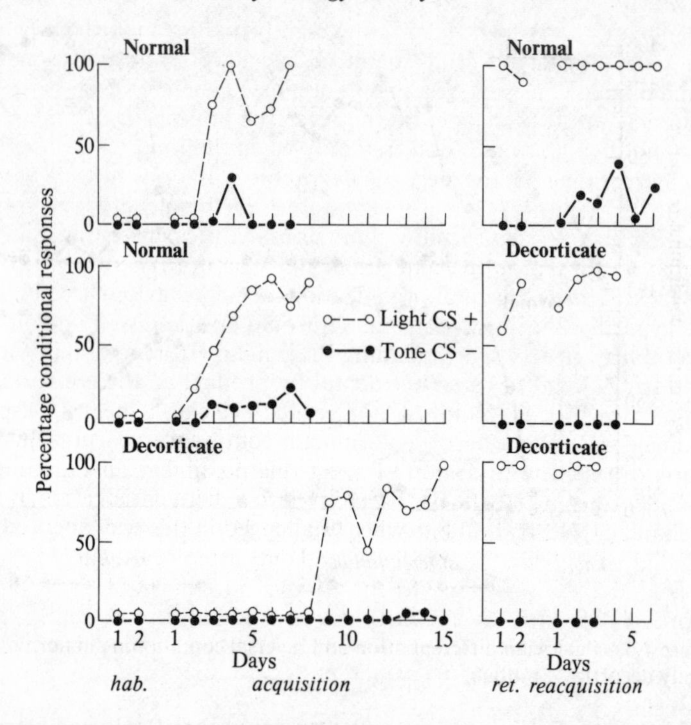

Figure 7.4 Retention of Pavlovian conditioning following complete removal of cortex. Group percentage of conditioned responses are shown for habituation, acquisition, retention and reacquisition phases. Following acquisition of the discrimination one group was given a pseudo-operation and the other group were decorticated.

to be attained analogous to a set of map co-ordinates. For these reasons it is likely that the cortex would be expected to play a greater role in this type of learning (Russell 1971).

Our early work on instrumental learning in the rat and rabbit had suggested that the removal of cortex resulted in a crippling impairment of this type of learning. For example decorticate rats were found to be incapable of genuine avoidance learning, where their performance was found to be indistinguishable from that of pseudoconditioning control animals (Russell 1971). Similarly, a decorticate rabbit that was found capable of barpress learning, did so in a way which was both inefficient and differently organized from the behaviour of normal animals (Oakley 1971). Subsequent experiments have been concerned to examine the reliability of these early studies and to explore the nature of the deficit.

The first study compared barpress learning in both normal and totally decorticate rabbits. Normal rabbits can be taught to barpress for food in one or two trials, and respond readily to the standard reinforcement schedules in the usual manner. The barpress response in the normal animal consisted of a highly organized chain of events, where the animal would first operate the lever the appropriate number of times and then go to the food tray only when the food was delivered. Such barpressing in the decorticate rabbit was only possible after extended training and was never very stable. Furthermore, the performance was characterized by many anomalous features suggesting that the learning was of a primitive and rudimentary nature. There was a complete lack of any sequential organization in the behaviour (see Figure 7.5). Typically, the decorticate animal would position itself in front of the food tray vigorously responding there in an effort to obtain food. Barpressing occurred as an accidental by-product of these efforts to push into the food tray and was not learned as a causal means. Despite prolonged training the decorticate animals continued to barpress in this apparently accidental fashion. To test this possibility an experiment was undertaken where the bar was moved to a different location in the test chamber. Normal rabbits when challenged in this way adapted by immediately searching for the lever, and only after locating it in its new position did they initiate their former instrumental behaviour. Decorticates in contrast never appeared to detect any change in the position of the lever. They continued to push and burrow in the food tray as before. Over time this resulted in a fresh adventitious conditioning of movements that randomly activated the bar in its new location (Oakley and Russell 1978, 1979).

Thus, at this juncture the main findings of these decortication studies is in close but not complete agreement with the split-brain studies. Taken together they suggest that the various types of learning are mediated at different control levels in the brain. However, subsequent research exploring the nature of the instrumental deficit in decorticate animals indicates that the neurological level of information processing is not determined by the learning paradigm *per se* as originally considered (Russell 1971).

The salient deficit in the instrumental learning of the decorticate is the animal's apparent inability to relate its actions to their consequences. A possible factor responsible for this impairment could be a failure to maintain a sequential ordering of the chain of responses that occur during normal barpress behaviour. As no chaining or sequential responding is entailed in Pavlovian conditioning this would account for the absence of a deficit with such tasks. Furthermore, it is clear that if the cortex is mainly responsible for response sequencing, then deficits would be expected in other behaviours as well as learning. For example, it is well known that decortication has no effect on female sexual behaviour in rats, rabbits, cats and dogs; whereas the same lesion in male animals renders them totally sexually inactive. As the male in all these species is both the initiator and controller of the mating sequence,

Normal

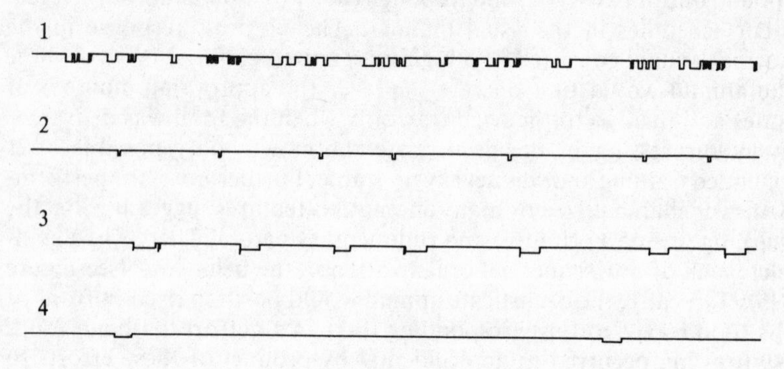

Decorticate

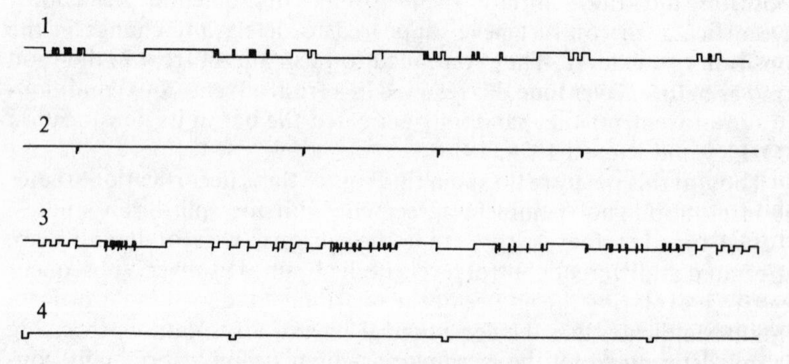

Figure 7.5 Kymograph records of the sequence of responding by individual normal and decorticate rabbits during FR8 performance. In both cases the frequency of barpresses are given in trace 1, the delivery of each food pellet in trace 2, and the tray responses in trace 3. A 30 s time marking is given by deflections in trace 4. The normal performance is ordered by first barpressing until the arrival of food pellets, which then produces a tray response. After a brief pause this cycle is repeated. The decorticate animal's behaviour is completely different and shows no such ordering of its responding. Instead, there is a continuous sequence of tray responding which is adventitiously accompanied by random lever presses that episodically produce rewards.

the explanation of the male dependency on cortex could be due to its sequential ordering function. Considering this lack of sequential ordering as the major cause of the decorticate animal's learning impairment, it is clear that the spatial separation of the bar and food tray in the test apparatus would compound and exaggerate their instrumental learning difficulty. Using the food tray door as a response manipulandum would not only minimize the sequential requirements of the task, it would also simplify it by abolishing the separation between the response and reward. Using this procedure Oakley and Morgan (1977) found that under these circumstances the decorticate learning deficit was completely attenuated. Unlike earlier reports (Oakley 1971; Oakley and Russell 1978, 1979) the instrumental responding was perfectly sequentially co-ordinated and also stable. Furthermore, the decorticate rat was found to tolerate intermittent reinforcement schedules as high as FR60 in the same way as the normal animal.

In reviewing the lack of any associative learning impairment following removal of cortex, attention was earlier drawn to the facilitating effect of this lesion on differential and reversal learning. This suggested that there was a significant reduction in attentional processes as a result of the loss of cortex. Further experiments have examined the possible contribution of this impairment to the instrumental learning deficit of decorticate animals. In particular it could be a major cause of their inability to acquire any 'causal understanding' of the consequences of their behaviour. The first study examined the possible beneficial effect of focusing the decorticate animal's attention on the response used to gain reward. The method used for this was to expose rabbits to extensive *response* discrimination training. The animals were trained to barpress in a two lever box, where one lever was correct and the other was ineffective. Both normal and decorticate rabbits were exposed to a series of response discrimination reversals. In all 15 reversals were given during this training phase. Normal animals showed a clear reversal learning set throughout the series. Not only did decorticate animals require extensive training to complete the series, but they also failed to show any reversal learning set. However, the effect of the response discrimination training was dramatic on later barpress performance. Despite a spatial separation between the bar and the food reward they showed entirely normal patterns of sequentially organized behaviour even under highly intermittent reward conditions (i.e. FR60). Control decorticate rabbits that were similarly tested without any prior response differentiation, showed the characteristic lack of sequential order in their performance and were also unable to tolerate intermittent reward (Oakley 1978).

Further work (Oakley and Russell 1980) has examined the role of response saliency in focusing the animal's attention on its actions. This used a response which takes advantage of the rat's natural tendency to explore objects by biting them. Using a method of successive approximations, rats were trained to pull a chain with their teeth as an instrumental response. Following this both normal and decorticate rats were exposed to high intermittent reward schedules (FR60). No deficit was seen in decorticates, either with respect to sequential organization or tolerance of periodic reinforcement.

A third alternative explanation for the decorticate learning impairment could be due to a loss of intrinsic cortical inhibitory control over lower centres. As a consequence the animal would become both hyper-reactive and hyper-emotional (Bard 1934) as well as easily distractable (Wade 1947). Bromiley (1948) first drew attention to the disruptive effects of emotional reactions due to shock motivation on decorticate learning ability. As we have seen, however, this does not always appear to be the case because in all of our Pavlovian conditioning experiments shock reinforcement was used. Thus, it is possible that there is an interaction with the type of learning and the disruptive effects of shock. To test this possibility Oakley (1979) made a comparison of the effect of shock and food motivation on decorticate learning of a runway response. Although decorticates could learn the runway task as well as normal rats, they were totally unable to acquire the same response under shock avoidance conditions, even when they had been successfully pretrained with food. These indicate that the inability to inhibit emotional reactions can seriously block all instrumental learning in the decorticate if the test situation entails emotional arousing features such as shock motivation.

The question is whether or not a similar inhibitory deficit operates to impede the animal's ability to eliminate 'errors' during instrumental learning. Given the beneficial effects of food motivation on decorticate learning in the runway, it was decided to examine the discrimination capacity of the decorticate rat. Using food reward, animals were trained on a simultaneous two-choice visual pattern task. Although the decorticate animals required extensive training, none the less they were able to reach the same discrimination criterion as normal animals (Oakley 1980). As no checks were made to determine whether or not the lesioned rats used the same response strategies as the normals, these results do not show inhibitory control in the decorticate. Accordingly a second experiment used a barpress task to examine the ability of decorticate rats to learn a successive brightness discrimination (GO NOGO) for food reward. Despite lengthy training no signs of discrimination were shown by the decorticate animals due to their inability to stop responding during each NOGO or S− period (Oakley and Russell 1979; Oakley and Russell 1980).

These findings suggest that the decorticate inability to acquire a successive discrimination was due to their inability to inhibit response tendencies during S−. However, differential Pavlovian conditioning, which is also a successive discrimination, has been repeatedly found to be independent of cortical function. In this case the absence of any deficit was not regarded as necessary evidence of response inhibition in the absence of cortex. It could equally well be interpreted as evidence for an attentional deficit, where only S+ stimuli were processed. This argument would account for the lack of decorticate deficit in a simultaneous discrimination, which could be solved by the animal using a simple S+ strategy where no processing of the S− stimulus need occur. The deficit that was found with the successive discrimination paradigm would strongly argue for a lack of behavioural inhibitory control, if it were not for the fact that the decorticate performance was highly irregular and unstable. Thus, the lack of discriminative learning could well be attributable to a sequential ordering deficit and not to an inhibitory one.

For these reasons a stringent investigation of the decorticate animal's ability to exert inhibitory control over its behaviour was undertaken. Advantage was taken of fairly recent developments in behavioural technology that distinguish between two principal types of inhibition. The first of these is *latent inhibition*, where the repeated exposure to the CS alone before conditioning results in a retardation of subsequent learning. This pre-exposure to the CS produces a loss of 'salience', and this attentional bias (i.e. a 'tuning-out' of the stimulus) must be overcome later in order for the learning to occur (Rescorla and Wagner 1972). The second form of behavioural inhibition is *conditioned inhibition*. This involves a discrimination paradigm where one stimulus is rewarded (S_1+) and the same stimulus in conjunction with an added cue is not (S_1+, S_1−). In order for a successive discrimination to be possible the animal must pay attention to the added cue. Thus, conditioned inhibition requires a discrimination where the animal must actively inhibit responses to the S+ when it is conjoined with an S− cue. A response strategy of processing the information solely with respect to the S+ would make it impossible to discriminate.

The role of the cortex was examined in both behavioural inhibition paradigms, using Pavlovian conditioning of the rabbit nictitating membrane (Moore, Yeo, Oakley and Russell 1980). For latent inhibition both normal and decorticate animals were first habituated to a brief tone. Following this, they were then given Pavlovian training to the same tone. Their rate of learning this task was then compared to control animals that had received no prior training to 'tune out' the tone. This procedure produced a marked retardation of learning only in normals, and no such latent inhibition was seen in the animals lacking cortex. A second experiment examined the learning ability of the decorticate in a conditioned inhibition paradigm. All animals were first exposed to a single stimulus paradigm where they were conditioned to a light stimulus (S_1+). After reaching criterion they were given the conditioned inhibition discrimination, where the positive stimulus remained as the light and the negative one was the same light combined with a tone (S_1+, S_2−). Training was continued until a 95% correct response level was attained in all animals. No differences were found between decorticate and normal rabbits; both acquired the discrimination at the same rate and to the same level. Thus, it would appear that the ability to actively inhibit responding is not dependent on the cerebral cortex. These results are decisive evidence against classical notions of the cortical inhibitory control of behaviour. By contrast, the findings of a deficit with regard to latent inhibition points to the importance of the cortex in the control of attentional processes.

Considering as a whole the research on cortical mechanisms of learning, it is clear that changes of learning paradigm *per se* do not index different control levels in the brain. The view that instrumental learning was processed by neocortical mechanisms and Pavlovian conditioning involved subcortical machinery is no longer plausible. Experiments investigating the role of the cerebral cortex in instrumental learning did not find that it provided any intrinsic 'computing' function. Instead, they drew attention to the cortical involvement in attentional processes and sequential ordering of information. Both of these processes play a more important role in any instrumental learning situation than they do in Pavlovian conditioning. In the latter, information order and stimulus acquisition are under experimenter control; they are not left for the animal to isolate from the test situation, as is the case for instrumental learning.

It could be argued that the objective of looking for separate representations of different types of learning in the brain is neither sensible nor profitable. The main reason for this is that the various types of learning refer either to different training paradigms or to test situations. They are in no way comparable to different types of visual behaviour that are identifiable in terms of their different underlying sensory processes, e.g. colour and stereoscopic vision. One can relate structure to function (process) when dealing with vision, but not when considering learning. Indeed, until the various types of learning are identifiable in terms of their different sensory process, it is hard to see how genuine progress can be made in understanding the underlying neurology. It would seem that for learning, as it was for vision, psychological constructs by themselves can never clarify fundamental brain mechanisms. Unless they are anchored to sensory processes or anatomical connections, they will merely obfuscate progress in our understanding of the organization of the differing control levels in the brain.

REFERENCES

Allman, J. 1977. 'Evolution of the visual system in the early primates.' In J. H. Sprague and A. N. Epstein (eds), *Progress in psychobiology and physiological psychology, 7.* New York: Academic Press.

Bard, P. A. 1934. 'On emotional expression after decortication with some remarks on certain theoretical views.' *Psychol. Rev. 41*, 309 – 29.

Bitterman, M. E. 1965. 'Phyletic differences in learning.' *Amer. Psychol. 20*, 396 – 410.

Brindley, G. S., Gautier-Smith, P. C., and Lewin, W. 1969. 'Cortical blindness and the functions of the non-geniculate fibres of the optic tracts.' *J. Neurol. Neurosurg. Psychiat. 32*, 259 – 64.

Bromiley, R. B. 1948. 'Conditioned responses in a dog after removal of neocortex.' *J. Comp. Physiol. Psychol. 41*, 102 – 10.

Bures, J., and Buresova, O. 1960. 'The use of Leao's spreading cortical depression in the interhemispheric transfer of memory traces.' *J. comp. physiol. Psychol. 53*, 558 – 63.

Bures, J., Buresova, O., and Fifkova, E. 1964. 'Interhemispheric transfer of a passive avoidance reaction.' *J. comp. physiol. Psychol. 57*, 326 – 530.

Cannon, W. B., and Britton, S. W. 1927. 'Studies on the conditions of activity in endocrine glands. XV Pseudoaffective medulliadrendl secretion.' *Amer. J. Physiol. 79*, 433 – 65.

Casagrande, V. A., Harting, J. K., Hall, W. C., Diamond, I. T., and Martin, G. F. 1972. 'Superior colliculus of the tree shrew: A structural and functional subdivision into superficial and deep structures.' *Science 177*, 444 – 7.

Culler, E. A., and Mettler, F. A. 1934. 'Conditioned behavior in a decorticate dog.' *J. comp. Psychol. 18*, 291 – 303.

Doty, R. E., and Negrao, N. 1973. 'Forebrain commissures and vision.' In R. Jung (ed.), *Handbook of sensory physiology*. Berlin: Springer-Verlag.

Dusser de Barenne, J. G. 1920. 'Récherches expérimentales sur les fonctions du système nervaux central, faites en particuliere sur deux chats dont le neopallium avait été enlévé.' *Arch. néerl. Physiol. 4*, 30 – 123.

Ebbesson, S. O. E., and Schroeder, D. M. 1971. 'Connections of the nurse shark's telencephalon.' *Science, 173*, 254 – 6.

Elliot Smith, G. 1910. 'Some problems relating to the evolution of the brain.' *Lancet 88*, 1 – 16, 147 – 53, 221 – 7.

Fox, R., Lehmkuhle, S. W., and Bush, R. C. 1976. 'Falcon visual acuity.' *Science 192*, 263 – 5.

Gazzaniga, M. S. 1970. *The bisected brain*. New York: Appleton-Century-Crofts.

Girden, E., Mettler, F. A., Finch, G., and Culler, E. 1936. 'Conditioned responses in a decorticate dog to acoustic, thermal, and tactile stimulation.' *J. comp. Psychol. 21*, 367 – 85.

Glickstein, M., King, R. A., Miller, J., and Berkley, M. 1967. 'Cortical projections from the dorsolateral geniculate nucleus of cats.' *J. comp. Neurol. 130*, 55 – 76.

Goltz, F. 1892. 'Der Hund ohne Grosshirn.' *Pflugers Arch. ges. Physiol. 51*, 570 – 614.

Graeber, R. C., Schroeder, D. M., Jane, J. A., and Ebbesson, S. O. E. 1972. 'The importance of telencephalic structures in visual discrimination learning in nurse sharks.' Soc. for Neuroscience. 2nd Ann. Meeting. Cited in R. B. Masterton (1978) (ed.) *Handbook of behavioural neurobiology 1: sensory integration*. New York: Plenum Press.

Hernandez-Peon, R., and Brust-Carmona, H. 1961. 'Functional role of subcortical structures in habituation and conditioning.' In A. Fessard, R. W. Gerard and J. Konorski (eds) *Brain mechanisms and learning*. Oxford: Blackwell.

Hodos, W., and Campbell 1969. '*Scala Naturae*: Why there is no theory in comparative psychology.' *Psychol. Rev. 76*, 337 – 50.

Hodos, W., and Karten, H. J. 1970. 'Visual intensity and pattern discrimination deficits after lesions of the ectostriatum in pigeons.' *J. comp. Neurol. 140*, 53 – 68.

Humphrey, N. 1970. 'What the frog's eye tells the monkey's brain.' *Brain Behav. Evol. 3*, 324 – 7.

Humphrey, N. 1974. 'Vision in a monkey without striate cortex: a case study.' *Perception 3*, 241 – 55.

Humphrey, N., and Weiskrantz, L. 1967. 'Vision in monkeys after removal of the striate cortex.' *Nature 215*, 595 – 7.

Jackson, J. Hughlings 1898. 'Relations of diff. divisions of the CNS to one another and to parts of the body.' *The Lancet 1*, 79 – 87.

Karplus, J. P., and Kreidl, A. 1914. 'Ueber Total extirpationen einer und beider Grosshirn hemisphaeren an Affen (Macacus rhesus).' *Arch. Anat. Physiol. Lpz. 38*, 155 – 212.

Karten, H. J., and Nauta, W. J. H. 1968. 'Organization retinothalamic projections in the pigeon and owl.' *Anat. Res. 160*, 373.

Kohn, B. 1967. 'Spreading depression and stimulus control of interhemispheric transfer.' *Neuropsychologia 5*, 275 – 86.

Lashley, K. S. 1929. *Brain mechanisms and intelligence*. Chicago: The University of Chicago Press.

Lashley, K. S. 1951. 'The problem of serial order in behaviour.' In L. A. Jeffress (ed.) *Cerebral mechanisms in behaviour*. New York: John Wiley.

Lebedinskaia, S. I., and Rosenthal, J. S. 1935. 'Reactions of a dog after removal of the cerebral hemispheres.' *Brain 58*, 412 – 19.

Levere, T. E. 1978. 'The primary visual system of the rat: A primer of its anatomy.' *Physiol. Psychol. 6*, 142 – 69.

Marquis, D. G. 1935. 'Phylogenetic interpretation of the functions of this visual cortex.' *Arch. Neurol. Psychiat. 33*, 807 – 15.

Meikle, T. H., Sechzer, J. A., and Stellar, E. 1962. 'Interhemispheric transfer of tactile conditioned responses in corpus-callosum sectioned cats.' *J. Neurophysiol. 25*, 530 – 7.

Mettler, F. A., Mettler, G. C., and Culler, E. A. 1935. 'The effects of total removal of the cerebral cortex.' *Amer. Med. Assoc. Arch. Neurol. Psychiat. 34*, 1238 – 49.

Moore, J. W., Yeo, C. H., Oakley, D. A., and Russell, I. S. 1980. 'Conditioned inhibition of the nictitating membrane response in neodecorticate rabbits.' *Beh. Brain Res.*, in press.

Oakley, D. A. 1971. 'Instrumental learning in neodecorticate rabbits.' *Nature 233*, 185 – 7.

Oakley, D. A. 1978 'Instrumental reversal learning and subsequent Fixed Ratio performance on simple and GO NOGO schedules in neodecorticate rabbits.' *Physiol. Psychol. 7*, 29-33.

Oakley, D. A. 1979. 'Neocortex and learning.' *Trends in Neurosciences 2*, 149 – 52.

Oakley, D. A. 1980. 'Improved instrumental learning in neodecorticate rats.' *Physiol. Behav. 24*, 357 – 66.

Oakley, D. A., and Morgan, S. C. 1977. 'Fixed ratio performance in neodecorticate rat.' *IRCS Med. Sci. 5*, 494.

Oakley, D. A., and Russell, I. S. 1972. 'Neocortical lesions and Pavlovian conditioning.' *Physiol. Behav. 8*, 915 – 26.

Oakley, D. A., and Russell, I. S. 1974. 'Differential and reversal learning in partially neodecorticate rabbits.' *Physiol. Behav. 13*, 221 – 30.

Oakley, D. A., and Russell, I. S. 1976. 'Subcortical nature of Pavlovian differentiation in the rabbit.' *Physiol. Behav. 17*, 947 – 54.

Oakley, D. A., and Russell, I. S. 1978. 'Performance of neodecorticate rabbits in a free-operant situation.' *Physiol. Behav. 20*, 157 – 70.

Oakley, D. A., and Russell, I. S. 1979. 'Instrumental learning on fixed ratio and GO NOGO schedules in neodecorticate rats.' *Brain Res. 161*, 356.

Oakley, D. A., and Russell, I. S. 1980. 'Effect of prior experience on barpressing in rats without cortex.' *Behav. Brain Res. 1*, 201 – 19.

Pasik, T., and Pasik, P. 1971. 'The visual world of monkeys deprived of striate cortex: effective stimulus parameters and the importance of the accessory optic system.' *Vision Res. Suppl. 3*, 419 – 35.

Passingham, R. E., and Ettlinger, G. 1974. 'A comparison of cortical functions in man and other primates.' *Int. Rev. Neurobiol. 16*, 233 – 99.

Pavlov, I. P. 1927. *Conditioned reflexes: an investigation of the physiological activity of the cerebral cortex* (translated by G. V. Awrep). Oxford: Oxford University Press.

Pinto-Hamuy, T., Santibanez-H, G., and Rojas, A. 1963. 'Learning and retention of a visual conditioned response in neodecorticate rats.' *J. comp. physiol. Psychol. 56*, 19 – 24.

Poltyrew, S., and Zelioney, G. 1930. 'Grosshirurinde und Assoziations funklion.' *Z. Biol. 90*, 157 – 60.

Rescorla, R. A., and Wagner, A. R. 1972. 'A theory of Pavlovian conditioning variations in the effectiveness of reinforcement and nonreinforcement.' In A. H. Black and W. F. Prokasy (eds) *Classical conditioning 11: Current Research and Theory*. New York: Appleton-Century-Crofts.

Ross, R. B., and Russell, I. S. 1964. 'Subcortical storage of classical conditioning.' *Nature 204*, 909 – 10.

Ross, R. B., and Russell, I. S. 1967. 'Lateralization and one-trial interhemispheric transfer of avoidance conditioning.' *Nature 214*, 210 – 11.

Rothman, H. 1923. 'Zusammenfassender bericht uber den Rothmannschen grosshirnalosen hund nach klinischer und anatomischer untersuchung.' *Z. ges. Neurol. Psychiat. 87*, 247 – 313.

Russell, I. S., and Ochs, S. 1961. 'One-trial interhemispheric transfer of a learning engram.' *Science 133*, 1077 – 8.

Russell, I. S., and Ochs, S. 1963. 'Localization of a memory trace in one cortical hemisphere and transfer to the other hemisphere.' *Brain 86*, 37 – 54.

Russell, I. S. 1966. 'Animal learning and memory.' In D. Richter (ed.) *Aspects of Learning and Memory*. London: Heinemann.

Russell, I. S. 1969. 'The role of the cortex in the acquisition and retention of a classically conditioned passive avoidance response.' *Physiol. and Behav. 4*, 575 – 81.

Russell, I. S. 1971. 'Neurological basis of complex learning.' *Brit. Med. Bull. 27*, 3, 278 – 85.

Russell, I. S., and Safferstone, J. F. 1973. 'Lateralization of brightness and pattern discrimination learning in the corpus callosum-sectioned rat.' *Brain Res. 49*, 497 – 8.

Russell, I. S. 1979. 'Brain size and intelligence: a comparative perspective.' In D. A. Oakley and H. S. Plotkin (eds) *Brain, Behaviour and Evolution*. London: Methuen Press.

Schneider, A. M. 1966. 'Retention under spreading depression.' *J. comp. physiol. Psychol. 62*, 317 – 19.

Schneider, A. M. 1967. 'Control of memory by cortical spreading depression: A case for stimulus control.' *Psychol. Rev. 74*, 201 – 15.
Schneider, G. E. 1969. 'Two visual systems: brain mechanisms for localization and discrimination are dissociated by tectal and cortical lesions.' *Science 163*, 895 – 902.
Sechzer, J. 1964. 'Successful interocular transfer of pattern discrimination in "split-brain" cats with shock-avoidance motivation.' *J. comp. physiol. Psychol. 58*, 76 – 80.
Snyder, M., and Diamond, I. T. 1968. 'The organization and function of the visual cortex in the tree shrew.' *Brain Behav. Evol. 1*, 244 – 88.
Sprague, J., and Meikle, T. 1965. 'The role of the superior colliculus in visually guided behavior.' *Exp. Neurol. 11*, 115 – 46.
Ten Cate, J. 1934. 'Austiche und optische reaktionen der katzen nach teilweiser und totaler exterpation des neopalliums.' *Arch. neerl. Physiol. 19*, 191 – 264.
Ter Braak, J. W. G., Schenk, V. W. D., and van Vliet, A. G. M. 1971. 'Visual reactions in a case of long-lasting cortical blindness.' *J. Neurol. Neurosurg. Psychiat. 34*, 140 – 158.
Travis, R. P., and Sparks, D. L. 1963. 'The influence of unilateral and bilateral spreading depression during learning upon subsequent learning.' *J. comp. physiol. Psychol. 56*, 56 – 9.
Wade, M. 1947. 'The effect of sedatives upon delayed response in monkeys following removal of the prefrontal lobes.' *J. Neurophysiol. 10*, 57 – 61.
Walls, G. L. 1939. 'Origin of the vertebrate eye.' *Arch. Ophthalmol. 22*, 452.
Walls, G. L. 1942. *The vertebrate eye and its adaptive radiation*. Bloomfield Hill, Mich.: Cranbrook Institute.
Ward, J. P., and Masterton, B. 1970. 'Encephalization and visual cortex in the tree shrew.' *Brain Behav. Evol. 3*, 421 – 69.
Ware, C. B., Casagrande, V. A., and Diamond, I. T. 1972. 'Does the acuity of the tree shrew suffer from removal of striate cortex?' *Brain Behav. Evol. 5*, 18 – 29.
Webster, K. E. 1973. 'Thalamus and basal ganglia in reptiles and birds.' *Symp. Zool. Soc. Lond. 33*, 169 – 203.
Weiskrantz, L. 1961. 'Encephalization and the scotoma.' In W. H. Thorpe and O. L. Zangwill (eds) *Current problems in animal behaviour*. Cambridge: Cambridge University Press.
Weiskrantz, L. 1963. 'Contour discrimination in a young monkey with striate cortex ablation.' *Neuropsych. 1*, 145 – 64.
Weiskrantz, L., and Cowey, A. 1970. 'Filling in the scotoma: A study of residual vision after striate cortex lesions in monkeys.' *Prog. Physiol. Psychol. 3*, 237 – 60.
Weiskrantz, L., and Cowey, A. 1971. 'Effects of striate cortex removals on visual discrimination.' *Brain Res. 31*, 376.
Wilson, M. 1978. 'Visual system: pulvinar-extrastriate cortex.' In R. B. Masterton (ed.) *Handbook of Behavioural Neurobiology*. New York: Plenum Press.
Zelioney, G. P. 1929. 'Effects de l'ablation des hémisphères cérébeaux.' *Rev. de Med. 46* (*Psychol. Abstracts* (1930) *4*, 717), 21.

Chapter 8

Experimental Studies of Intergroup Behaviour

HENRI TAJFEL

EXPERIMENTS AND THE REALITIES OF SOCIAL CONFLICTS

> 'The strength of (social psychology) and the main feature distinguishing it from other social sciences were traditionally seen in its use of experimental methods of research. The aim was, some forty years ago, to create a reliably scientific approach to human social behaviour. This developed in due course into experimental social psychology which overwhelmingly dominated (and still does) the research and writing in the subject. But what started as an exciting new venture became over the years, as is often the case, a complacent and unquestioned old routine. It is therefore not surprising that the "experimental" tradition found itself at the receiving end of most of the attacks directed in the last ten years or so at the *kind* of research done by social psychologists' (Tajfel 1978a, p. ix).

It is, however, interesting that these attacks were mainly concerned with the inadequacies of the experimental studies of *interpersonal* behaviour. It has been said again and again that the contrived arrangements of laboratory experiments distorted out of all recognition the reality and richness of genuine human encounters. They created, it was argued, an Alice-in-Wonderland world of their own which produced very little of interest or value, could not add to our common experience and even distorted it; methods of research needed to be closer to genuine articulations by the social actors of their experiences. It is not the aim of this chapter to enter this controversy. It is mentioned here solely because both the 'old' and the 'new' social psychologies seem to share their relative lack of interest in the dynamics and functioning of the relations between human *groups* as contrasted with their preoccupation with what happens between individuals. It is because of this common lack of interest that the experimental social psychology of intergroup behaviour has not become a direct target of the attacks against the experimental methods, although, by implication, it was undoubtedly included in them.

The purpose of the present brief and selective review of some recent experimental studies of intergroup behaviour is threefold: (i) to provide an account of the recent revival of interest in what has been a long-neglected area of social psychology; (ii) to show that, in this particular area, experimental studies are and will have to remain *one* of the indispensable tools of further research; and, (iii) to take stock, very briefly, of the present position and of the major requirements for further new developments.

It is possible to conceive of the psychological study of social interaction as containing a broad range of interests which can be simply defined, as it moves from one to the other of its extremes, in terms of the *numbers* of people who are the target of research. Thus, we have at one extreme the study of processes that are inherent in the individual, as in the case of cognitive dissonance, although they do intervene in many important ways in social interaction. From here we move to the study of interpersonal or dyadic relationships that has been at the core of many important developments in the subject in the last twenty years or so. Small groups – containing a few people who are in direct interpersonal contact – represent the next step in the range. From here, we move to the study of the relations between two or more such small groups. These relations are still affected by direct interpersonal involvements, both within each of the small groups and between members of the different groups. And finally, at the extreme of the range, there remains the social psychology of relations between large-scale human groups or categories, be they social, national, ethnic, racial, political or religious. As we move from the dyadic relationships to those between small groups, and finally to large social categories, an important question arises: how much of the behaviour displayed in the encounters between members of small groups or, even more so, of large social categories is determined by interpersonal processes, and how much of it is due to the structure of the relations between the groups involved?

This question must be discussed in terms of two transitions which concern two different segments of the range we have just described. The first transition is from interpersonal to inter-small group behaviour; and the second is the transition from small groups, which still remain interpersonal, to the large-scale social categories.

The first of these transitions has long been the major theme in the work of Sherif. As he wrote in one of his later books, 'The word "group" in the phrase "intergroup relations" is not a superfluous label. Our claim is the study of relations between groups and intergroup attitudes of their respective members. We therefore must consider both the properties of the groups themselves and the consequences of membership for individuals. Otherwise, whatever we are studying, we are not studying intergroup problems' (Sherif 1966, pp. 61 – 2).

Although Sherif appears to state here what should seem to be obvious, the tradition of studying intergroup relations as if they were an extension of individual and interpersonal processes has been, and still is, powerful in social psychology. Much of Sherif's work was based on the view that the structure and dynamics of relations between groups determine and direct, in all relevant situations, the course of personal encounters between people belonging to the different groups. The alternative perspective has been to consider the encounters between individuals that take place in the framework of issues posed by relations between groups as no more than a special category of other interpersonal encounters.

A good example of this perspective can be found in some approaches to the study of intergroup negotiations and bargaining in which are involved representatives of the groups in conflict. Stephenson and his colleagues have done, over the years, a great deal of work on these issues (e.g. Morley and Stephenson 1977; Stephenson 1978; Stephenson *et al.* 1976). The interpersonal emphasis of much of the work in this field has recently led Stephenson to feel that he had to stress once more that, '. . . in collective bargaining, interpersonal exchange between the participants is not the subject at issue, but is incidental to the dispute between the parties' (Stephenson 1980). This he contrasted with the assumption still prevailing in some quarters that, 'the intergroup or collective nature of the negotiation' is just one factor superimposed on, 'individual or interpersonal bargaining.' 'The fallacy in such reasoning is exposed when we realize that in collective bargaining the individuals would not be there but for the existence of a dispute which transcends their interpersonal relationship' (Stephenson 1980). A recent review by Druckman (1977) of studies on intergroup bargaining provides a good example that Stephenson is not tilting at windmills. Many of these studies assume, 'that role (i.e. group) obligations impinge – more or less detrimentally – on an otherwise interpersonal negotiation'.

These interpersonal perspectives upon collective bargaining or intergroup negotiations are but one example of an approach to problems of intergroup relations, which is still frequently found in social psychology. This neglects the need for a psychological analysis of the social context within which take place many encounters between individuals. Although such encounters may superficially appear to be personal, they are structured and directed by a wider and extra-personal set of determinants. The example of negotiations will have to do for this brief survey of some present developments in the study of intergroup relations. More detailed discussions of a number of other similar issues which are still often conceived in 'inter-individual' terms can be found in, e.g. Billig (1976) and Tajfel (1978b, 1979).

The transition from interpersonal behaviour to behaviour between members of small groups represents a shift in theoretical perspectives. This is needed in order to establish a correspondence between the nature of the intergroup problems and the requirements of the research concerning them. There exists a second transition, which requires yet another shift of perspectives. The nature of personal interactions between individuals still affects in *some* measure the relations between small and restricted groups, be they 'natural' or created in social psychological experiments. When one approaches the issues of intergroup behaviour that derive from tensions or conflicts between large-scale social categories, such as ethnic or national groups, personal interactions become, in many situations, even less important in determining the individuals' reciprocal attitudes and their manner of behaving towards each other.

One of the major features of encounters between members of different social categories is the *interchangeability* of the individuals who take part in them. In other words, behaviour towards members of an outgroup is often, in such cases, to a large extent determined by that membership rather than by any individual characteristics of the people involved. It is this interchangeability which casts the shadow of anonymity upon the 'outsiders', and thus it is directly relevant to the study of what is often called 'depersonalization'. As I wrote elsewhere, 'when in conditions of racial discrimination people find it difficult to obtain accommodation or employment, it is not because they are ugly or handsome, short or tall, smiling or unsmiling, but because they are "black"' (Tajfel 1978b, pp. 27–8).

The question then arises about the ways in which social psychologists can study phenomena of this kind. Field studies of conflicts, tensions and prejudices are one of the obvious solutions, and many such studies are in existence. They have evident advantages, such as their closeness to social reality and the possibility of getting to know 'in depth' the attitudes and experiences of selected individuals (e.g. Weinreich 1979). But their findings need to be seen *in combination* with the results of research aiming at a more contrived and artificial isolation of one or another of the causal factors that may be involved. It is here that experimentation becomes a crucial adjunct to the field studies of intergroup processes, without in any sense being conceptually prior to field research or being able to compete with it in its closeness to raw social reality. It is not the role of such experiments to *simulate* social reality; it is unlikely that they could ever achieve this. Their value lies in the possibility they offer of providing hints about the theoretical links between the innumerable strands that compose the maze of the world of real social conflicts; and thus, experimental studies can help to guide and direct the difficult selection of empirical questions on which must be based any adequate field study of intergroup behaviour. Experiments of this kind have two fundamental and inherent limitations: in time and in numbers. They cannot reproduce the complex history of any instance of conflict or tension between social groups; nor can they mobilize or reproduce the massive membership of multigroup clashes and encounters in complex social systems. But it is possible to contrive research on some selected aspects of these systems and to establish theoretical links from there to the half-hidden and closely interlocking complexities of natural social situations.

The next section of this chapter will be concerned with a selection of such experimental studies, centring around a few of the issues which may turn out to be important for our further understanding of intergroup behaviour at large.

THE INTERCHANGEABLE INDIVIDUALS

The characteristic of intergroup behaviour stressed in the previous section of this chapter was that, as one moved towards larger groups of individuals engaged in some form of conflict or competition, their reciprocal behaviour was increasingly determined by the structure of the relations between these groups. This does not, of course, apply to *all* social behaviour of the people concerned; the intergroup determination is limited to those social encounters and interactions that are perceived by the participants as being in some ways relevant to the relations between the groups to which they respectively belong. Some of Sherif's studies provided a good example of this shift from the interpersonal to the intergroup context of behaviour. In some of these studies (e.g. Sherif and Sherif 1953), the first stage of the activities in a holiday camp did not involve a division into competing groups. When such a division was introduced after about a week, 'care was taken to separate close friends and to place them into opposing groups' (Billig 1976, p. 303). This did not prevent the development of intergroup antagonisms in the subsequent stages of camp activities. It was the intergroup conflict that structured the behaviour of the boys, and not their previous friendships across the groups' boundaries.

This kind of finding enables us to state a simple but fairly general proposition: the stronger is an individual's affiliation with a social group, the more it is likely that, in a variety of situations, his behaviour towards members of other groups will show uniformities that are largely independent of the individual differences between the members of the outgroup. Stated in this bare form, the proposition is, of course, much too general. The variety of situations must be specified and analysed in terms of the nature of the outgroup, of its relations with the ingroup and of the classes of social situations that may be involved. Nevertheless, the general proposition provides a useful pointer towards research concerned with the conditions in which certain categories of other people become, in a sense, anonymous and irrelevant *as* individuals. This kind of research is important not only for theoretical reasons; it is directly relevant to many social situations, too familiar to need illustrating or exemplifying, in which strongly drawn boundaries between groups seem to create forms of behaviour towards outsiders that are hardly conceivable, in usual circumstances, within an ingroup, large or small.

It seems, however, that an explicit conflict of interests (real or imaginary) between groups is not the only necessary condition for the appearance of many forms of discriminatory intergroup behaviour. It is not the purpose of this chapter to outline the substantial number of theoretical considerations that lead one to expect that this kind of behaviour can also occur in a variety of intergroup situations which do not appear, on the face of it, competitive or fraught with conflict. These outlines are available elsewhere (see p. 122 for some of the references). We can do no more here than select a few empirical variables which seem particularly relevant to this treatment '*en masse*' or 'interchangeably' of people from social categories other than one's own.

Social Categorization and Social Competition

Can intergroup discrimination occur when groups are not in an explicit conflict of interests and their relationship is not based on previous hostility? It was to answer these questions that some studies were conducted from which all factors were carefully eliminated, other than a simple and clear-cut *division* between two groups based on a trivial difference between them (Tajfel *et al.* 1971). The following criteria guided the experimental procedures: there was no face-to-face interaction either within the 'groups' or between them; anonymity of group membership was preserved; the intergroup responses requested of the subjects were not in any way related to the original criterion for the intergroup division; these responses were not directly related to a personal gain or loss for the subjects making them; a strategy of not differentiating between the groups would have been more rational and advantageous to *all* the subjects, independently of their group membership; there was no previous hostility between the groups; the responses were not trivial, in the sense that they consisted of decisions awarding amounts of money to two anonymous *other* subjects from the 'ingroup' or from the 'outgroup' (Tajfel *et al.* 1971, pp. 153–4). The results showed a clear-cut differentiation in favour of the ingroup, even when this meant, in some cases, that in order to preserve a difference between the groups favouring one's own group, the subjects had to award less money to members of the ingroup than would have been otherwise possible. These results have since been replicated in various ways in a large number of other studies conducted in several countries with subjects ranging in age from 7-year-old children (Vaughan 1978a) to young adults (e.g. Doise *et al.* 1972). A review of some of these studies can be found in Brewer (1979).

There is little doubt that the anonymity of group membership (and thus, depersonalization) had something to do with the appearance of intergroup discrimination in these 'minimal' situations. In this way, these highly contrived experimental procedures paradoxically rejoin the reality of some social situations in which behaviour towards certain people is largely affected by their social label (or sometimes, as Goffman 1971, put it, stigma) and not by their other characteristics. Wilder (1978) recently reported a series of experiments in which a decrease in this 'deindividuation', as he called it, of members of the outgroup led to a corresponding decrease in the bias shown against them.

Although anonymity of membership may contribute to intergroup discrimination, it cannot, by itself, explain its occurrence. Hostile attitudes and discrimination have traditionally been seen as consequences of an intergroup conflict of interests, real or imaginary. Most of the earlier studies on the subject, such as those of Sherif, explored in detail various aspects of these conflicts. There is now, however, an accumulating body of evidence showing that such conflicts are not the *only* necessary conditions for intergroup bias to occur. As Brewer (1979) put it, 'it appears . . . that ingroup bias does occur in the absence of explicit competitive interdependence between groups'. But, as she adds, 'the absence of implicit competitive orientation . . . is difficult to establish'. Indeed, the evidence that such an implicit competition exists has been provided in a large number of recent studies.

It has already been mentioned that in the initial 'minimal categorization' experiments of Tajfel *et al.* (1971), obtaining a *relative* gain for the ingroup was often more important for the subjects than increasing the absolute amounts of gain. This was also the case in a study by Billig and Tajfel (1973) in which the criteria for categorization into groups were even more flimsy than those used in the earlier experiments. Brewer and Silver (1978), using a simplified version of the distribution matrices employed in the previous studies, found the same maximization of, 'relative gain in favour of the ingroup over choices maximizing absolute ingroup gain or other alternatives' (Brewer 1979). Co-action rather than explicit conflict seemed sufficient to cause here this discriminatory intergroup behaviour or attitudes (as also shown in the studies of, for example Allen and Wilder 1975; Dann and Doise 1974; Janssen and Nuttin 1976; Kahn and Ryen 1972; Rabbie *et al.* 1974; Rabbie and Wilkens 1971; Ryen and Kahn 1975). As might be expected, the introduction in such conditions of explicit competition increases still further the amount of bias.

The question then arises about the nature and determinants of this implicit competitive orientation. Two different views about it have recently been formulated. Neither of them denies the overriding importance of objective conflicts of interests in intergroup behaviour and attitudes; but they also both agree that this competitive interdependence is by no means the whole story. Very briefly stated, the first of these views (as represented in, e.g. Doise 1978) is an elaboration closely based on some earlier ideas about the functioning of social categorizations (cf. Tajfel 1959, 1972; Eiser and Stroebe 1972). It makes use of these views to argue that such categorizations, when applied by individuals to social groups, are a necessary *and* sufficient condition for intergroup bias and discrimination to occur. As Doise wrote, 'Differentiation of aspects of the social reality occurs in association with other differentiations relevant to the same reality . . . Category differentiation gives rise to behavioural, evaluative and representational differentiations . . . When there is differentiation at one of these three levels . . . there is a tendency for corresponding differentiations to be made at the other levels' (1978, p. 152).

This view is based on the general idea that, 'the categorization process not only enables the individual to organize his subjective experience of the social environment but also, and perhaps more importantly, constitutes a process by which social interaction is structured, differentiates among, and shapes individuals' (Doise 1978, p. 151). In other words, the introduction by the experimenters of a categorization of subjects into 'groups' in several of the experiments mentioned earlier was sufficient to create the ingroup biases that were observed, and no other variables need to be postulated in order to explain their existence.

Although these initial 'minimal categorization' experiments were designed to ascertain whether social categorization *per se* can elicit intergroup bias and they produced findings that this indeed was the case, later theoretical and research developments led to the elaboration of the second of the two views mentioned above. It has been argued (e.g. Tajfel 1974, 1978b; Tajfel and Turner 1979; Turner 1975, 1980; see also, e.g. Brown 1978a; Caddick 1978; Eiser 1980, for extensive reviews) that, although social categorization is a necessary condition for these intergroup phenomena to occur, it is not a sufficient condition. What was needed in addition was that the individuals' group membership be relevant in some ways to their positive or negative self-images. This leads to a search for a positive social identity through group membership, and, in turn, this search can only be conducted and its outcomes assessed through engaging in, or *creating*, social comparisons with other groups. These comparisons are selective, both in their choice of groups appropriate as objects of comparison and of dimensions on which these intergroup comparisons are made. A positive outcome of such a process would be the achievement, creation or preservation of a positive distinctiveness of the ingroup from the outgroup. From this general basis, a number of hypotheses were formulated concerning the conditions, modes and varieties of social actions attempting to achieve this distinctiveness, these differentiations of the ingroup from the outgroups. The aim was to provide an explanation of the general ingroup bias *and* of the importance to the subjects of the ingroup's *relative* gain over the outgroup, which was found in many studies. The theory provided at the same time the point of departure for a large number of new studies, in the laboratory and in the field (see Tajfel 1978c, for some of the reports). In this survey we can do no more than outline some of the experimental attempts to support the 'pure' categorization view and those that tried to show that the social identity requirements for engaging in certain kinds of intergroup social comparisons were a *sine qua non* condition for intergroup discrimination.

Turner (1975, 1978a) assumed that, 'where an intergroup situation allows a positive self-evaluation on *some* dimension, then the individual confronting this situation will define himself in social terms relevant to that dimension . . . ' (1975, p. 17). This was, according to him, the case in the initial minimal categorization experiments where distribution of amounts of money to members of ingroup and outgroup was the *only* such dimension available to the subjects. In his own experiments, Turner enabled each subject, in some of the conditions, to make distributions (of money or valueless points) between himself and either a member of the ingroup or of the outgroup. When such a distribution came first in the order of tasks, there was no evidence that the members of the ingroup were being treated any better than members of the outgroup. When, however, this task was *preceded* by choices concerning two *other* people, one from the ingroup and one from the outgroup, the subsequent choices between self and others did show a clear difference, in the sense that less was awarded to self at the expense of a member of the ingroup than of the outgroup. In other words, group membership – when it was made more salient at the beginning of the study – led the subjects to make choices between themselves and a member of the ingroup, which represented a direct sacrifice in the amounts they could have awarded to themselves. This was so despite the fact that, as Turner (1978a) wrote, the self is by no means a 'minimal' category, while the others – both from the ingroup and the outgroup – remained anonymous throughout the study.

Turner's contention is further supported by his data that results of the same kind were even clearer when valueless points were being distributed by the subjects rather than amounts of money. What seems to matter here is the ingroup's *relative* position on a dimension on which a differential between the groups exists or can be created. In more general terms, 'social competition', as the term is used by Turner, refers to attempts to achieve gains in relative distinctiveness on a dimension of comparison which is *commonly* valued by the separate groups. In this way, studies of this kind represent an experimental paradigm which is of direct theoretical relevance to the presently ubiquitous issues of 'differentials'. It will be clear, however, from the preceding discussion that social competition, i.e. the achievement of positive distinctiveness on criteria that are consensually valued in a multigroup social context, is only one of the possible modes of action open to groups to achieve, preserve or defend, through the outcomes of social comparisons of various kinds, a positively valued social identity (or personal integrity) of their members. As already mentioned, other possibilities of this kind are discussed elsewhere within a more general theoretical framework.

The evidence for the alternative position, favouring 'pure' categorization as a determinant of intergroup bias, comes from a study by Deschamps and Doise (1978). They found that their results did, 'not confirm the view that there exists a preference for establishing distinctions between oneself and others as compared with the establishment of differentiations between one's own membership category and another one. On the contrary, it seems that, at least for the boys in our study, the two types of discrimination are inherently connected. When one of them appears . . . so does the other; and they are both absent' in another experimental condition (pp. 154 – 5). As Deschamps and Doise imply, according to Turner's argument the two kinds of discrimination (self-other and ingroup-outgroup) should vary inversely, since the possibility of engaging in one makes the other less functionally relevant. The issue remains to some extent unresolved, although there exists now more recent evidence from a study by Oakes and Turner (1980) that the opportunity offered to subjects to establish a difference in favour of their own group through intergroup discrimination directly enhances their self-esteem. These findings would seem to support Turner's position since the enhancement of self-esteem occurs on measures which are unrelated to the nature of the favourable difference that the subjects have been able to establish in the experiments, and it does not appear when there is no possibility to engage in intergroup discrimination.

This issue of social categorization and social competition is one only of the many theoretical problems on which work is now continuing in the recent revival of interest in the social psychology of intergroup relations. The differentials remain a crucial element in many of the social and industrial conflicts of today. There is no doubt that the socio-economic and political objectives of groups in conflict must be given priority in any discussion of these conflicts. But it is also true that such discussions will remain incomplete until and unless the social psychological processes of intergroup categorization and comparison, not always directly related to objective gains, are accorded their due place in the total picture (see Brown 1978b, for a particularly clear example from real life; cf. also Skevington 1980).

Social comparison is the process that provides the links between various forms of categorization of human beings into social groups and the forms of individual and collective actions towards outgroups. It can be assumed that some general social labels, even when they are frequently used, remain fairly neutral and socially inactive; so long as the various differences between the groups involved are not endowed with strong value connotations. The origins and development of these value connotations cannot be discussed here, although they are amongst the crucial social psychological issues in intergroup relations (cf., e.g. Milner 1975; Tajfel 1978b). We shall attempt, however, a brief review of some recent studies of one of the underlying processes. This concerns the effects on social comparisons of an increase in people's awareness that they are members of a group which is immersed in an interacting system involving other groups as well as their own.

Social Comparison and Group Membership

Social categorization cannot be considered as a static variable which somehow leads people to behave in a constant and uniform manner towards those who are classified as outsiders. The conditions of interaction between groups, and the relevance of a group membership to an individual vary from situation to situation, from one period of time to another, and from one outgroup to another. The individual and social significance of the membership of a group (and, consequently, the importance of the presence of *other* groups) vary continuously. Therefore, an individual's affiliation with a group and the functional relevance of social comparisons with other groups, or even with the same group from one situation to another, enter into a continuously changing dynamic relationship.

There are at least three separate lines of evidence that, in this diversity of conditions, an increase in the awareness of one's group membership determines the nature of intergroup comparisons, and thus, has predictable effects on intergroup attitudes and behaviour. They are as follows: (i) the findings that individuals acting as members of a group, or representing a group, tend to be more competitive than they are in similar situations in which they act as individuals in relation to other individuals; (ii) studies showing the effects of an experimentally produced increase in the salience of a social categorization; and finally, (iii) results of some of the studies concerned with attitudes towards their own group of children from various ethnic or racial minorities. In briefly outlining these studies, their results and their general significance we leave it to the reader to pursue further any of these issues in the references provided.

In an experiment by Billig and Tajfel (1973), it was shown that a categorization of people into 'groups' on an explicitly random basis induced more discrimination against anonymous outsiders than did equally anonymous inter-individual dissimilarities. But this finding raises issues concerning the relative effects of inter-individual similarities and intergroup categorizations on prejudice (see Rokeach 1960) which cannot be discussed here (see Brown 1978a, for a detailed review and analysis). There exists, however, a good deal of evidence concerning the effects on attitudes and behaviour of group membership, when intergroup disagreements are compared with inter-individual differences or disagreements. For example Stephenson *et al.* (1976) found that differences in attitudes about the raising of the age of compulsory school attendance led to less bias against those of another opinion when they were considered as a collection of individuals than after they had been divided into two separate groups. Wilson and his collaborators showed in a number of studies (e.g. Wilson and Katayani 1968) that subjects in pairs make more competitive choices in a game than when they compete individually.

There is also a good deal of evidence (see, e.g. Morley and Stephenson 1977; Stephenson 1978 for reviews) that people acting as representatives of groups tend to show more competitive actions and attitudes than is the case in inter-individual negotiations.

All these studies share one characteristic: they show the effects of group categorizations superimposed on individual characteristics in situations which involve some kind of conflict or competition. These effects seem to consist of a bias against the 'other', which is stronger in the case of intergroup than inter-individual relations. But situations of explicit conflict of competition are, once again, not the only necessary condition for showing the powerful effects of categorizing people into groups. It is apparently sufficient simply to make people more aware of the *presence* or potential presence of another group to elicit ingroup bias. A technique of this kind was first used by Doise and Sinclair who, in one condition, asked, 'group members to describe themselves without mentioning any other group' (1973, p. 140); in a second condition, the same request was made but an outgroup was 'evoked', in the sense that the subjects knew that they would have to describe it afterwards. Using groups of apprentices and *collégiens* (i.e. approximately grammar-school pupils) in Geneva, Doise and Sinclair found that the induced awareness of another relevant group led the *collégiens* to evaluate their own group much more favourably than was the case in the non-comparison condition; the apprentices showed a trend in the same direction which did not reach statistical significance. A similar method was used in a study by Doise *et al.* (1978) on Swiss linguistic groups with results showing a clear tendency to accentuate ingroup similarities when relevant outgroups were brought symbolically into the situation. Van Knippenberg (1978) refined and improved the method in his recent study of engineering students from two Dutch educational institutions of unequal social and academic prestige. His complex results cannot be described here, but they also showed clear effects of increasing the salience of a social categorization. Similar results were obtained from studies of ethnolinguistic groups (see Bourhis *et al.* 1979; Bourhis and Giles 1977) in Belgium and Wales.

Thus, the first of the three groups of studies mentioned above focuses on situations in which groups rather than individuals disagree. The second line of evidence, just discussed, is based on strengthening the salience of an existing intergroup categorization in experimental or controlled semi-natural situations. The third source of data comes from studies on the self-images of children from minority groups. There are many such studies, the first of which were conducted in the thirties in the United States (see Milner 1975, for a detailed review). The consensus of data that emerged from them was that minority children (particularly those from racial minorities) tended, in specially devised tests, to show preference for stimuli (such as dolls, etc.) representing the dominant 'white' outgroups over those representing their own group. Some of these results were criticized on methodological grounds (e.g. Greenwald and Oppenheim 1968). There is little doubt, however, that most of the apparent discrepancies in the findings can be attributed to the functioning of a process, which has repeatedly been referred to in this chapter. In relation to the studies on minority children, this can be stated as follows: the intensity of 'ingroup devaluation' shown in these tests by children from racial minorities seems to be directly related to the degree of *explicitness* of comparisons with the outgroup which is built into the methods of testing. This fits in with data on desegregated schools in the United States obtained by Katz in the sixties who concluded (Katz 1968) that anticipated comparisons with whites affected adversely the level of performance of black pupils. The outcomes of these comparisons are in the direction opposite to the findings from the first two groups of studies described above (although some of the data from the study by van Knippenberg 1978, are consonant with the minority group data). In the case of these first two groups of studies, an increased salience of group membership or of social categorization led to an increase in ingroup bias or outgroup discrimination. In the case of the children studies, an increased salience of comparisons with the dominant outgroup led to what has come to be known as a more marked 'ingroup devaluation'.

In discussing these findings, we can thus return to the major theme of this chapter. The identity of minority children (as distinct from their conceptions of self based on individual interactions within their own group) is based on unfavourable comparisons with the majority. The nature of these comparisons is affected by the innumerable economic, social, political, ideological and linguistic influences in the society-at-large. It is therefore hardly surprising that when comparisons with the dominant outgroup are made more salient, be it in natural conditions or in controlled studies, young children are reduced to express aspects of their social identity through the only channels of comparison which are open to them. These negative self-images are by no means the only ones in existence; there exist many positive alternatives (see Tajfel 1978d), and the negative ones change quickly in the wake of social change (see Vaughan 1978b). Either way, they provide one further example of the importance of social intergroup comparisons in the general structure of social psychological processes underlying intergroup relations.

CONCLUSION

This brief survey has discussed a few aspects of intergroup relations with some of the experimental studies related to them. After a fairly long period of relative inactivity, there has been in the last few years an upsurge of interest and revival of research into many social psychological issues of intergroup behaviour. Some of these issues which are quite fundamental were not even mentioned in this chapter. They include, for example, the problems of status relationships (e.g. Brown 1978b; van Knippenberg 1978; Moscovici and Paicheler 1978; Turner and Brown 1978), of power and subordination (e.g. Deschamps and Personnaz 1980; Ng 1977, 1980), of stability and change in the relations between social groups (e.g. Rabbie *et al.* 1974; Rabbie and Wilkens 1971; Vaughan 1978a,b), of competition and co-operation between groups which are similar or dissimilar (e.g. Brown 1978a; Turner 1978a; Turner, Brown and Tajfel 1979), of the perceived legitimacy or illegitimacy of a social multigroup system (e.g. Caddick 1978, 1980). A substantial amount of work on all these problems has recently been done and is continuing at present. Much of this work remains in the form of social psychological experimentation. The view defended in this chapter was that, however artificial or contrived much of this experimental work may appear to be, it has a substantial and continuing role to play in our further understanding of one of the most crucial social problems of our day. Social psychological experiments will not solve these problems, and they are not meant to do this. However, fruitful social psychological theories, seeking to combine their evidence from *both* the laboratory and the natural conditions of human social interaction, can undoubtedly contribute to a further unravelling of this tangled and difficult set of issues.

REFERENCES

Allen, V. L., and Wilder, D. A. 1975. 'Categorization, belief similarity and intergroup discrimination.' *J. Pers. Soc. Psychol. 32*, 971 – 7.

Billig, M. 1976. *Social psychology and intergroup relations. European monographs in social psychology*, no. 9. London: Academic Press.

Billig, M., and Tajfel, H. 1973. 'Social categorization and similarity in intergroup behaviour.' *Eur. J. Soc. Psychol. 3*, 27 – 52.

Bourhis, R. Y., and Giles, H. 1977. 'The language of intergroup distinctiveness.' In H. Giles (ed.) *Language, ethnicity and intergroup relations. European monographs in social psychology*, no. 13. London: Academic Press.

Bourhis, R. Y., Giles, H., Leyens, J.-P. and Tajfel, H. 1979. 'Psycholinguistic distinctiveness: language divergence in Belgium.' In H. Giles and R. St Clair (eds) *Language and social psychology*. Oxford: Blackwell.

Brewer, M. B. 1979. 'Ingroup bias in the minimal intergroup situation: a cognitive-motivational analysis.' *Psychol. Bull. 86*, 307 – 41.

Brewer, M. B., and Silver, M. 1978. 'Ingroup bias as a function of task characteristics.' *Eur. J. Soc. Psychol. 8*, 393 – 400.

Brown, R. J. 1978a. 'Competition and co-operation between similar and dissimilar groups.' Unpubl. Ph.D. dissertation, Univ. of Bristol.

Brown, R. J. 1978b. 'Divided we fall: an analysis of relations between sections of a factory workforce.' In H. Tajfel (ed.), *op cit*.

Caddick, B. F. J. 1978. 'Status, legitimacy and the social identity concept in intergroup relations.' Unpubl. Ph.D. dissertation, Univ. of Bristol.

Caddick, B. F. J. 1980. 'Equity theory, social identity and intergroup relations.' *Review of personality and social psychology*, in press.

Dann, H. D., and Doise, W. 1974. 'Ein neuer methodologischer Ansatz zur experimentellen Erforschung von Intergruppen-Beziehungen.' *Zeitschrift fur Sozialpsychologie 5*, 2 – 15.

Deschamps, J.-C., and Doise, W. 1978. 'Crossed category membership in intergroup relations.' In H. Tajfel (ed.), *op cit*.

Deschamps, J.-C., and Personnaz, B. 1980. 'Etudes entre groupes "dominants" et "dominés": importance de presence du hors-groups dans les discriminations evaluatives et comportementales.' *Soc. Sci. Info.*, in press.

Doise, W. 1978. *Groups and individuals: explanations in social psychology*. Cambridge: Cambridge University Press.

Doise, W., Csepeli, G., Dann, H. D., Gouge, C., Larsen, K., and Ostell, A. 1972. 'An experimental investigation into the formation of intergroup representations.' *Eur. J. Soc. Psychol. 2*, 202 – 4.

Doise, W., Deschamps, J.-C., and Meyer, G. 1978. 'The accentuation of intracategory similarities.' In H. Tajfel (ed.), *op cit*.

Doise, W., and Sinclair, A. 1973. 'The categorization process in intergroup relations.' *Eur. J. Soc. Psychol. 3*, 145 – 57.

Druckman, D. (ed.) 1977. *Negotiations: social psychological perspectives*. London: Sage Publications.

Eiser, J. R. 1980. *Cognitive social psychology*. London: McGraw Hill.

Eiser, J. R., and Stroebe, W. 1972. *Categorization and social judgement. European monographs in social psychology*, no. 3. London: Academic Press.

Goffman, E. 1971. *Relations in public*. London: Allen Lane,

Greenwald, H. J., and Oppenheim, D. B. 1968. 'Reported magnitude of self-misidentification among Negro children: artifact?' *J. Pers. Soc. Psychol. 8*, 49 – 52.

Janssen, L., and Nuttin, J. 1976. 'Frequency perception of individual and group successes as a function of competition, coaction and isolation.' *J. Pers. Soc. Psychol. 34*, 830 – 6.

Kahn, A., and Ryen, A. H. 1972. 'Factors influencing bias towards one's own group.' *International Journal of Group Tensions 2*, 33 – 50.

Katz, I. 1968. 'Factors influencing Negro performance in the desegregated school.' In M. Deutsch, I. Kahn and H. R. Jansen (eds) *Social class, race and psychological development*. New York: Holt, Rinehart and Winston.

van Knippenberg, A. 1978. *Perception and evaluation of intergroup differences*. University of Leiden.

Milner, D. 1975. *Children and race*. Harmondsworth: Penguin Books.

Morley, I. E., and Stephenson, G. M. 1977. *The social psychology of bargaining*. London: George Allen & Unwin.

Moscovici, S. and Paicheler, G. 1978. 'Social comparison and social recognition: two complementary processes of identification.' In H. Tajfel (ed.), *op cit*.

Ng, S. H. 1977. 'Structural and non-structural aspects of power distance reduction tendencies.' *Eur. J. Soc. Psychol. 7*, 317 – 45.

Ng, S. H. 1980. *The social psychology of power. European monographs in social psychology*. London: Academic Press, in press.

Oakes, P., and Turner, J. C. 1980. 'Social identity, social competition and self-esteem in the minimal group paradigm.' *Eur. J. Soc. Psychol.*, in press.

Rabbie, J. M., Benoist, F., Oosterbaan, H., and Visser, L. 1974. 'Differential power and effects of expected competitive and co-operative intergroup interaction on intragroup and outgroup attitudes.' *J. Pers. Soc. Psychol. 30*, 46 – 56.

Rabbie, J. M., and Wilkens, G. 1971. 'Intergroup competition and its effects on intragroup and intergroup relations.' *Eur. J. Soc. Psychol. 1*, 215 – 34.

Rokeach, M. 1960. *The open and closed mind*. New York: Basic Books.

Ryen, A. H., and Kahn, A. 1975. 'Effects of intergroup orientation on group attitudes and proxemic behaviour.' *J. Pers. Soc. Psychol. 31*, 302 – 10.

Sherif, M. 1966. *Group conflict and co-operation: their social psychology*. London: Routledge and Kegan Paul.

Sherif, M., and Sherif, C. W. 1953. *Groups in harmony and tension*. New York: Harper and Row.

Skevington, S. 1980. 'Intergroup relations and social change within a nursing context.' *Brit. J. Soc. Clin. Psychol.*, in press.

Stephenson, G. M. 1978. 'The characteristics of negotiation groups.' In H. Brandstatter, J. H. Davis and H. Schuler (eds) *Social decision processes*. New York: Sage Publications.

Stephenson, G. M. 1980. 'Intergroup bargaining and negotiation.' In J. C. Turner and H. Giles (eds) *Intergroup behaviour*. Oxford: Blackwell, in press.

Stephenson, G. M., Skinner, M. R., and Brotherton, C. J. 1976. 'Group participation and intergroup relations: an experimental study of negotiation groups.' *Eur. J. Soc. Psychol. 6*, 51 – 70.

Tajfel, H. 1959. 'Quantitative judgement in social perception.' *Brit. J. Psychol. 50*, 16 – 29.

Tajfel, H. 1972. 'La catégorisation sociale.' In S. Moscovici (ed.) *Introduction à la psychologie sociale I*. Paris: Larousse.

Tajfel, H. 1974. 'Social identity and intergroup behaviour.' *Soc. Sci. Info. 13*, 65 – 93.

Tajfel, H. 1978a. Foreword to the English edition. In W. Doise 1978. *Groups and individuals: explanations in social psychology*. Cambridge: Cambridge University Press.

Tajfel, H. 1978b. 'The psychological structure of intergroup relations.' Part I in H. Tajfel (ed.), *op cit*.

Tajfel, H. (ed.) 1978c. *Differentiation between social groups: studies in the social psychology of intergroup relations. European monographs in social psychology*, no. 14. London: Academic Press.

Tajfel, H. 1978d. *The social psychology of minorities*. London: Minority Rights Group.

Tajfel, H. 1979. 'Individuals and groups in social psychology.' *Brit. J. Soc. Clin. Psychol.*, in press.

Tajfel, H., Flament, C., Billig, M., and Bundy, R. 1971. 'Social categorization and intergroup behaviour.' *Eur. J. Soc. Psychol. 1*, 149 – 78.

Tajfel, H., and Turner, J. C. 1979. 'An integrative theory of intergroup conflict.'

In W. G. Austin and S. Worchel (eds) *The social psychology of intergroup relations*. Monterey, Calif.: Brooks/Cole.

Turner, J. C. 1975. 'Social comparison and social identity: some prospects for intergroup behaviour.' *Eur. J. Soc. Psychol. 5*, 5 – 34.

Turner, J. C. 1978a. 'Social categorization and social discrimination in the minimal group paradigm.' In H. Tajfel (ed.), *op cit*.

Turner, J. C. 1978b. 'Social comparison, similarity and ingroup favouritism.' In H. Tajfel (ed.), *op cit*.

Turner, J. C. 1980. 'The experimental social psychology of intergroup behaviour.' In J. C. Turner and H. Giles (eds) *Intergroup behaviour*. Oxford: Blackwell, in press.

Turner, J. C., and Brown, R. J. 1978. 'Social status, cognitive alternatives and intergroup relations.' In H. Tajfel (ed.), *op cit*.

Turner, J. C., Brown, R. J., and Tajfel, H. 1979. 'Social comparison and group interest in ingroup favouritism.' *Eur. J. Soc. Psychol. 9*, 187 – 204.

Vaughan, G. M. 1978a. 'Social categorization and intergroup behaviour in children.' In H. Tajfel (ed.), *op cit*.

Vaughan, G. M. 1978b. 'Social change and intergroup preferences in New Zealand.' *Eur. J. Soc. Psychol. 8*, 297 – 314.

Weinreich, P. 1979. 'Cross-ethnic identification and self-rejection in a black adolescent.' In G. Verma and C. Bagley (eds) *Race, education and identity*. London: Macmillan.

Wilder, D. A. 1978. 'Reduction of intergroup discrimination through individuation of the outgroup.' *J. Pers. Soc. Psychol. 36*, 1361 – 74.

Wilson, W., and Katayani, M. 1968. 'Intergroup attitudes and strategies in games between opponents of the same or different race.' *J. Pers. Soc. Psychol. 9*, 24 – 30.

Chapter 9

Hormones and Sexual Behaviour

DAVID M. VOWLES

INTRODUCTION

In attempting to unravel the complex relations between hormones and sexual behaviour a number of different kinds of questions may be asked.

The causal relationship. It is a common observation that an organisms' sexual sensitivity or responsiveness (and feelings and emotions in humans) changes from time to time, e.g. with the seasons, with age, or as a result of prior behaviour. These changes in sexual activity may in some cases be correlated with the activity of sex hormones, and it is important to establish which hormones are involved.

The mechanisms involved. When it has been established that hormones affect sexual activity, the question of the nature of the mechanism whereby these effects are caused immediately arises. Commonly, one asks how hormones may affect tissues in the brain or the body to produce behavioural changes.

The development of sex. Some of the changes in sexual activity may occur in an orderly fashion over the life history of an individual, starting from the fertilized ovum and culminating in the sexually mature performance of the adult. The analysis of these changes, both morphological, physiological and psychological leads to a better understanding of normal sexual behaviour, and of sexual aberrations arising from some fault in the developmental pattern.

The genetic background. One potential source of variability between the sexual activities of different individuals is their genetic makeup. The most obvious being the XX chromosome pair for women and the XY pair for men, although the duplication or omission of one of the sex chromosomes, or individual mutations, may lead to abnormalities. In addition, we must be concerned with the way in which the genetic programme affects the development referred to in the previous section.

Phylogeny and adaptiveness. In the past 50 years it has been only too common for psychologists to regard the laboratory rat as providing a stereotype for human sexual behaviour, although which species should be the more offended is debatable. However, it is now clear that the patterns of sexual behaviour and their underlying physiology can differ widely between different species, and the study of the way in which these patterns are adapted to the life styles and environment of the species forms an important new branch of the study of sexual behaviour. The phylogenetic history of the sexual behaviour may throw important light on the biological inheritance of the species. At the very least it is clear that extrapolation from even chimpanzees to man is dangerous.

Cultural factors. All the questions above may be asked both about people and the lower animals, although the ethics and methods of investigation may differ. However, in human societies the cultural factors may assume a role at least as important as the biological. In the widest sense we must therefore be concerned with the influence of social, legal, cultural and political systems in their effect upon behaviour, the mechanisms underlying them, and how their development may be guided.

For a good general reference to the physiological psychology of sex the reader is referred to Carlson (1978). A wider study of the biological aspects of reproduction is given in an admirable series of short books by Austin and Short (1972 – 76). In the present essay the three particular aspects of sex that will be discussed are the causal relationships between hormones and behaviour, the mechanisms underlying these, and sexual differentiation and development. Important light has been thrown on these by three technical developments: the ability to assay directly the presence and concentration of specific hormones in small quantities of blood and tissue; the understanding of the way in which different hormones are synthesized and broken down and their relationships to each other; and the ability to localize specific hormones in particular areas and cells in the brain and other tissues. These developments enable us to examine directly, and within individuals, the relationship between hormones and sex drive, and the mechanisms involved in these relationships. For reasons of brevity only mammalian studies will be discussed, and in particular primate, including human, work.

THE CAUSAL RELATIONSHIPS

The basic question in studying these relationships is to determine what behaviour is correlated with the presence of which hormones, and if there is any quantitative relationship between hormone levels and sexual activity. Perhaps the best way to introduce the modern picture is to parody the classical descriptions that might have been found in standard texts 20 years ago.

The Early Picture

Sexual behaviour seems to depend upon two types of hormones, the gonadotrophins originating from the pituitary gland under the control of the hypothalamus, and the steroid hormones androgen (testosterone) and oestrogen originating from the gonads under the influence of the gonadotrophins.

In the male, two gonadotrophins are produced. These are released into the blood stream and absorbed by the testes, where they produce two different effects: the first stimulates the formation of spermatozoa; the second, interstitial cell stimulating hormone (ICSH), stimulates the Sertoli cells to produce the male sex hormone – an androgen called testosterone. The output of the gonadotrophins is tonic, causing a steady output of sperm and testosterone. Seasonal factors such as light and warmth may result in an increased output of gonadotrophins, and hence growth of the gonads, and in the male increase in the sperm production and androgen.

In the female, there are three gonadotrophins produced by the pituitary. These are affected by the steroids produced by the ovary, and the negative feedback system involved produces cyclic changes in physiology and behaviour. The first gonadotrophin, follicle stimulating hormone (FSH), acts upon the ovary to stimulate growth and maturation of one of the follicles (or more in some species). This leads first to development of the ovum itself, but also causes the thecal cells lining the follicle to secrete the female sex hormone oestrogen. This acts back upon the hypothalamus to cause the pituitary to inhibit the output of FSH and to stimulate the output of the second gonadotrophin, luteinising hormone (LH). This leads to the stimulation of some yellow tissue in the follicle in the ovary – the corpus luteum – which secretes the second steroid hormone – progesterone. This acts to prepare the uterine wall for implantation of the ovum in preparation for pregnancy, to maintain the output of LH, and together with oestrogen brings the animal into behavioural oestrus, making her attractive to the male by means of pheromones or other factors, and receptive to the male to permit him to mate. A surge of LH and progesterone causes release of the ovum ready for fertilization. In some species this occurs reflexly as a result of mating, and in others without such stimulation. If fertilization occurs, the uterine wall becomes thickened and highly vascularized forming the endometrium for the support and nutrition of the developing embryo, and it starts to produce its own gonadotrophins and steroids for the maintenance of pregnancy and the inhibition of further ovulatory activity. The pituitary also starts to secrete the third gonadotrophin – prolactin – that initiates the growth of the mammary glands and the development of maternal milk. If no fertilization occurs, two changes take place resulting in the end of the old ovulatory cycle and the initiation of the next. First, the atretic follicle no longer produces oestrogen so that the pituitary begins to secrete FSH again, and to reduce its synthesis of LH, which in its turn leads to the degeneration of the corpus luteum and a decline in progesterone. The endometrium can no longer be maintained and is sloughed off together with the unfertilized ovum passing to the outside in the form of a discharge of cellular tissue, blood and mucus – the menses. This completes the menstrual cycle. In some species the endometrium is merely reabsorbed without bleeding, and in others ovulation and implantation occur reflexly as a result of stimulation during mating.

In classical endocrinology the establishment of a genuine hormonal effect relied upon three steps. First, extirpation of the organ suspected to give rise to the hormone should lead to the disappearance of the effect. Secondly, hormone therapy by injecting extracts of the suspected endocrine gland should restore the lost function. Thirdly, purified extracts are used to identity the specific nature of the hormones involved. In the case of sexual behaviour it was early established that removal of the ovaries led to a decline in sexual behaviour, and that this could be re-established by injections of oestrogen and progesterone (which seemed to act synergistically). However, in the male (Young 1961) although similar effects were observed following castration and testosterone therapy, the decline in sexual behaviour following castration was affected by a number of other factors. First, the higher the phylogenetic level of the species the longer the decline took: in the male stickleback sexual behaviour disappeared within 2 – 3 days; in rhesus monkeys, a few months; and in man, several years, and might then not be complete. Since most of the volume of ejaculate is from the prostate gland this would explain the continued sexual activity of old men when the testes' output of sperm and testosterone has markedly declined. Secondly, the earlier in life castration occurs and the less sexual experience the individual has the more rapid the decline in sexual activity. Thus, a randy old tom cat may continue to mate for several months while a young inexperienced male may stop within 2 – 3 weeks.

This kind of evidence established a clear link between hormones and sexual behaviour. However, the field was bedevilled by two particular difficulties. First, the concentration of natural endogenous hormones was too small to be measured (nowadays it is known to be in terms of nanograms per millilitre) – the preparation of the first milligram of oestrogen required several tons of fresh sows' ovaries from a sausage factory. Secondly, the application of exogenous hormones in hormone therapy (whether natural extracts or synthetic) was in high concentration and grossly unphysiologic if it was to produce any effect. There was some evidence that blood levels of testosterone correlated to some extent with male sexual behaviour in rodents (see Young 1961) but only within narrow and artificial limits. It was not known whether the hormonal extracts, made from blood, organs, or urine were the active principle or just precursors or breakdown products of the active hormones, nor whether the hormones need to be bound to particular chemical molecules in order to penetrate and effect, for example, neural tissue. Thus, recent work on identifying the metabolites of hormones, their concentration in blood and tissue and the interference with their synthesis by drugs and by techniques of immunization against them, has led to rapid progress in these areas. However, it should be stressed that the simplistic account of hormonal – behaviour interactions given above is a caricature, and that many variations and inconsistencies were already evident before modern developments; some of these will be referred to and clarified later.

The Metabolism of Sex Hormones

The metabolic pathways for the synthesis of progesterone, testosterone and oestrogen are shown in Figure 9.1. It has been known for some time that these substances were closely related in their chemical structure. What is novel is the demonstration that there are a number of naturally occurring progestagens, androgens and oestrogens, and that these are synthesized one from another in the body. The process of aromatization to convert testosterone to oestrogen is particularly significant since it had been assumed that the former was the male and the latter the female sex hormone. Indeed, two problems immediately arise concerning the specificity of action of hormones:

(1) When there are a number of similar substances, e.g. androstenedione, testosterone and 19-OH testosterone, do these all act as androgens in the same way, or do they have separate functions? Both findings have been demonstrated; thus, all three have effects on increasing male sex drive but in the order testosterone, androstenedione, 19-OH testosterone: and the first is very much more potent than the others. In sexual differentiation, however, (see later) androstenedione is as active as testosterone in inducing the neural mechanisms of male behaviour but does not inhibit female mechanisms, while 19-OH testosterone is more effective at masculinizing the external genitalia. (Goldfoot *et al.* 1969; Ward 1974; see also Herbert 1977 for a more general discussion). Likewise, the progesterones have similar functions to each other, but also differ: in primates, 17α-OH progesterone occurs in a surge prior to ovulation and ordinary progesterone occurs during the postovulatory premenstrual period, with different physiological and psychological consequences (see later).
(2) Since hormones may be converted into each other in the body this

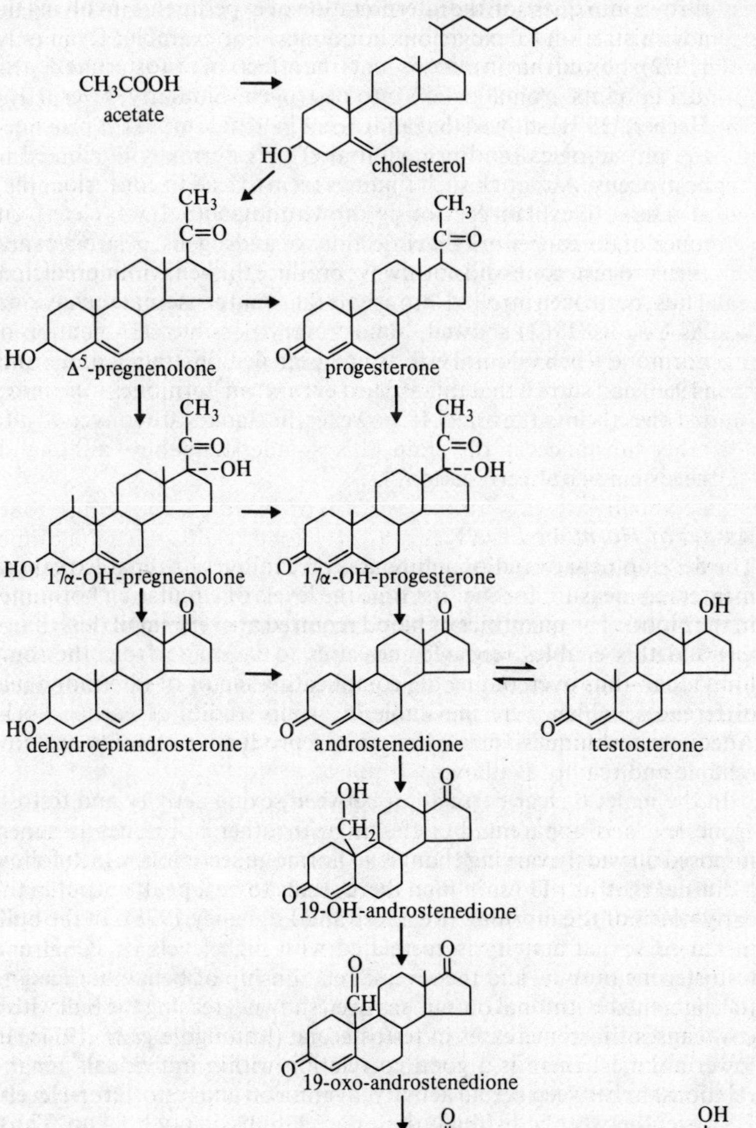

CH_3COOH acetate → cholesterol

Δ^5-pregnenolone → progesterone

17α-OH-pregnenolone → 17α-OH-progesterone

dehydroepiandrosterone → androstenedione ⇌ testosterone

19-OH-androstenedione

19-oxo-androstenedione

oestrone ⇌ oestradiol-17*β*

Figure 9.1 The main routes of biosynthesis of androgens, oestrogens and progesterone from acetate and cholesterol.

throws into question the interpretation of experiments involving the administration of exogenous hormones. For example, Ryan *et al.* (1972) showed that in male rodents the effects of testosterone depended upon its aromatization into oestrogen. Similarly, Everitt and Herbert (1971) showed that androgens in female monkeys produced the physiological and behavioural effects normally attributed to oestrogens. Although such findings seem to lead to confusion, they also serve to explain previously known anomalies. It was clear from much of the early work that injections of androgens, oestrogens and even progesterones did not always produce the behaviour predicted. Thus, oestrogen injected into a male rat could cause male behaviour. As Young (1961) showed, almost every possible combination of hormone – behavioural effects had been demonstrated, and Fisher (1966) had shown that this applied even when hormones were injected directly into the brain. If, however, hormones are converted into other substances in the brain, this is understandable – although it needs empirical verification.

Assays of Hormone Levels

The development of radioimmunoassay techniques has enabled experimenters to measure for the first time the levels of circulating hormones in the blood. The quantities of blood required are very small (less than 1 ml) and this enables repeated measures to be made from the same individual, thus overcoming the complicating factor of interindividual differences, which were inevitable in group studies of earlier work. Adequate techniques for all the main reproductive steroids are now reliable and readily available.

In the male, a clear correlation between sexual activity and testosterone levels is apparent, but this as with other hormones is superimposed on widely varying changes in hormone secretion, which follow a diurnal rhythm. Thus, in man there seems to be a peak output in the early hours of the morning (Reinberg and Lagogney 1978). In the bull, increased sexual activity is correlated with high levels of ICSH and testosterone output, and the reverse relationship of behaviour leading to heightened hormonal output has been shown – teasing the bull with a cow causes sharp increases in testosterone (Katongole *et al.* 1971). In lower animals, there is a good correlation within individuals for the relationship between sexual activity, aggression and testosterone levels. However, between individuals these correlations do not hold up. Thus, Gordon *et al.* (1976) examined testosterone levels in a free-living colony of rhesus monkeys over 3 years. They found seasonal fluctuations in the hormone, which had not previously been reported in laboratory colonies. In grouped data, there was a significant positive correlation between testosterone levels and all measures of sexual activity and aggression, and a negative correlation with play. However, in the case of the individual no such correlation could be obtained, whether the hormone was assayed before or after the observed sexual activity, and there was no correlation with rank order.

A number of studies have been made on human males to investigate the relationship between sexual behaviour, aggressive behaviour and testosterone levels. (Persky *et al.* 1976; Doering *et al.* 1974; Meyer-Bahlberg 1976; Kraemer *et al.* 1976). These have used normal subjects, criminals sentenced for crimes of violence and various psychopathological patients. As measures of behaviour they used criminal records, diaries of sexual activities, adjective tests lists, mood questionnaires and so on. The major finding to emerge from these studies was the great variability in hormone levels between individuals and general failure to establish any really significant correlations between any of the factors studied. This leaves the role of testosterone in human males fairly problematical, which perhaps correlates with the variable effects of castration when it has been used to reduce levels of sexual behaviour and crimes of violence (Money 1961).

In females, the hormone assays have revealed very clearly the hormonal changes associated with the oestrus or menstrual cycles. One clear fact to emerge is the difference in different species. In Figures 9.2 and 9.3 the rat and the human situation can be compared. The primate results are similar to humans and only these will be discussed here.

In the past it had been somewhat naively assumed that the female played a passive role, merely becoming receptive to the male during her behavioural oestrus. While this quite well fits the picture in the rat, it is clear that the female has a much more active role to play in other animals. A little introspection or observation might indeed have suggested this in humans some time ago. Beach (1976) has reviewed the case to suggest that a female's sexual behaviour must be separable into at least three activities:

Receptivity – her willingness to accept the male,
Proceptivity – her willingness actively to solicit the male,
Attractivity – her ability to attract the male.

This kind of approach has been well analysed in some elegant work by Michael and his colleagues (Michael *et al.* 1972; Baum *et al.* 1977). Studying a colony of rhesus monkeys, they devised a combination of ethological measures of behaviour with the performance of an operant task. Thus, if a female was attractive to a male, he could be made to operate a door in order to approach and attempt to mate with her; receptivity was measured by her acceptance of the male, and proceptivity by the female working to open a door to allow a male access. One of the major factors to emerge was the wide individual variability between different males and females, and the existence of strong individual sexual preferences. However, on the hormonal side, it appeared that oestrogens, while increasing a female's attractiveness due to pheromones in

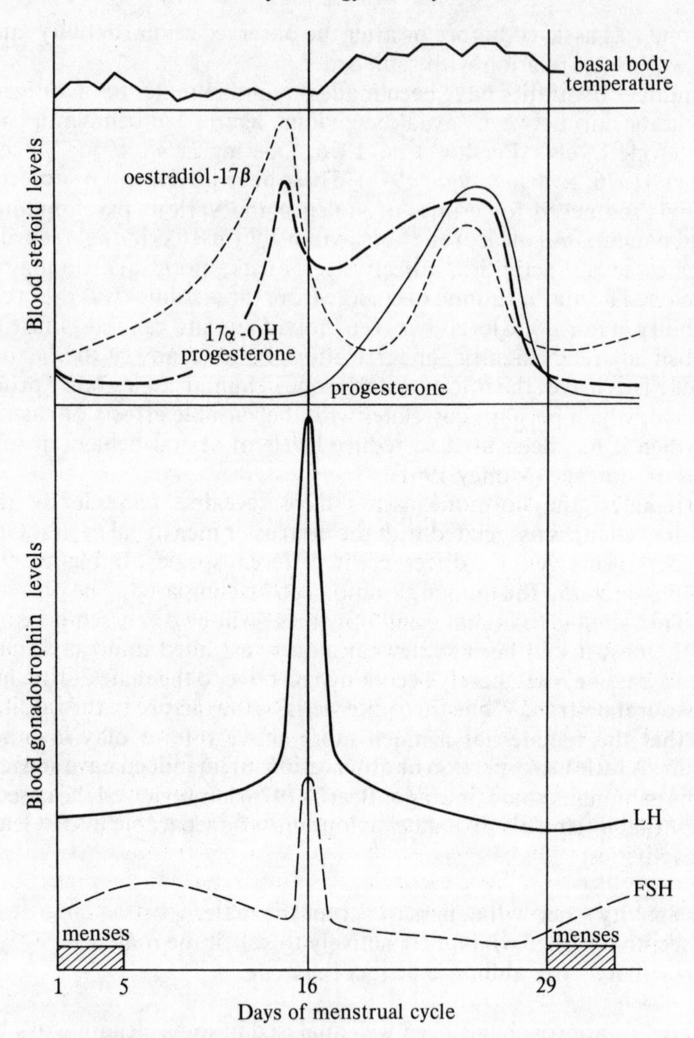

Figure 9.2 Hormone changes in the human menstrual cycle.

her vaginal secretions, did not increase her proceptivity, but did increase receptivity. Progesterone, on the other hand, decreased receptivity and tended to reduce attractivity possibly due to the inhibition of oestrogen secretion. Proceptivity, however, seemed to be increased by androgens, which are also known to be high around ovulation and during behavioural oestrus. The androgens could originate in both the ovaries and the adrenal glands.

This latter finding could fit well with the suggestions from some time ago that in women the 'sex' hormone associated with the libido was

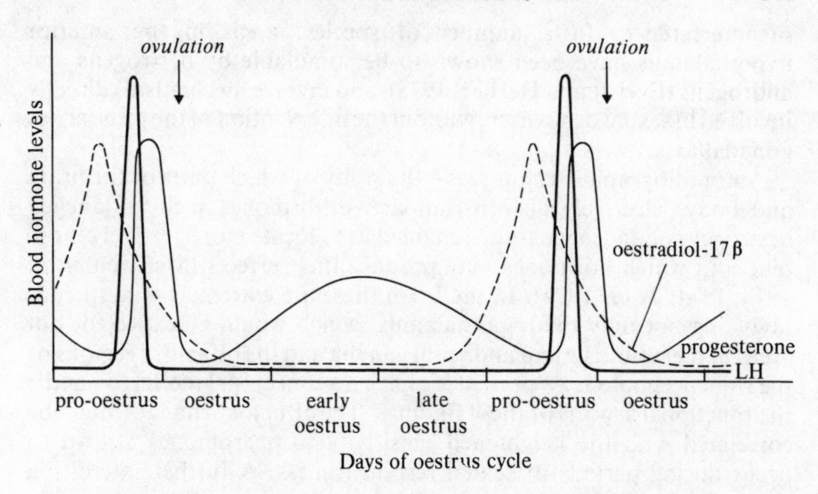

Figure 9.3 Hormone changes in the oestrous cycle of the rat.

androgen rather than oestrogen (Money 1961). It is well established that in women sexual activities may persist at a high level after ovariectomy or after the menopause, but disappear after adrenalectomy – when they can be restored by androgen therapy. In view of these findings it is not surprising that studies attempting to correlate sexual activities and mood in women with oestrogen or progesterone levels have had little success (Persky 1974): indeed even the classical symptoms and causes of premenstrual tension in normal women seem to be called into question. In a later study Persky (1978) studied couples as an interacting pair, obtaining ratings of attraction and gratification. In this preliminary study there did seem to be a correlation of such high ratings with androgens in both sexes. Studies of male homosexuals or lesbians have revealed no obvious hormonal abnormalities, although a very high level of testosterone has been reported in a small sample of Hungarian transsexual women (Sipova and Staka 1976).

THE NEURAL MECHANISMS

One classical debate around the topic of sexual behaviour centred on the question as to whether hormones produced their effects on sexual behaviour by acting upon peripheral structures or on neural mechanisms of the brain. Certainly hormones can affect peripheral structures such as sense organs on the penis (Beach and Levinson 1950). Equally clearly, there are central nervous mechanisms in the brain stem (particularly the hypothalamus) and the limbic system, which when stimulated or lesioned affect sexual responsiveness. Hypo- or hypersexuality can be produced according to the technique employed and the location of interference. In a number of species, areas in the anterior hypothalamus have been shown to be stimulable by oestrogens and androgens (Everitt and Herbert 1975), and involve mechanisms directly involved in sexual behaviour, without the intervention of the pituitary – gonadal axis.

Autoradiographic techniques – the study of which parts of the brain and body selectively absorb radioactive hormones such as labelled oestrogens or androgens – has enabled us to locate more precisely those places in which hormones may produce their effects (McEwen *et al.* 1974; Pfaff *et al.* 1974). In the brain these are extremely widespread, involving not only the hypothalamus, which would be expected, but areas in the limbic system and basal ganglia and the olfactory regions of the rhinencephalon. At present we have no conceptual model to handle the functional aspects of these findings. The olfactory changes might be correlated with the heightened sensitivity to pheromones known to occur during periods of sexual responsiveness. A further interesting finding is that in female rats the skin on the back and flanks normally grasped by the male during mounting selectively absorbs oestrogen, and results in increased size and sensitivity of the somatic receptive fields. Similarly, selective absorption of the hormone into the spinal cord may be correlated with the facilitation of the lordosis reflex. It is quite clear that central, spinal and peripheral mechanisms are affected by hormones, but how this is reflected in behaviour is not yet established.

The selective absorption of hormones into specific cells implies that these cells possess specific receptor sites to receive and bind the hormone molecule within the cell. There is some evidence that this binding affects the messages sent out by the DNA in the cell to modify or initiate the protein synthesis of the cell. Thus, a mechanism exists whereby the effect of the hormone can outlast its original existence. Since the lifetime of hormones secreted into the blood stream is very short – a matter of minutes only – this could provide the basis for the long-term effects of hormones on behaviour, even in the presence of considerable fluctuation as revealed in the plasma assays.

SEXUAL DIFFERENTIATION

Perhaps the longest lasting effect that a hormone is known to produce is that of testosterone upon the developing foetus or neonate. Since the classical work of Pfeiffer in the thirties, and Harris and Levine in the fifties, it has been repeatedly confirmed in rodents that there is a particular sensitive period in development in which a brief exposure to testosterone ensures that the brain develops mechanisms which make it permanently male in both its behaviour and physiology. If androgens are not present, the individual develops as a female irrespective of its genetic sex. In the genetic male, there is a small, brief spurt of testosterone from the testes which produces this effect. In females, the masculinization can only be produced by exogenous testosterone.

Since this classical work a number of additional findings have come to light which may be summarized as follows:

(1) The sensitive period varies in different species – being postnatal in rats, prenatal in guinea pigs and at different periods during foetal life in monkeys and humans (Goy 1970). It seems probable that these sensitive periods correspond with the brain growth spurts described by Dobbin and Smart (1974), during which the brain is particularly sensitive to chemical and nutritional influences.
(2) In the brain a distinction must be made between the suppression of female mechanisms and the facilitation of male mechanisms. These seem to occur at slightly different times, and may possibly involve different androgens (Goldfoot *et al.* 1969; Ward 1974; Jost 1973).
(3) Sensitive periods also exist in the development of the internal and external genitalia (Jost 1973). The suppression of the female genitalia and the development of the male genitalia proceed in a definite sequence, and are irreversible. They may also be influenced by the presence or absence of testosterone. But they are not causally related to the other aspects of differentiation.
(4) The changes in the brain produced by testosterone seem to involve a suppression of the receptor sites for oestrogen and an opening up of receptor sites for androgen (McEwen 1974; Goldman 1974). These are relatively permanent and result not in the abolition of the neural mechanisms for female behaviour during masculinization, but in reducing its relative sensitivity.
(5) The masculinization of genetic females in primates, including humans, does not appear to be as drastic as in lower animals (Goy 1970; Money and Ehrhardt 1972).

Limitations of space have not allowed us to deal here with the problems of the growth of sexual differences and gender identities in humans. It is clear, however, that on the biological side there is a complex series of developmental steps, any one of which could potentially go wrong. It is therefore unwise to predict a pathology of sex or a remedy based solely on physiology, or morphology or psychology, or even the genotype.

The field of hormones and sexual behaviour is developing with great rapidity. New techniques have revealed a situation far more complex than previously thought, but pregnant with possibilities.

REFERENCES

Austin, C. R., and Short, R. V. *Reproduction in mammals*. Cambridge: Cambridge University Press.

1. 'Germ cells and fertilisation.' 1972.
2. 'Embryonic and foetal development.' 1972.
3. 'Hormones in reproduction.' 1972.
4. 'Reproductive patterns.' 1972.
5. 'Artificial control of reproduction.' 1972.
6. 'The evolution of reproduction.' 1976.

Baum, M. J., Everitt, B. J., Herbert, J., and Keverne, E. B. 1977. 'Hormonal basis of proceptivity and receptivity in female primates.' *Archiv. Sex. Behav. 6*, 173–92.

Beach, F. A. 1976. 'Sexual attractivity, proceptivity and receptivity in female mammals.' *Horm. Behav. 7*, 105–38.

Beach, F. A., and Levinson, G. 1950. 'Effects of androgen on the glans penis and mating behaviour of the castrated male rat.' *J. exp. Zool. 114*, 159–71.

Carlson, N. R. 1978. *Physiology of behaviour*. London: Allyn and Bacon.

Dobbing, J., and Smart, J. L. 1974. 'Vulnerability of the developing brain and behaviour.' *Brit. Med. Bull. 30*, 164–8.

Doering, C. H., Brodie, H., Kraemer, H., Becker, H., and Hamburg, D. A. 1974. 'Plasma testosterone levels in men.' In R. Friedman, R. Richart and R. Vande Wiele (eds) *Sex differences in behaviour*, 413–32. New York: John Wiley.

Everitt, B. J., and Herbert, J. 1971. 'The effects of dexamethasone and androgens on sexual receptivity in female monkeys.' *J. Endrocrinology 51*, 575–88.

Everitt, B. J., and Herbert, J. 1975. 'The effects of implanting testosterone into the c.n.s. of female monkeys.' *Brain Res. 86*, 109–20.

Fisher, A. E. 1966. 'Chemical and electrical stimulation of the brain of the male rat.' In R. A. Gorski and R. K. Whalen (eds) *Brain and behaviour: brain and gonadal function*. UCLA.

Goldfoot, A., Feder, H. H., and Goy, R. W. 1969. 'Development of bisexuality in the male rat treated neonatally with androstenedione.' *J. comp. physiol. Psychol. 67*, 41–5.

Goldman, B. D. 1974. 'The hypothalamic-pituitary-gonadal axis and the regulation of cyclicity and sexual behaviour.' In F. O. Schmitt and F. G. Worden (eds), *The Neurosciences: Third Study Program*. Cambridge, Mass.: MIT 587–91.

Gordon, T. P., Rose, R. M., and Bernstein, I. S. 1976. 'Seasonal rhythms in plasma testosterone levels in the rhesus monkey.' *Horm. and Behav. 7*, 229–43.

Goy, R. W. 1970. 'Early hormonal influences on the development of sexual and sex related behaviour.' In F. O. Schmitt (ed.) *The Neurosciences: Second Study Program*, 196–206. Cambridge, Mass.: MIT.

Herbert, J. 1977. 'Hormones and behaviour.' *Proc. R. Soc. Lond. B. 199*, 425–43.

Jost, A. 1973. 'Sexual differentiation in rabbits.' *Recent Prog. Brain Res. 29*.

Kraemer, H. C., Becker, H. B., Brodie, H. K. H., Doering, C. H., Moos, R. H., and Hamburg, D. A. 1976. 'Orgasmic frequency and plasma testosterone levels in normal human males.' *Archiv. Sex. Behav. 5*, 125–32.

Katangole, C. B., Naftolin, F., and Short, R. V. 1971. 'The effect of sexual excitement on testosterone levels in the bull.' *J. Endocrinol. 50*, 457.

McEwen, B. S., Denef, C. J., Gerlach, J. L., and Plapinger, L. 1974. 'Chemical studies of the brain as steroid hormone target tissue.' In F. O. Schmitt and F. G. Worden (eds) *The Neurosciences: Third Program*, 599 – 620. Cambridge, Mass.: MIT.

Meyer-Bahlburg, H. F. L. 1977. 'Sex hormones and male homosexuality in comparative perspective.' *Archiv. Sex. Behav. 6*, 297 – 325.

Michael, R. P., Zumpe, D., Keverne, E. B., and Bonsall, R. W. 1972. 'Neuroendocrine factors in the control of primate behavior.' *Recent Prog. Horm. Res. 28*, 665 – 706.

Money, J. 1961. 'Components of eroticism in man.' *J. Nerv. Ment. Dis. 132*, 239 – 48.

Money, J., and Ehrhardt, A. A. 1972. *Man and woman, boy and girl.* Baltimore: Johns Hopkins University Press.

Persky, H. P. 1974. 'Reproductive hormones, moods and the menstrual cycle.' In R. C. Friedman, R. M. Richart and R. L. Vande Wiele (eds) *Sex differences in behaviour*, 455 – 76. New York: John Wiley.

Persky, H. P., Lief, H. I., Strauss, D., Miller, W. R., and O'Brien, C. A. 1978. 'Plasma testosterone level and sexual behavior of couples.' *Archiv. Sex. Behav. 7*, 157 – 73.

Pfaff, D. W., Diakow, C., and Zigmond, R. E. 1974. 'Neural and hormonal determinants of female mating behaviour in rats.' In F. O. Schmitt and F. G. Worden (eds) *The Neurosciences: Third Study Program*, 621 – 49. Cambridge, Mass.: MIT.

Reinberg, A., and Lagogney, M. 1978. 'Circadian and circannual rhythms in sexual activity and plasma hormones in five human males.' *Archiv. Sex. Behav. 7*, 13 – 30.

Ryan, R. K., Naftolin, F., Reddy, V., Flores, F., and Petro, Z. 1972. 'Oestrogen function in the brain.' *Am. J. Obstet. Gynecol. 114*, 404 – 60.

Sipova, I., and Starka, L. 1976. 'Testosterone levels in transsexual women.' *Archiv. Sex. Behav. 6*, 477 – 85.

Ward, I. L. 1974. 'Sexual behaviour and differentiation.' In R. C. Friedman, R. M. Richart and R. L. Vande Wiele (eds) *Sex differences in behaviour*, 3 – 18. New York: John Wiley.

Young, W. C. 1961. 'The hormones and mating behaviour.' In W. C. Young (ed.) *Sex and internal secretions*, 1173 – 239. Baltimore: Williams and Wilkins.

Chapter 10

Behaviour Therapy

M. PHILIP FELDMAN

The chapter on 'Behaviour Modification' (Kiernan 1978) in *Psychology Survey No. 1* was concerned entirely with remedial work with the mentally handicapped and their parents and the educational development of normal children in school settings. Considerations both of space and special interest excluded many other areas of this enormous field. In this chapter I will concentrate largely on behavioural approaches to the psychological problems of adults with only a brief reference to work with young offenders.

HISTORY

Occasional clinical articles in the behaviourist tradition had appeared for many years, for example the now famous report on children's fears by Mary Cover Jones (1924a,b), but the major development came in the 1950s due to a combination of influences (see Yates 1970, for a detailed account). Many in the growing profession of clinical psychology had received a thorough training in the experimental method and that approach was now extending, with some success, into more complex human behaviours. At the same time, they were increasingly dissatisfied, both with the mounting evidence of the inadequacy of the conventional psychiatric approach to psychological problems (for example the 'disease model' fitted poorly the vast range of non-psychotic problems) and with the limited nature of their own role (psychometric testing, or in a minority of cases psychotherapy in the psychodynamic tradition). Questions were being asked about the efficacy of psychotherapy; the resulting evidence (Eysenck 1952) although controversial, fed the growing discontent. In response to these influences behaviour therapy research developed in South Africa (Wolpe 1958) and in Britain (e.g. Jones 1956; Eysenck 1960). Developments in the USA soon overtook those elsewhere in breadth and depth and the leadership in the behaviour therapies is now firmly American.

The generic term, *behaviour therapy*, has been associated with a theoretical approach to psychological problems with its roots in the experimental psychology of Pavlov and Hull as developed by Wolpe (1958). *Behaviour modification*, as a generic term, has tended to refer to theory and techniques in the tradition of Skinner. Today, the two terms are used, almost interchangeably, to refer to clinical theory and method stemming, very broadly, from many areas of *experimental* work on behaviour, including social and cognitive psychology.

BASIC CONCEPTS

The Concern with Behaviour

The emphasis in treatment by behaviour therapy is always on the behaviour of which the client complains ('client' is used increasingly rather than 'patient' and is in itself an important shift away from the disease model). Although for purposes of exposition, conventional descriptive diagnoses such as 'depression' are used in this chapter, the objective of the behaviour therapist is not to give a diagnosis and prescribe a standard remedy but instead, 'the problem behaviors and the desired objectives have to be defined with clear behavioral referents. Next it is necessary to describe the exact circumstances provoking the problem behaviors and to identify the conditions maintaining them. In the light of this information the particular behavior-change operations most likely to produce the desired objectives must be selected' (Mischel 1968, p. 235).

Again, for purposes of exposition, I shall describe a number of techniques but in practice the more expert behaviour therapists (as opposed to those working from a 'cook book') will design a procedure appropriate to each problem of each individual; the common element is that the procedures have their origins in the experimental tradition, now widely interpreted to include research on covert as well as overt behaviour. Thus, there is an increasing emphasis on the fact that many problems of overt behaviour are maintained in part by the client 'talking to himself' about his difficulties. Other problems are largely, even wholly, 'internal' (for example repeated obsessional ruminations). Finally, an important contribution to behavioural treatment is made by words as controlling stimuli, both for external actions by the client relevant to the targets of treatment and for internal events, for example positive as opposed to negative, self-statements (see Mahoney 1974).

The emphasis of behaviour therapists on the crucial importance of *current* environmental antecedents and consequences in designing an appropriate method of changing behaviour does not imply that biological influences play no part in the origin of psychological problems. Indeed, some individuals may be more pre-disposed biologically than others to develop either a specific psychological problem or a whole range of such problems. However, information of this kind is only relevant to the psychological problems of a given individual, as opposed to the advance of knowledge about people in general, if it has implications for the treatment of that individual by biological means. This is the case for certain groups of problems such as the schizophrenias but for a whole range of non-psychotic problems, including increasingly many examples of depression (see below), psychological difficulties are treated by psychological methods.

The Rights of the Client

Behaviour therapists assume that most clients can report accurately both the nature of their problem and what changes they seek. In contrast, the psychodynamic tradition has tended to the view that the expressed concerns of 'patients' often mask unconscious conflict revealed only in distorted form and that their objectives are frequently unrealistic, because of the same distortions. Thus, far from behaviour therapy reducing human freedom – a frequently made charge (e.g. Glover 1959) – it is at the very least as concerned to extend the individuals' control over his own life as any of the other psychological approaches to therapy and its increasingly good record of success is helping to make this concern effective in practice. But powerful approaches *can* be both abused (employed towards undesirable ends) and misused (applied incompetently). Both problems are true of all applications of scientific research. The onus is on the profession that supplies the service and the public that consumes it both to demand high standards of professional competence and to set clear objectives. The latter is particularly important: the main principles are that the client as the key interested party gives his fully *informed consent* and that any treatment shall seek to bring the *maximum benefit to the client* both by increasing access to positive consequences and by decreasing negative consequences, as defined in both cases by the client (Feldman 1976a). Problems arise in the case of young children and the mentally handicapped, they have to be 'spoken for' by legal guardians, preferably subject to monitoring on behalf of clients by independent agencies. Another special case is that of convicted offenders. Should they have their socially damaging behaviour changed irrespective of their own aims? The consensus is increasingly that therapy aimed at behaviours legally defined as undesirable should be offered on a voluntary self-referral basis and only to two groups: those who feel in danger of committing an offence and those who have already served a legally imposed penalty (see Feldman 1977 for a more detailed discussion).

METHODS

The following is a summary, and arbitrary, list of some of the major principles of treatment by the behaviour therapies. In the treatment of any one client it is common for more than one principle to be used.

Increasing, Restoring or Acquiring Behaviours

(1) Planned exposure to the feared object, situation or person. This is typically used for problems in which the behaviour is already present in the repertoire of the client but is no longer performed, or only at a level seriously inconveniencing to daily life. The exposure may be in imagination or in reality, may be gradual (termed desensitization) or rapid (flooding) and may or may not be preceded by the behaviour concerned being modelled by someone else, preferably similar to the client in some important way. This broad approach has been particularly frequent in the behavioural treatment of phobias.
(2) Positive training in relevant skills, previously either absent from the clients repertoire, or present at such a low level as seriously to impair the performance of the skill concerned. There is much emphasis on the detailed analysis and specification of the behaviour concerned, on the modelling and practice of specified segments and the gradual transition from easier to more difficult segments. Transition is assisted by immediate feedback of results and positive reinforcement for progress. Examples of this broad principle include training in social and sexual skills.

Decreasing Behaviours
Helping the client to reduce or to cease altogether behaviours he sees as damaging in some important respect.

(1) The application of an aversive consequence for the performance of the undesired behaviour (termed punishment).
(2) Helping clients to identify and so avoid the environmental cues which elicit the undesired behaviours.
(3) Time-Out. This means that if the unwanted behaviour occurs the client is removed from positive consequences.
(4) Response-cost. Following the performance of the undesired behaviour the client gives up a proportion of the positive reinforcements already received.
(5) Extinction. There are no external consequences, positive or negative, for performing the undesired behaviour. Lack of external consequences tends to result in reduced performance.

Among the problems to which the behaviour reduction principles have been applied are weight control, particularly overeating, drug and alcohol abuse, gambling and several minority sexual behaviours. In general, such procedures are most effective when combined with the systematic provision of alternative positive behaviours.

Other Major Principles

(1) The token economy. This is a large scale *system* of reinforcers

applicable to a wide range of behaviours, which can be readily distributed or removed. The medium of exchange is not money but a system of tokens which can be exchanged later for a range of goods and services. This approach is widely used in group settings such as the chronic wards of psychiatric hospitals, particularly to restore dormant behaviour to normal levels, or to bring seriously disruptive behaviour under control – as in a residential institution for young offenders. It is desirable to transfer control as soon as possible to the natural reinforcers that occur in the real world, such as social approval and disapproval.

(2) Self-management or self-control. There is an increasing tendency to teach clients simple behavioural principles so that after the therapist has managed the early part of treatment they can take over setting their own goals and monitoring their own performance. A variation on this is to involve families or friends as treatment managers (Kiernan 1978, described parental involvement in some detail). The self-management principle is applicable to all the major approaches to treatment, both positive and negative and to a very wide range of problems. Because professional behaviour therapists are both relatively expensive and thinly spread, involving clients and significant others in treatment is going to grow in importance, as is the training of other professionals who then supervise clients directly. The role of the behaviour therapist becomes one of initial consultant and occasional monitor.

Features Common to all Effective Methods

(1) Generalization. It is crucial to arrange for the newly acquired, restored, or reduced behaviours to generalize across the full range of relevant situations and not remain confined to the typically limited range used in treatment. It requires the specification of those situations and the planned practice in them of the relevant desired behaviours or alternatives to the undesired behaviours.

(2) Social influence. The early behaviour therapists tended to play down the importance of the therapeutic relationship (the mutual evaluation of therapist and client) and instead emphasized the technical competence of the therapist as the only variable crucial to success. Technical competence will be wasted unless clients both remain in therapy and carry out the 'homework' assignments so crucial to the behavioural approach. More recently, behaviour therapists have come to share the long-held awareness of psychotherapists of the importance of the therapeutic relationship and to study ways in which this can be made maximally effective (Feldman 1976b).

APPLICATIONS

Phobias

About 2 people per 1000 suffer from phobias disabling enough to impair every-day life seriously (Agras *et al.* 1969). If this is correct it would mean about 100 000 potential phobic clients in a country the size of Britain. The most clinically reported phobia is agoraphobia, the fear of open or public places. Untreated phobias tend to improve in only about 40% of cases (Agras *et al.* 1972). The first and most thoroughly studied behaviour therapy technique is that of desensitization (Wolpe 1958). It has three major components: a graduated hierarchy of anxiety provoking scenes presented in order from least to most distressing; training in deep muscle relaxation prior to presentation of scenes; visualizing each scene while relaxed. Many hundreds of studies (see for example, Davison and Wilson 1973) have researched these components separately and in combination. The crucial factor (if any) seems to be that of *exposure*, preferably in reality as well as in imagination. A series of controlled trials (McConaghy 1970) suggests strongly that desensitization is superior to a variety of psychotherapeutic procedures. Comparisons with alternative behavioural methods, including reinforced practice, participant modelling and flooding are less clear cut.

Reinforced practice (e.g. Leitenberg and Callahan 1973) emphasizes repeated graduated practice, instructions to arouse expectation of gradual success, immediate and precise feedback of performance, and social approval for small gains in performance. Modelling stems from the important researches of Bandura (e.g. 1977) into observational learning. The evidence is now very powerful that observing other peoples behaviour and its consequences have all the effects of learning by direct experience, including losing a range of fears. The clinical use of participant modelling (reviewed by Rachman 1976) involves a model (who may be the therapist) demonstrating the desired behaviour to the client, followed by a joint performance (typically with the client holding the model's hand) and then by the client carrying out the act alone.

Flooding has its origin in a considerable animal literature (Baum 1970). It involves prolonged exposure to high levels of the anxiety provoking stimuli and *preventing* the client from avoiding them. Therapists, though surprisingly not clients (Marks *et al.* 1971), sometimes find the procedure unpleasant and difficult to carry out, but it has achieved some very rapid successes.

Obsessions

There are two major types of obsessional difficulty: ruminations and rituals. The first is covert and hence not visible, the second is all too observable – often involving the repetition of acts, such as hand washing and checking, for many hours on end. Obsessional problems are not common – accounting for about 1% of the total population of psychiatric patients – but are exceptionally disabling and have a poor record for spontaneous improvement without help. The results of treatment by a variety of non-behavioural methods have been unsatisfactory. Only 30% of those reported by 13 outcome studies reviewed by Goodwin *et al.* (1969) were rated even as 'improved' – a less stringent requirement than 'problem free'.

Systematic desensitization has proved largely ineffective with obsessional problems (Cooper *et al.* 1965). The crucial advance was made by Meyer (1966) who used two major elements: preventing the rituals from taking place, while at the same time exposing the client to the thoughts and situations that normally evoke them. Instead, the client is encouraged to carry out the range of behaviours typically prevented by the ritual (for example, touching objects which conceivably might be dirty). Several controlled studies (e.g. Hodgson and Rachman 1972) have now confirmed Meyer's original report. Effective treatment requires prolonged contact between client and therapist in the settings in which the behaviour occurs, often the client's home.

Depression

The available evidence (Mendels 1970) tends to support the view that depression takes two major forms, although with much overlap: endogenous and reactive. The former seems more related to biological causes and consequences (a slowing in physical activity, loss of weight, etc) and the latter to environmental causes and psychological consequences. Physical treatments such as electro-convulsive therapy (ECT) and drugs seem reasonably effective for the more endogenous type of depression, less so with the more reactive; hence the development of psychological therapies for the latter. A behavioural approach to depression, with implications for therapy, has been suggested by, amongst others, Moss and Boren (1972). They argued that the major environmental conditions associated with depressive behaviour are insufficient positive reinforcement (e.g. a salesman no longer obtaining sales with previously successful behaviours) and aversive control (punishing consequences, such as loss of income, for the type of failure experienced by the salesman; followed by first escape, then avoidance of the situation – the task of selling). The behavioural treatment that follows from such an analysis is exemplified by Burgess (1968) and consists of two elements. The first emphasizes the extinction of 'depressive behaviour' by ignoring the clients statements of depressed mood, etc. The second seeks to restore the reduced or absent performance of positive responses (e.g. seeking sales) by re-training in the task, using a gently ascending order of difficulty, and much positive feedback for the successful completion of each small step. Controlled trials of such behavioural methods for depression are yet to be reported but preliminary reports are promising.

Seligman (1975) has presented a detailed account, stemming from animal studies, of depression viewed as *learned helplessness* – environmental events and their consequences lead the individual to believe that he has lost control over important aspects of his life. The results are that former responses are no longer made, and a change in mood occurs in the downward direction typical of depression. The implication of this theory for therapy is that the effective methods are those that restore the rate of responding, particularly responding which leads to reliable positive reinforcement. The most effective behavioural method would be a combination of Burgess's approach, described above, and a considerable initial effort to stimulate the client to produce responses of any kind, however simple.

Sexual and Marital Problems

The monumental studies of Masters and Johnson (1966) have provided new information of major importance on human sexual responses and problems of response. The same researchers have originated methods of treatment which, together with associated improved versions, have opened up major possibilities of help for those suffering from a range of sexual difficulties (Masters and Johnson 1970). The number of such individuals is unknown – no systematic surveys have been carried out – but the heavy demand on the increasing number of therapists offering behavioural methods of help indicates that the size of the problem is very considerable.

The focus of help is most often on the couple rather than either partner alone. Treatment usually includes the 'sensate focus' together with additions relevant to the specific problem. The basic assumption is that sexual enjoyment will follow if fear can be eliminated. Following a detailed assessment of sexual history and attitudes the couple practice mutual touching to give pleasure, beginning with non-sexual areas of the body and proceeding finally to sexual areas and to intercourse – attempts at which are forbidden until the full hierarchy of touching has been completed. The treatments of male impotence and female difficulties of orgasm have specific additional features.

Success in problems of sexual response depends only in part on the careful analysis of the problem and the matching to it of an appropriate method of treatment. There is good evidence that it also requires a satisfactory non-sexual *marital relationship*. In addition, many couples whose sexual relationships are still relatively good seek help because the non-sexual side is in increasing disarray. An excellent account of the behavioural approach to marital distress and therapy is given by Patterson *et al.* (1976). Relationships are maintained as long as both members supply enough positive reinforcement to each other. When this is no longer the case the result is a mounting cycle of either angry exchanges or silent withdrawal. Behavioural intervention emphasizes helping the couple in pinpointing (describing in precise terms the behaviours of the other that are positively reinforcing and vice versa), communicating (exchanging information equally) and problem solving (developing skills in planning, negotiation and compromise) in order to set and achieve targets for changes in each others' behaviour. The aim of the therapist is gradually to transfer responsibility and to fade out of the picture. This method exemplifies particularly well the typical emphasis of behaviour therapies on active client participation and self-management. Evaluative studies (e.g. Patterson *et al.* 1975) are promising.

Social Difficulties

Many clients complain of difficulties with social relationships, either separately or in combination with a range of psychological problems associated with deficits in many verbal and non-verbal social skills (Trower *et al.* 1978). The list of skills includes observing (e.g. getting information), performing (e.g. listening, speaking, 'turn-taking', greeting and parting) and such cognitive elements as planning and problem solving. There is much use of videotape recording and feedback by 'trainers'. Both modelling and guided practice are likely to be important. It is vital to arrange for generalization to the full range of situations in which the social difficulties occur. Skills training can produce positive changes in short-term social behaviour. Evaluative studies to date suggest that the field is very difficult, yet promising (Marzillier 1978).

Problems of Eating and Drinking

Problems of eating. Anorexia nervosa is a rare problem, seemingly confined to young females and characterized by voluntary restriction of food, loss of weight and amenorrhea (delayed or absent periods). It is more appropriately described as 'weight phobia'. Behavioural approaches have been largely within the operant tradition, gains in weight receiving prompt feedback of the improvement, social attention, and a range of positive reinforcements. So far treatment has been confined to in-patients and the results reported to date have been very satisfactory (Stunkard 1975).

In contrast, *overweight* (relative to insurance norms) is very widespread and is a major health problem. Stimulus control procedures seem much the most powerful of those used by behaviour therapists. Treatment begins with an analysis of the environmental cues that elicit and control eating behaviours (for example a particular room, certain times of day, etc). The client is asked to separate eating from other pleasurable activities, to avoid buying high calorie foods, to eat small portions and to eat slowly and not to 'clean' the plate. The aim is to restrict the range and frequency of cues associated with eating. A number of studies have repeated and extended the good results originally reported by Stuart (1967). The best results of all are obtained when stimulus control is supplemented by self-management (the client sets the target and monitors progress, etc. Mahoney 1972).

Alcoholism. The social and personal costs of dependence on alcohol includes child neglect, occupational absenteeism and inefficiency, road casualties, and increased proneness to a variety of illnesses. Considerable emphasis is now placed on early intervention and on the social and psychological aspects of the problem rather than delaying help for so long that physical problems predominate and obscure the need for psychological methods of help. The most effective behavioural approaches are those that employ a broad-spectrum of methods to train the client in social and vocational skills so as to cope with his problems effectively rather than by recourse to alcohol. For some alcoholics, controlled drinking has become an attainable treatment goal and an alternative to that of abstinence, formally the only outcome considered satisfactory (Sobell and Sobell 1973).

Juvenile Offenders

The range of traditional methods of coping with young offenders has proved so ineffective as to raise the possibility that they may even be doing more harm than good. Psychotherapeutic approaches which emphasize setting up personal relationships with offenders have been tried for many years but with little success so far as preventing reconviction – the key test of efficacy – is concerned (Feldman 1977). Behavioural approaches began in the 1960s, the most thorough and carefully reported being the Achievement Place (AP) programme developed in Kansas (Phillips 1968). Boys aged 12 – 14 who have carried out minor offences live in small groups with a pair of experienced foster parents. The boys undergo a complex programme based on token economy principles, but also there is much self-government and great attention is given to skills and achievements in the outside world, both social and educational. It seems clear that a stay in Achievement Place achieves substantial benefits in educational attainment and social skills (Braukman *et al.* 1975). What of legally related indices? We still await a fully controlled trial but some results are now available (Feldman 1977, p. 259 – 60). Two years after release the reconviction rate of a group of AP boys was only 19% as against 50% of those placed either on probation or committed to a conventional institution. The authors point out that the boys were not randomly assigned to each group, so that the results may have been due either to, 'a population effect or to a treatment effect'. Delinquency is an example of a problem from which the 'client' may both lose and benefit (crime brings both material and social return). The objectives of client and therapist may be very different. Of all the areas of work reviewed in this chapter that of crime is likely to prove the most complex and difficult (see Feldman 1977).

CONCLUDING COMMENT

During the past 20 years the development of behaviour therapy has dramatically transformed and enlarged the role of the clinical psychologist and improved the chances of effective help being given to a wide range of psychological problems. The field of behaviour therapy – itself only one segment of clinical psychology – is served by scores of textbooks (good introductions are those by Bootzin 1975; Bellack and Hersen 1977) and at least half a dozen specialist journals, the best known of which are: *Behaviour Therapy* and *Behaviour Research and Therapy*. There has been an increasing emphasis on controlled studies, using both group and single case designs, concerned with clinical populations. A period of analogue studies, carried out on American female undergraduates (Bernstein and Paul 1971) and of uncontrolled single cases, seems likely to have passed. A major current development is in cognitive aspects of behavioural problems and treatment (Mahoney 1974) an emphasis shared, of course, with psychotherapy. In turn, the adherents of psychotherapy are increasingly concerned with experimental studies and quantitative methods (Garfield and Bergin 1978).

REFERENCES

Agras, W. S., Chapin, H. N., and Oliveau, D. C. 1972. 'The natural history of phobia.' *Arch. Gen. Psychiat. 26*, 315 – 17.

Agras, W. S., Sylvester, D., and Oliveau, D. 1969. 'The epidemiology of common fears and phobias.' *Comprehensive Psychiatry 10*, 151 – 6.

Bandura, A. 1977. *Social learning theory*. Englewood Cliffs, NJ: Prentice-Hall.

Baum, M. 1970. 'Extinction of avoidance responding through response prevention (flooding).' *Psychol. Bull. 74*, 276 – 84.

Bellack, A. S., and Hersen, M. 1977. *Behaviour therapy: an introductory text book*. Baltimore: Williams and Wilkins.

Bernstein, D. A., and Paul, G. L. 1971. 'Some comments on therapy analogue research with small animal phobias.' *J. Behav. Ther. Exp. Psychiat. 2*, 223 – 39.

Bootzin, R. R. 1975. *Behaviour modification: an introduction*. New York: Winthrop.

Braukmann, C. J., Fixsen, D. L., Phillips, E. L., and Wolf, M. M. 1975. 'Behavioural approaches to treatment in the crime and delinquency field.' *Criminology 13*, 299 – 33.

Burgess, E. P. 1968. 'The modification of depressive behaviours.' In R. D. Rubin, and C. M. Franks (eds) *Advances in behaviour therapy*, 193 – 200. New York: Academic Press.

Cooper, J. E., Gelder, M. G., and Marks, I. M. 1965. 'Results of behaviour therapy in 77 psychiatric patients.' *Brit. Med. J. 1*, 1222 – 5.

Davison, G. C., and Wilson, G. T. 1973. 'Processes of fear reductions in systematic desensitization: cognitive and social reinforcement factors in humans.' *Behav. Ther. 4*, 1 – 21.

Eysenck, H. J. 1952. 'The effects of psychotherapy: an evaluation.' *J. Consult. Psychol. 16*, 319 – 24.

Eysenck, H. J. (ed.) 1960. *Behaviour therapy and the neuroses*. Oxford: Pergamon.

Feldman, M. P. 1976a. 'The behaviour therapies and society.' In M. P. Feldman and A. Broadhurst (eds) *The experimental bases of the behaviour therapies*, 405 – 34. London: John Wiley.

Feldman, M. P. 1976b. 'Social psychology and the behaviour therapies.' In M. P. Feldman and A. Broadhurst (eds) *The experimental bases of the behaviour therapies*, 227 – 68. London: John Wiley.

Feldman, M. P. 1977. *Criminal behaviour: a psychological analysis*. London: John Wiley.

Garfield, S. L., and Bergin, A. E. 1978. *Handbook of psychotherapy and behaviour change*, 2nd edn. New York: John Wiley.

Glover, E. 1959. 'Critical notice of Wolpe's "Psychotherapy by reciprocal inhibition".' *Brit. J. Med. Psychol. 32*, 68 – 74.

Goodwin, D. W., Guze, S. B., and Robins, E. 1969. 'Follow-up studies in obsessional neuroses.' *Arch. Gen. Psychiat. 20*, 182 – 7.

Hodgson, R. J., and Rachman, S. 1972. 'The effects of contamination and washing in obsessional patients.' *Behav. Res. and Ther. 10*, 111 – 17.

Jones, H. G. 1956. 'The applications of conditioning and learning techniques to the treatment of a psychiatric patient.' *J. Abnorm. and Soc. Psychol. 56*, 414 – 20.

Kiernan, C. C. 1978. 'Behaviour modification.' In B. Foss (ed.) *Psychology survey no. 1*. London: George Allen & Unwin.

Leitenberg, H., and Callahan, E. 1973. 'Reinforced practice and reduction of different kinds of fears in adults and children.' *Behav. Res. and Ther. 11*, 19 – 30.

McConaghy, N. 1970. 'Results of systematic desensitization with phobias re-examined.' *Brit. J. Psychiat. 117*, 89 – 92.

Mahoney, M. J. 1974. 'Research issues in self-management.' *Behav. Ther. 3*, 45 – 63.

Marks, I., Boulougouris, J., and Marset, P. 1971. 'Flooding versus desensitization in the treatment of phobic patients: a cross-over study.' *Brit. J. Psychiat. 119*, 353 – 75.

Marzillier, J. S. 1978. 'Outcome studies of skills training: a review.' In P. Trower *et al. Social skills and mental health*, 103 – 32. London: Methuen.

Masters, W. H., and Johnson, V. E. 1966. *Human sexual response*. Boston: Little, Brown.

Masters, W. H., and Johnson, V. E. 1970. *Human sexual inadequacy*. Boston: Little, Brown.

Mendels, J. 1970. *Concepts of Depression*. New York: John Wiley.

Meyer, V. 1966. 'Modification of expectations in cases with obsessional rituals.' *Behav. Res. and Ther. 4*, 273 – 80.

Mischel, W. 1968. *Personality and assessment*. New York: John Wiley.

Moss, G. R., and Boren, J. J. 1972. 'Depression as a model for behavioural analysis.' *Comprehensive Psychiatry 13*, 581 – 90.

Patterson, G. R., Hops, H., and Weiss, R. L. 1975. 'Interpersonal skills training for couples in the early stages of conflict.' *J. Marriage and the Family*, 295 – 303.

Patterson, G. R., Weiss, W. G., and Hops, H. 1976. 'Training of marital skills: some problems and concepts.' In H. Leitenberg (ed.) *Handbook of behaviour modification and behaviour therapy*, 242 – 54. Englewood Cliffs, NJ: Prentice-Hall.

Phillips, E. L. 1968. 'Achievement Place: token reinforcement procedures in a home style rehabilitation setting for pre-delinquent boys.' *J. App. Behav. Anal. 1*, 213 – 23.

Rachman, S. J. 1976. 'Observational learning and therapeutic modelling.' In M. P. Feldman and A. Broadhurst (eds) *The experimental bases of the behaviour therapies*, 193 – 226. London: John Wiley.

Seligman, M. E. P. 1975. *Helplessness*. San Francisco: W. H. Freeman.

Sobell, M. B., and Sobell, L. C. 1973. 'Individualized behaviour therapy for alcoholics.' *Behav. Ther. 4*, 49 – 72.

Stuart, R. B. 1967. *Behavioural research and therapy: behavioural control of overeating 5*, 357 – 65.

Stunkard, A. J. 1975. '*Anorexia nervosa*.' In J. P. Sanford (ed.) *The science and practice of clinical medicine*. New York: Grune and Stratton.

Trower, P., Bryant, B., and Argyle, M. 1978. *Social skills and mental health*. London: Methuen.

Wolpe, J. 1958. *Psychotherapy by reciprocal inhibition*. Stanford: Stanford University Press.

Yates, A. 1970. *Behaviour therapy*. New York: John Wiley.

Chapter 11

Mathematical Thinking

G. BRIAN GREER

The main emphasis of this review is on experimental studies of mathematical thinking, though, as will be clear, this cannot be divorced entirely from discussion of the learning and teaching of mathematics. For convenience, the material has been divided into three sections. The first two deal with experimental studies, in relation to the mathematical content and the underlying cognitive processes respectively. The final section is a brief critique of Piagetian views on mathematical thinking.

RESEARCH IN VARIOUS CONTENT AREAS

Number

Much if not most of the research on number concepts relates to Piaget's work.* Piaget describes the development of number concepts within his usual conceptual framework of operational thinking. The natural numbers have two aspects: ordinal, related to seriation operations, and cardinal, related to class operations. According to Piaget, a true concept of number emerges as an integration of these two aspects. He stresses also the importance of the insight (attained at the age of 5 or 6) that the number of objects in a set is invariant under spatial transformations, as tested by the familiar number conservation task.

Piaget's account of the development of number concepts has been severely criticized in recent years. For example, Gelman's research on preschool children implies that they have much more numerical competence than Piaget credits them with (Gelman 1978; Gelman and Gallistel 1978). Gelman and Gallistel provide a detailed account of the development of number concepts in 2- to 5-year-olds. In particular, they have analysed: (i) the development of counting, not as a simple skill to be rote learned, but as a complex system of operations and principles

*In discussing Piaget's work, the primary sources will not be cited (there is no difficulty in tracing them from secondary sources). It need hardly be added that the scope of Piaget's research and the complexity of his philosophical views can only be hinted at in this review.

which develops gradually, and (ii) the increasing sophistication of young children's numerical reasoning.

By way of contrast, the model presented by Schaeffer, Eggleston and Scott (1974) views understanding of number in terms of a hierarchical integration of skills, namely: (i) counting, (ii) the cardinality rule (that the last number named when counting denotes the number of objects in a set), (iii) acquisition of more objects (the ability to give, take, or ask for more objects), (iv) judgements of relative numerosity, (v) pattern recognition of small numbers, (vi) use of one-to-one correspondence. Although the six skills have been empirically tested, this model appears to be based on *a priori* logical analysis, rather than being empirically derived.

Understandably, research on number concepts has been concentrated on the natural numbers, with very little attention being given to the negative integers (but see Lunzer, Bell and Shiu 1976, discussed in the next subsection) and the rational, real, imaginary and transfinite numbers. Imaginary and transfinite numbers are particularly interesting from the psychological and epistemological point of view because they are pure constructs, which cannot be linked directly to experience. Fischbein, Tirosh and Hess (1979) carried out a developmental study of intuitions about infinity, using questions like this:

> Consider the set of natural numbers $N = \{1, 2, 3, 4, \ldots\}$
> and the set of even numbers $D = \{2, 4, 6, 8, \ldots\}$
> Question: Which of the two sets contains more elements?
> Explain your answer.

They found a strong tendency to misapply 'finitist' arguments (e.g. that a proper subset always has fewer elements) to problems involving infinity, and that mathematical education had little effect on such incorrect intuitions.

Arithmetic

Many process models for simple arithmetical calculations have been proposed in recent years: these are discussed in the next section. For such models to be viable, it must be assumed that people, by and large, adopt a common approach to such tasks. By contrast, Ginsburg (1977) deals largely with 'case-studies' and shows clearly the variety of strategies used by children in elementary arithmetic.

Lunzer, Bell and Shiu (1976) pointed out that numbers model aspects of the real world in various ways (cf. Freudenthal 1973, pp. 170 ff) and studied the development of different conceptions of number, paying particular attention to problems of major pedagogical importance: the relation between addition and subtraction, and the extension of understanding from the natural numbers to negative numbers. They concluded (p.v.) that the development of number models proceeds through the following sequence: (i) numbers as counters, for modelling how many objects there are in a set, (ii) numbers as objects in their own right, which can be manipulated symbolically, (iii) numbers for measuring visually apparent magnitudes, (iv) numbers as displacements (e.g. on a number line model), (v) understanding of negative integers as inverse elements for the corresponding positive integers.

Algebra

Gelman and Gallistel (1978, pp. 227 – 37) make a distinction between arithmetical reasoning (reasoning about specific numerosities), and algebraic reasoning (reasoning which is independent of numerosities). For example, they characterize Piaget's conservation of number task as requiring algebraic reasoning. The same distinction can be seen in the work of Collis (1978). In one study, he used a range of items varying along two dimensions:

(1) Concrete or formal content. Compare these three items:

$$8+4-4=?$$
$$4283+517-517=?$$
$$a+b-b=?$$

The first involves small numbers, so can be worked out directly ($8+4=12$, then $12-4=8$). This is more difficult with large numbers, and impossible with algebraic symbols (second and third items).

(2) Operational structure. An item such as:

$$a+b-b=?$$

can be solved by immediate 'closure' since $b-b$ can be replaced by 0. By contrast, an item of the form:

$$a+b=(a+c)+(b-?)$$

involves the ability to cope with 'lack of closure', an important construct in Collis' theory.

Collis presents developmental data for these tasks and relates the results to the Piagetian concrete and formal operational stages. Halford (1978) has also considered how Piagetian theory might be related to developmental stages in mathematical thinking.

In another study, Collis traced developmental changes in the ability to work with an unfamiliar abstract system, based on the operation $*$, defined by $a*b=a+2b$. He found that from about 8 years of age children substituted a familiar operation ($+$ or $\times$) for $*$ and that only the oldest children tested (17-year-olds) predominantly worked, or at least attempted to, within the system as defined.

Krutetskii's (1976) extensive study included many algebraic problems.

For example, in one series of tasks, the form of the tasks was kept constant, but numerical parameters were one by one replaced by symbols, thus providing a series of tasks varying along the concrete-abstract dimension. In another type of task, subjects were taught formulae such as $(a+b)^2 = a^2 + 2ab + b^2$ then tested for generalization to increasingly complex cases of the same form, e.g. $(\frac{1}{3}a^m + \frac{1}{7}b^n)^2$. Striking differences were found between mathematically able, average and inept pupils in the ability to ignore surface features and perceive the constant underlying structure of such expressions.

Geometry

Historically, geometrical problems were used extensively in studies of problem-solving, being particularly appropriate for the Gestalt approach to problem-solving, and for the study of heuristic processes. Relatively little work along these lines has appeared recently; a few examples will be found in Wickelgren's (1974) book.

Developmental work on geometrical concepts has been dominated by Piaget's research, summarized conveniently by Holloway (1967a,b). Indeed, there has been very little research apart from his, which is rather surprising (Dodwell 1971). From Piaget's epistemological viewpoint, geometrical concepts are integrally bound up with concepts of space. His emphasis is on representation of space, rather than perception of space; this is characteristic of his constructivist views. He has interpreted his findings as indicating an ontogenetic development from topological to projective to Euclidean representations, which, as he stresses, reverses the historical order of formalization of the corresponding branches of geometry.

Probability

Piaget's contribution in this area has been briefly outlined by Inhelder (1977). Characteristically, Piaget links the mathematical aspects with the broader epistemological issues such as causality, and relates them to the development of operational thinking. For example, he believes that a concept of randomness develops relatively late (at about 6 or 7 years of age) and only when complementary concepts of order have developed (i.e. concrete operational thought). At the formal operational stage, the concept of probability based on relative frequencies is grasped, as well as the idea of a probability distribution (which is linked to the emergence of combinatorial thinking).

Fischbein (1975) has recently reviewed two major lines of research: that based on Piagetian developmental research and that based on the 'probability learning' paradigm. In probability learning, the subject predicts on each trial which of a number of possible outcomes (usually two) will occur and then observes the outcome that is determined randomly, but with fixed unequal probabilities for the different outcomes. Under these circumstances human subjects consistently produce 'probability matching', i.e. the proportions of predictions of outcomes asymptotically match the probabilities of occurrence. In reviewing evidence of probability matching in children, Fischbein states that, 'the results of probability learning experiments argue strongly in favour of the view that preschool children adapt their predictions to the probabilities of events' (1975, p. 118). This conclusion seems questionable, since probability matching is predicted by very simple conditioning models (as Fischbein himself discusses).

Fischbein stresses the role of intuition in probability, an aspect also studied by Tversky and Kahnemann (1974). They analysed the performance of adult subjects on probabilistic problems which they are unable to solve formally. In such circumstances, subjects show systematic biases in their errors, which Tversky and Kahnemann have interpreted in terms of a number of 'heuristics'.

'Piagetian' Studies

A lot of current educational research on mathematical learning, particularly in the United States, is broadly inspired by Piagetian theory. Two collections of studies along these lines are those edited by Rosskopf (1975) and Steffe (1975). They cover a wide variety of topics; Rosskopf's book includes studies of the concepts of bilateral symmetry, area measure, limit, function, various topological concepts, and understanding of some forms of logical inference. The degree to which these studies are genuinely Piagetian in approach varies. For example, in Thomas's (1975) investigation, the author states at the outset that he was not dealing with a general concept of function but with the learning of the material in a formal course on functions. Moreover, the 'stages' he defined were very different from typical Piagetian stages; they were defined in advance, and in operational terms.

The studies in Steffe's book are more directly related to Piagetian topics: equivalence and order relations, classification and seriation, conservation. They mainly consist of training studies. In summarizing the findings, Lovell concluded that, 'it remains uncertain whether there will be any real improvement in operativity as the result of narrowly based experiences' (1975, p. 182), a point also made by Sinclair, 'A child's reactions to a few Piagetian tasks will enable a well-trained psychologist to give a fair description of that child's intellectual level; but teaching the solutions of these same Piagetian tasks to a group of children does not mean that the children will thereby attain the general intellectual level of the child who can solve the tasks independently.' (1971, pp. 1 – 2).

COGNITIVE PROCESSES UNDERLYING MATHEMATICAL THINKING

Process Models

Performance on simple arithmetical tasks is an ideal field for mathematical models. Several process models for addition (e.g. Svenson, Hedenborg and Lingman 1976; Groen and Resnick 1977), and subtraction (Woods, Resnick and Groen 1975; Svenson and Hedenborg 1979), have appeared in recent years. These are typically based on analysis of response latencies, and mainly restricted to manipulation of single-digit numbers. At an early stage in the development of this approach, it was the tendency to look for unitary models – with aggregated data it was always possible to fit the data (more or less) with such a model. More recent versions have taken more account of:

(1) Individual differences in subjects;
(2) The fact that different computational methods are used for different classes of problem. For example, Svenson and Hedenborg's (1979) model postulates that in subtracting *N* from *M* the answers are quickly retrieved, reproductively, from memory for the special cases $M=N$, $N=1$ and $M=2N$, but that in other cases reconstructive processes operate.

In models which assume different processes for different classes of items, flow diagrams represent the initial classification of item type as a series of decisions. As Svenson *et al.* (1976) acknowledge, this is an inherent disadvantage of this type of representation; the initial classification is unlikely to be the sequential process that the diagram implies. They also recommend strongly that the straightforward modelling approach should be complemented by getting subjects to report on their own solution processes.

Studies of more complex mental calculations include Hollnagel's (1978) experiment (performed on himself) involving multiplication of integers of up to three digits. He interpreted his results in terms of an information-processing system consisting of:

(1) A number of registers for storing numbers;
(2) A control system controlling the operations performed on the stored numbers;
(3) A higher-order control system controlling, in particular, the scheduling of time between rehearsal of the numbers in (1) and carrying out the operations in (2).

Hitch (1978) also studied multi-digit problems, by assessing reported strategies.

Process models of more complex thinking tend to take the form of computer programs. As one example of this approach may be cited the simulation by Baylor and Gascon (1974) of a weight seriation task.

Related to the 'process model' approach is a fundamental theoretical question, with important implications. S-R bonds no longer figure prominently in discussions of mathematical learning, but to what extent can the learning of mathematics be reduced to hierarchic integration of concepts, skills (e.g. Schaeffer *et al.* 1974) or rules (Scandura 1977)? This view of mathematical learning is prevalent in the United States, and is reflected in an approach to curriculum planning based on task analysis, operationally defined educational objectives, and tests to see if those objectives have been reached (see, for example Resnick 1976). A trenchant attack on this 'atomistic philosophy' has been made by Freudenthal (1978, Ch. 3). Many other writers also feel that such an approach presents a drastically oversimplified picture of mathematical learning and thinking. Gelman and Gallistel's (1978) treatment of counting as opposed to that of Schaeffer *et al.* (1974) has already been discussed. Likewise, Ginsburg's (1977) analysis of children's arithmetical behaviour may be contrasted with some of the simple process models that have been proposed. (The revised process model put forward by Svenson *et al.* 1976 makes a concession in this direction by including a frame for 'idiosyncratic strategies').

Memory

Some of the studies discussed in the previous subsection were largely concerned with the role of working memory (storage, rehearsal and decay of numbers and intermediate results) and long-term memory (use of algorithms) and their interaction. One of Hitch's findings, for example, was that interim results tend to be forgotten if not used immediately. A model assuming decay of information in working memory fitted his data reasonably well.

Ashcraft and Battaglia (1978) used a different procedure, in which adult subjects were presented single-integer additions, which had to be judged true or false. For incorrect additions, reaction times increased as the discrepancy between the presented answer and the correct result decreased; reaction times for correct additions were the quickest. They interpreted these results as supporting the view that the information is retrieved from memory rather than produced by a reconstructive counting process.

As Reed and Johnsen (1977) point out, a major trend in memory research over recent years is the increasing emphasis on memory for meaningful material. Their study investigated what subjects remembered after solving a version of a well-known problem: the missionaries and cannibals problem. Subjects solved the problem twice, but only half of the subjects knew that they would be required to do so more than once. Performance on the second solution improved more for these subjects than the others and the results suggested that this was due to better memory for general information such as strategies or subgoals.

Retention of mathematical information was one aspect studied by Krutetskii (1976, especially Ch. 14). He found clear differences between mathematically capable and mathematically inept pupils in this respect:

> 'Most capable pupils remember the type and the general character of the operations of a problem they have solved, but they do not remember a problem's specific data or numbers. Incapable pupils, on the other hand, usually recall only specific numerical data or specific facts about a problem.
>
> . . . the essence of a mathematical memory consists in the generalized recollection of typical schemes of reasoning and of operations. As for a memory for specific data, for numerical parameters, it is "neutral" with respect to mathematical ability' (Krutetskii 1976, p. 299).

Perceptual Processes

The role of perceptual processes in mathematics is most obvious in geometry, yet there has been little research into this (Dodwell 1971). Geometrical thinking is usually mediated by diagrams, but so may many other types of mathematical thinking (consider, for example the use of Venn diagrams). Fischbein (1977) describes a visual solution of the following problem:

> On a farm there are hens and rabbits. Altogether there are 13 animals possessing 36 legs. How many hens and how many rabbits are there on the farm?

This may be solved by drawing 13 bodies with 2 legs each, then adding legs 2 by 2 until the total number of legs reaches 36. Fischbein points out that such a visually mediated solution would be much less likely if the problem was phrased in terms of coins of different denominations. Krutetskii (1976, p. 156) specifically studied this aspect with a series of problems varying in the degree of visuality.

It has often been remarked that mathematicians differ in the extent to which they rely on diagrams and imagery. Despite the recent upsurge of interest in imagery, relatively little work specifically relating to mathematics has appeared as yet. In one interesting experiment, Hayes (1974) found that subjects presented visually with elementary mathematical tasks used a great deal and variety of imagery, which was almost always perceived as being integrated with the visually presented material, in what Hayes termed 'hybrid images'.

Problem-solving

A useful survey of mainly mathematical problems, classified in terms of general problem-solving strategies, has been provided by Wickelgren (1974).

More specific aspects of problem-solving, which are relevant to mathematical thinking, are currently receiving attention from cognitive psychologists. Of particular interest is the relationship between formally identical problems presented under different guises (Hayes and Simon 1977; Luger and Bauer 1978). It has repeatedly been found that such problems can vary enormously in difficulty, and that transfer between isomorphic problems is typically weak or non-existent. Such findings raise interesting questions about the extent to which subjects extract the logical or mathematical structure of problems. Halford (1975) did find that subjects could abstract the underlying structure in a task based on the three-element group, and use it to achieve near-optimal transfer between isomorphic problems, but his tasks differed only in the symbols used.

A related topic of interest is the way in which verbally presented material is transformed into mathematical form (e.g. as a set of algebraic equations). Rosenthal and Resnick (1974) looked at some linguistic effects in the verbal presentation of arithmetic problems. Robinson and Hayes (1978) studied the performance of both human subjects and a computer program (which did not do very well) in abstracting relevant information from verbally stated arithmetic problems, which also contained irrelevant information.

Both lines of research just discussed illustrate a general interest in internal representations of problems and translations between them (cf. also Fischbein's example discussed above).

PIAGET ON MATHEMATICS

Piaget's work is extremely important in the developmental study of mathematical thinking. Its influence on mathematical education seems to be growing (e.g. Halford 1978; Brown 1979). Piaget himself has always been more interested in epistemological questions (e.g. Piaget 1972) than in the educational applications of his theory. He is a constructivist, i.e. he believes that mathematics results from the activity of the intellect rather than existing independently of the mathematical thinker, merely awaiting discovery. He believes that this ancient philosophical debate, 'can be stated today in psychological terms and even in terms of child psychology' (Piaget 1972, p. 118), and that the results of his psychological research support his philosophical position.

Piaget's position has not gone unchallenged. Some of its fundamental problems have been clearly analysed by Feldman and Toulmin (1976). In particular, they point to the difficulty of relating the theory to the data, '. . . the actual observed behaviour of subjects has to be passed through a filter of scientific interpretation before we can see whether it in any way supports or fails to support the theoretical claims in question' (Feldman and Toulmin 1976, p. 413).

Such interpolated interpretation opens the way for major

disagreements regarding the theoretical implications of the data. By way of illustration, we may take a familiar example: conservation of number. The basic experiment has often been replicated and there is no argument about the findings. However, there is a great deal of disagreement about the interpretation of success on this task as a criterion of understanding of the concept of number. Bryant (1974, Ch. 8) has criticized the design of the experiment; using modified tasks, he showed that children as young as 4 years of age could maintain relative judgements after spatial transformations of arrays, if the transformed arrangement did not provide a misleading cue. Gelman and Gallistel (1978) share Bryant's misgivings, 'Failure to pass the Piagetian number-conservation test cannot by itself be taken as proof that preschoolers lack number-invariance rules.'

Freudenthal (1973, especially Appendix I) has severely criticized Piaget's views on early number concepts (as well as many other aspects of Piaget's views on mathematics). For example, he objects to Piaget's, 'habit of borrowing mathematical terminology and applying it with quite divergent meanings'. An example of this was noted by Feldman and Toulmin (1976) in complaining that Piaget and Inhélder, 'deliberately blur the distinction between topology and Euclidean geometry' in describing the ontogeny of geometrical concepts as beginning with topological concepts: this point has been elaborated by Kapadia (1974).

As all of these writers point out, one factor which demands that these criticisms be thoroughly ventilated is the 'discovery' of Piaget by those involved in mathematical education. As a result of this Piaget is invoked as an authority to justify pedagogical decisions, such as the recent fashion for introducing number via class concepts rather than counting (see Freudenthal 1973, Ch. 11; Macnamara 1975; Lunzer, Bell and Shiu 1976) or the suggestion that topology should be taught to young children (Kapadia 1974). Books such as that by Copeland (1974) advocate uncritically a direct assimilation of Piagetian theory to mathematical teaching. However, other writers have been much more cautious: the problems have been clearly stated by Steffe:

> 'In fact, few attempts have been made toward the identification of relationships between the cognitive operations demanded by the mathematical systems. For example, (1) if a child is or is not in possession of cognitive operations normally attributed to the grouping structures vis-a-vis Piaget, what does this say about his knowledge or acquisition of the integers, of the rational numbers of arithmetic, or even the rational number system? Or, (2) if a child does or does not possess the proportionality scheme or the INRC group, what does this say about his knowledge of acquisition of measurement, of the rational numbers or finite algebraic systems?' (1975, p. 3).

There is no doubt that Piaget's work is highly relevant to mathematical education: these criticisms warn against an uncritical or superficial acceptance of it.

REFERENCES

Ashcraft, M. H., and Battaglia, J. 1978. 'Cognitive arithmetic: evidence for retrieval and decision processes in mental addition.' *J. exp. Psychol.: Hum. Learn. and Mem. 4*, 527 – 38.

Baylor, G. W., and Gascon, J. 1974. 'An information processing theory of aspects of the development of weight seriation in children.' *Cog. Psychol. 6*, 1 – 40.

Brown, M. 1979. 'Cognitive development and the learning of mathematics.' In A. Floyd (ed.) *Cognitive development in the school years*. London: Croom Helm.

Bryant, P. E. 1974. *Perception and understanding in young children*. London: Methuen.

Collis, K. F. 1978. 'Operational thinking in elementary mathematics.' In J. A. Keats, K. F. Collis and G. S. Halford (eds) *Cognitive development*. London: John Wiley.

Copeland, R. W. 1974. *How children learn mathematics*. New York: Macmillan.

Dodwell, P. C. 1971. 'Children's perception and their understanding of geometrical ideas.' In M. F. Rosskopf, L. P. Steffe and S. Taback (eds) *Piagetian cognitive-development research and mathematical education*. Proceedings of Conference at Columbia University, Oct. 1970. Reston, Virginia: National Council of Teachers of Mathematics.

Feldman, C. F., and Toulmin, S. 1976. 'Logic and the theory of mind.' In W. J. Arnold (ed.) *Nebraska Symposium on motivation: conceptual foundations of psychology. Current theory and research in motivation, 23*. Lincoln: University of Nebraska Press.

Fischbein, E. 1975. *The intuitive sources of probabilistic thinking in children*. Dordrecht: Reidel.

Fischbein, E. 1977. 'Image and concept in learning mathematics.' *Educ. Studies in Maths 8*, 153 – 65.

Fischbein, E., Tirosh, D., and Hess, P. 1979. 'The intuition of infinity.' *Educ. Studies in Maths 10*, 3 – 40.

Freudenthal, H. 1973. *Mathematics as an educational task*. Dordrecht: Reidel.

Freudenthal, H. 1978. *Weeding and sowing*. Dordrecht: Reidel.

Gelman, R. 1978. 'Counting in the pre-schooler: what does and does not develop.' In R. S. Siegler (ed.) *Children's thinking: what develops?* Hillsdale, NJ: Lawrence Erlbaum.

Gelman, R., and Gallistel, C. R. 1978. *The child's understanding of number*. Cambridge, Mass.: Harvard University Press.

Ginsburg, H. 1977. *Children's arithmetic: the learning process*. New York: Van Nostrand.

Groen, G., and Resnick, L. B. 1977. 'Can preschool children invent addition algorithms?' *J. educ. Psychol. 69*, 645 – 52.

Halford, G. S. 1975. 'Effect of structure on learning and transfer: a possible link between learning and thinking.' *Australian J. Psychol. 27*, 3, 237–50.

Halford, G. S. 1978. 'An approach to the definition of cognitive developmental stages in school mathematics.' *Brit. J. educ. Psychol. 48*, 298–314.

Hayes, J. R. 1974. 'On the function of visual imagery in elementary mathematics.' In W. G. Chase (ed.) *Visual information processing*. New York: Academic Press.

Hayes, J. R., and Simon, M. A. 1977. 'Psychological differences among problem isomorphs.' In N. J. Castellan, Jr., D. B. Pisoni, and G. R. Potts (eds) *Cognitive theory 2*. Hillsdale, NJ: Lawrence Erlbaum.

Hitch, G. F. 1978. 'The role of short-term working memory in mental arithmetic.' *Cog. Psychol. 10*, 302–23.

Hollnagel, E. 1978. 'An information processing analysis of mental multiplication.' *Scand. J. Psychol. 19*, 63–72.

Holloway, G. E. T. 1967a. *An introduction to the child's conception of geometry*. London: Routledge and Kegan Paul.

Holloway, G. E. T. 1967b. *An introduction to the child's conception of space*. London: Routledge and Kegan Paul.

Inhelder, B. 1977. 'The development of the concepts of chance and probability in children.' In W. F. Overton and J. M. Gallagher (eds) *Knowledge and development 1*. New York: Plenum Press.

Kapadia, R. 1974. 'A critical examination of Piaget-Inhelder's view on topology.' *Educ. Stud. in Maths. 5*, 419–24.

Krutetskii, V. A. 1976. *The psychology of mathematical abilities in school children*. Chicago: University of Chicago Press.

Lovell, K. 1975. 'Summary and implications.' In L. P. Steffe (ed.) *Research on mathematical thinking of young children*. Reston, Virginia: National Council of Teachers of Mathematics.

Luger, G. F., and Bauer, M. A. 1978. 'Transfer effects in isomorphic problem situations.' *Acta Psychologica 42*, 121–31.

Lunzer, E. A., Bell, A. W., and Shiu, C. M. 1976. *Number and the world of things*. Report of Shell Centre for Mathematical Education, Nottingham University.

Macnamara, J. 1975. 'A note on Piaget and number.' *Child Develop. 46*, 424–9.

Piaget, J. 1972. 'Mathematical structures and the operational structures of the intellect.' In W. E. Lamon (ed.) *Learning and the nature of mathematics*. Chicago: SRA.

Piaget, J. 1973. 'Comments on mathematical education.' In A. G. Howson (ed.) *Developments in mathematical education*. Cambridge: Cambridge University Press.

Reed, S. K., and Johnsen, J. A. 1977. 'Memory in problem solutions.' In G. H. Bower (ed.) *The psychology of learning and motivation 11*. New York: Academic Press.

Resnick, L. B. 1976. 'Task analysis in instructional design: some cases from mathematics.' In D. Klahr (ed.) *Cognition and instruction*. Hillsdale, NJ: Lawrence Erlbaum.

Robinson, C. S., and Hayes, J. R. 1978. 'Making inferences about relevance in understanding problems.' In R. Revlin and R. E. Mayer (eds) *Human reasoning*. New York: John Wiley.

Rosenthal, D. J. A., and Resnick, L. B. 1974. 'Children's solution processes in arithmetic word problems.' *J. educ. Psychology 66*, 817 – 25.
Rosskopf, M. F. (ed.) 1975. *Children's mathematical concepts: Six Piagetian studies in mathematics education*. New York: Teachers' College Press.
Scandura, J. M. 1977. 'Structural approach to instructional problems.' *Amer. Psychol. 32*, 33 – 53.
Schaeffer, B., Eggleston, V. H., and Scott, J. L. 1974. 'Number development in young children.' *Cog. Psychol. 6*, 357 – 79.
Sinclair, H. 1971. 'Piaget's theory of development: the main stages.' In M. F. Rosskopf, L. P. Steffe and S. Taback (eds) *Piagetian cognitive-development research and mathematical education*. Proceedings of Conference at Columbia University, Oct. 1970. Reston, Virginia: National Council of Teachers of Mathematics.
Steffe, L. P. (ed.) 1975. *Research on mathematical thinking of young children*. Reston, Virginia: National Council of Teachers of Mathematics.
Svenson, O., and Hedenborg, M. L. 1979. 'Strategies used by children when solving simple subtractions.' *Acta Psychologica 43*, 477 – 89.
Svenson, O., Hedenborg, M. L., and Lingman, L., 1976. 'On children's heuristics for solving simple additions.' *Scand. J. Educ. Res. 20*, 161 – 73.
Thomas, H. L. 1975. 'The concept of function.' In M. F. Rosskopf (ed.) *Children's mathematical concepts*. New York: Teacher's College Press.
Tversky, A., and Kahnemann, D. 1974. 'Judgment under uncertainty: heuristics and biases.' *Science 185*, 1124 – 31.
Wickelgren, W. A. 1974. *How to solve problems*. San Francisco: Freeman.
Woods, S. S., Resnick, L. B., and Groen, G. J. 1975. 'An experimental test of five process models for subtraction.' *J. educ. Psychol. 67*, 17 – 21.

Chapter 12

The Social Psychology of Unemployment

COLIN FRASER

MARIENTHAL, AN EXTREME CASE?

Marienthal, an Austrian village about thirty-five minutes by train and then a couple of miles on foot from Vienna, was an unusual village in one important respect. It had grown up, not around a church or a market, but around a textile factory. By the late 1920s, Marienthal consisted of about 500 families, and the great majority of men in the village, as well as a number of the women, worked in the factory. But the world recession hit the village cruelly. In a period of barely 9 months, up to February 1930, the factory went from peak employment to complete closure, and then quickly to partial demolition. Initially, 60 men were retained for demolition and maintenance work. By January 1932 only 6 men in the village had maintenance jobs at what remained of the factory.

In 1930 a group of social scientists from the University of Vienna undertook a study of this unemployed community, in which more than three-quarters of the families had no income other than unemployment benefits. They conducted a sympathetic, perceptive, yet intensive investigation of the effects of unemployment on the activities of daily living of the villagers. The outcome was the appearance, in German in 1933, of the monograph by Jahoda, Lazarsfeld and Zeisel that has become a classic amongst attempts to document and understand the consequences of unemployment for individuals and for families.

Most of this essay will consist of a selective review of the evidence about such effects. My strategy will be to start with the well-documented 1930s and then move on to the, as yet, less well studied 1970s. The effects on the unemployed will be my main focus. Subsequently I will briefly consider a number of additional social psychological issues which relate to those effects. For example, assumptions about, or representations of, unemployment apparently held by many of the employed, the implications of unemployment for the meaning and practices of work, unemployment amongst particularly vulnerable social groups and the study of poverty.

What did Jahoda and her colleagues observe? Let me summarize their findings under seven, somewhat arbitrary headings, chosen partly because they cover many of a family's recurring activities and concerns and partly because these topics have also been discussed with regard to unemployment in other places at other times. The headings start with overtly material consequences and move on to less material ones; as psychologists, we should not become so engrossed in the study of self-esteem that we ignore starvation.

Finances. Despite the fact that wages in the area had already been low, unemployment brought consistent reductions in income. The system of paying unemployment relief and assistance made this a necessity. Unemployment relief was payable for a period of about 6 months, then discretionary emergency assistance could be provided for a further period of up to a year. The maximum relief permissible was 80% of wages in the last week of work; in turn, the maximum emergency assistance possible was 80% of the relief. There were numerous ways in which families failed to be eligible for maximum benefits, but even if they were, within 6 or 7 months of unemployment, the most they could receive was slightly less than two-thirds of their previous, generally low, wages. Many families were even worse off. From the figures in the report, I estimate, in a necessarily rough and ready way, that the plight of an unemployed Marienthal family of, say, 2 parents and 3 children might be compared to that of a similar British family having to live, in 1979, on less than £20 per week, i.e. between one-half and two-thirds of the weekly maintenance grant of a university student.

Material aspects of life-style. Obviously drastic economies of all sorts were absolutely essential. Standard items of food, such as coffee and butter were replaced by cheaper alternatives. Carbohydrates dominated at meal-times. Only 30% of families had meat on at least 2 days per week, and over 90% of that meat was either horse-meat or rabbit. On the day before the fortnightly payments of unemployment benefits, approximately half of the schoolchildren took either dry bread or nothing at all for their lunch at school. Even so, so much of a family's budget had to go on food – perhaps up to 90% – that any other substantial item of expenditure, such as shoe repairs, became a major problem.

Physical well-being. There was evidence of an overall decline in health standards, despite the equally horrifying fact that there was actually improvement, at least in the short-run, in the health of some adults, namely those who had been prone to tuberculosis as a result of their working conditions in the mill. Even the children suffered, despite the willingness of the unemployed families to spend a disproportionate amount of their income on milk for their children. One-third of the children under 14 were rated, during the study, as being in poor general health. Only 8% of the children had teeth unaffected by caries. There were signs of an inverse correlation between ill-health and family income.

Emotional state. There were many specific reports of emotionality, upsets, fearfulness and the like. Many of the men, in particular, manifested a blunted sense of time relations. 'Apathy', 'despair', 'depression' were terms frequently used to describe the unemployed. The investigators attempted to classify the overall state of the 100 families for whom they had detailed information. They concluded: 16 families were 'unbroken', i.e. they remained positive, even optimistic, in attitudes and emotions; 48 were 'resigned', i.e. they had accepted the realities of unemployment but were still coping well with organizing the necessities of everyday life; 11 were 'in despair', i.e. although still attempting to cope with the necessities of daily living, emotionally they were 'broken'; 25 were 'apathetic', i.e. they had given up all attempts to cope either emotionally or practically. Over one-third of the families, then, were regarded as psychologically 'broken'. The emotional well-being of the families showed a positive correlation with the amount of weekly income.

Personal relationships. In some cases, the crisis appears to have actually improved marital relations, by, for example, leaving husbands free to help around the house or forcing them, through financial pressures, to give up drinking. But those were exceptions. The more general picture was one of an increase in minor quarrels and of reports of withdrawal from social relations and friendships. So there was some, though by no means dramatic, evidence of increased interpersonal strains and difficulties. In fact, close personal relationships appear to have held up more effectively than many other facets of individual and family life.

Social interests and activities. In general, these decreased markedly. Clearly, some of the decrease, such as visits to Vienna or to the theatre, reflected financial pressures. But almost all formal social organizations experienced a decline in membership and participation, even when financial outlay was not involved. Inexpensive or free informal activities, such as visiting friends or going for walks, also declined in popularity. The fate of the village library is instructive. Just before the factory closure, the library, fortuitously, had expanded considerably. Its small borrowing charges were abolished. Yet borrowing dropped markedly, mainly in terms of the number of borrowers, but even in terms of the number of books per remaining borrower. The unemployed did not even feel like reading.

Political activities. The unemployment, poverty and shattered lives led to no increase in political action. Quite the reverse. There had been a history of political involvement in Marienthal, but all three of the major political organizations suffered marked losses in membership. Since membership fees for the unemployed were nominal, it is unlikely that the primary reason for such loss was financial, a point supported by the fact that the cheaper but more political newspaper lost more readers in the village than the dearer but entertainment oriented one. A striking demonstration of the fact that those who remained politically active tended to be from the minority of people still in work was provided by the Young Socialist Workers, who retained 37 members, of whom only 7 were unemployed. 'When one of their officers lost his job, he resigned from his position and decided to give up politics entirely' (Jahoda *et al.* 1933, p. 41).

It is clear, then, that for the families, and individuals, of Marienthal the effects of unemployment were pervasive. Whether we consider their health or emotional state or interest in the world around them, the unemployed suffered severely. To a considerable extent, the suffering appears to have been the result of financial hardship. But, as we saw, it is too simple to believe that the lack of money explained all the suffering. If the state of Austria in 1930 had been able to do what, to the best of my knowledge, no state has yet done, namely ensure that unemployment brings no financial loss whatsoever, it is conceivable that the unemployed in Marienthal would have remained less than normally content. For, typically, a job does more for an individual than provide financial support for self and family. One of the original Marienthal investigators Professor Marie Jahoda has recently (1979) suggested that work helps meet at least five enduring non-material needs: 'First among them is the fact that employment imposes a time structure on the working day; secondly, employment implies regularly shared experiences and contacts with people outside the nuclear family; thirdly, employment links an individual to goals and purposes which transcend his own; fourthly, employment defines aspects of personal status and identity; and finally, employment enforces activity.'

In the light of these points in addition to the existence of financial hardship, it is possible to begin to understand more readily some of the striking phenomena reported in Marienthal: the common disorientation in time; the apparent lethargy; the inability to organize one's life to make some positive use of unsought leisure; the loss in self-confidence and self-esteem; the guilt and shame experienced by people out of work because of events for which they were not responsible and over which they had no control.

EVIDENCE FROM THE 1930s

Was Marienthal a horrifying yet quite atypical extreme case, from which we can learn little of general relevance? Or did Marienthal highlight consequences of unemployment which were, in fact, much more general if sometimes taking an attenuated form? Quite apart from the moving accounts of unemployment provided by novelists and others (Greenwood 1933; Orwell 1937), there is an abundance of empirical evidence to help us assess the significance of that 'weary community'. A number of major studies were conducted in Britain alone, including Bakke's (1933) detailed investigation of 'the unemployed man', carried out mainly in Greenwich, and a survey of over 1000 unemployed, in six contrasting geographical areas, carried out on behalf of the Pilgrim Trust (1938).

The last-named, overtly moralistic volume, with its Preface by Lord Macmillan and Introduction by the then Archbishop of York, does not strike one as an avowedly radical document, but many of its findings and conclusions are reminiscent of Marienthal. The investigators found, for instance, that families dependent on unemployment assistance had incomes that were only 60% of the estimated wages they would reasonably have been expected to earn. Just under one-third of the families in the survey were found to be living in what was described as, 'deep or moderate poverty' and another third at a bare 'subsistence level'. 'There [was] little doubt that many unemployed men [were] undernourished' (p. 134) and there was, 'a marked increase in the number of women suffering from anaemia, neurasthenia and other conditions arising directly as a consequence of malnutrition and nervous strain' (Pilgrim Trust 1938, p. 139). The investigators repeatedly commented on the widespread existence of states such as, 'a sort of nerviness or listlessness', 'feeling of uselessness', 'depression and apathy'. 'The majority of the long-unemployed men had not the heart for clubs or activities of other kinds . . . ' (p. 148), instead there were problems of isolation; 'I keep myself to myself' (Pilgrim Trust 1938, p. 286). In poorer wards during the slump, there were without exception downward trends in borrowings from public libraries. About political attitudes and activities the report said nothing.

That similarities with Marienthal were not confined to a few regions in Britain is clear from Garraty's (1978) recent and impressively wide-ranging review of unemployment and its consequences. All of his evidence, from many countries, points to the fact that the unemployed suffered financially. Particularly in countries, such as the United States in the early thirties, that did not have nationally organized systems of unemployment relief, 'there were many cases of severe malnutrition and some of starvation' (Garraty 1978, p. 174). As early as December 1930, milk consumption in New York City had dropped by 1 000 000 quarts per week below the previous normal level. In France, the unemployed person's consumption of meat, dairy products and vegetables was much lower than that of workers. 'In Budapest in the early thirties hundreds of homeless unemployed professional workers were living in an army barracks, and eating left-overs in the university cafeteria until the dean ejected them on the ground that they were having, "a prejudicial effect, morally, on the students".' (Garraty 1978, p. 177). Unemployment, evictions and bad housing conditions led to the rise of shanty-towns on the edges of large cities in countries as diverse as Argentina, Australia, France and the United States. Continental and North American social scientists, and writers, recorded amongst unemployed populations, 'bleak, downcast eyes', 'the depressed look', 'lowered morale and broken spirits', 'sheep-like apathy', 'tendency to avoid social contacts', 'general loss of pride', 'deep humiliation'.

Garraty (1978) also discusses the political attitudes and activities of the unemployed. It was not difficult to find critical and angry beliefs and opinions being expressed; it was much more difficult to find evidence of their leading to more than 'mere talk'. Similarly, Eisenberg and Lazarsfeld (1938) concluded that the empirical evidence showed that unemployed people did tend to become more critical of the economic system, more antagonistic in their feelings towards employers, and more favourable to a change of government, but there were few signs of these attitudes being acted upon. Garraty (1978) points to the apparent absence of any major and sustained political movement, in any country, amongst the unemployed themselves and he presents evidence, from a number of countries, of the lack of recruitment amongst the unemployed to radical political parties of either left or right. There were of course specific protests, such as rent strikes, mass meetings and marches, but these appear to have been occasional and non-cumulative. In retrospect, even the high points of action and protest, namely the large marches, may have been less militant than they have been portrayed. When 8000 marchers in Washington in 1932 heard that their 'bonus bill' had just been rejected by the Senate, they accepted their leaders' advice to do two things, first to sing 'America', and then to go home. And one of the biggest protest marches in Britain, in 1934, ended in the presentation of a petition to the Houses of Parliament, formulated in appropriately subservient terms, '[We] humbly desire to represent that great suffering has been caused to the unemployed ...' What was requested was, 'employment at trade union rates' or 'decent maintenance', not revolutionary social change.

EVIDENCE FROM THE 1970s

As yet, the consequences of current and recent unemployment have been somewhat less well documented and it is certainly harder to arrive at the panoramic view that can be painted for the thirties. For those reasons, I shall concentrate on the limited body of evidence that pertains to Britain in recent years. Some of this evidence comes from presentations of selected case studies. Gould and Kenyon (1972) provide one set; Marsden and Duff (1975) is a weightier, much more systematic exemplar. At the other extreme are relatively large-scale surveys, such as Hill *et al.*'s (1973) research in three English towns or Daniel's (1974) national survey, which is a mine of relevant information. Field's (1977) valuable compendium falls somewhere between the extremes. Most of that evidence, however, was gathered when unemployment was lower than it currently is.

Over 40 years, many features of life in Britain have changed. How relevant, or irrelevant, are the findings of Marienthal and the thirties for Manchester or Middlesborough today? Let us look at the recent evidence with the same seven headings in mind.

With regard to finances, Hill *et al.* (1973) found that about 75% of their samples of the unemployed had incomes which were clearly lower than their last week's wages. Seventy-one per cent of Daniels' (1974) sample reported that unemployment had been either 'very bad' or 'quite bad' for them personally, and, of those, 72% expressed concern about 'lack of money' and related financial problems. These are findings one would expect, since our system of unemployment benefits is designed to ensure, in the great majority of cases, financial loss, compared to income from employment. The financial 'elite' of the unemployed are the minority who, for all of 6 months, are eligible for both flat-rate unemployment benefit and earnings related supplement, but for both sources of income combined there is an upper limit of 85% of average previous weekly earnings. In cases of hardship, supplementary benefit can be claimed which, if granted, is designed to bring claimants and their families up to a far from luxurious 'State poverty line'. Thus, to avoid financial loss through unemployment, it would be necessary either to have been working for exceedingly low wages or to benefit from a quite atypical set of circumstances. In one enquiry, the Department of Employment and the Supplementary Benefits Commission estimated that only between 1 and 2% of the unemployed were obtaining more from benefits than they might have obtained from work and another 6% were receiving roughly equivalent incomes. In Field's (1977) words, '. . . losing one's job is still a major cause of poverty in this country.'

Daniel (1974) found that financial difficulties arose quite frequently in connection with food, day-to-day living expenses, gas, electricity and heating bills, clothes for children, always buying second-hand clothes, paying the rent or mortgage, amongst other things. Marsden and Duff (1975) described families for whom both quantity and quality of food was a problem, and others where food standards were being maintained only by scrimping on clothing and basic furniture. Marshall (1972) reported that 29% of unemployed men receiving supplementary benefit claimed their families had insufficient blankets for winter and 51% claimed their children wore second-hand shoes. (In 1976, just over 45%

of the unemployed were receiving supplementary benefits and the percentage was increasing steadily year by year). Although this latter claim was higher amongst the unemployed than amongst unmarried mothers, separated wives, sick claimants, and widows, it could be argued that second-hand shoes are better than no shoes at all. Perhaps one index of the improved position of the unemployed, compared with the thirties, is that the percentage of their children going barefoot has dropped detectably!

Reports of malnutrition and problems of physical health have not been common recently, although Marsden and Duff (1975) have described problems associated with eating and sleeping. But complacency may be premature. Professor Harvey Brenner, an American medical researcher, has recently extended to this country his ambitious studies of the health correlates of unemployment and according to newspaper reports has claimed that, in England and Wales over a 5-year period, each increase of 1% in the conventionally calculated unemployment rate has been associated with 40 000 additional deaths. And, with regard to mental health, various studies conducted outside Britain have related unemployment to neuroticism, nervous breakdown, and depression, as well as to marital strain (Headlam 1978).

Over half of Daniel's (1974) sample expressed negative personal feelings, such as boredom, depression and feelings of failure. Marsden and Duff (1975) reported individual cases of bad temper and irritability. In a study of the psychological well-being of redundant steel-workers, Warr (1978) reported significant differences between employed and unemployed groups regarding positive and negative affect and the likelihood of both general and specific anxieties. Reports of lowered self-esteem and lack of self-confidence associated with unemployment remain common. Wedderburn's (1971) conclusion that, 'unemployment involved not only a loss of dignity for the individual: his whole life lost meaning,' might have come from the Marienthal investigation rather than from a study of more recent redundancies at Rolls Royce.

Marsden and Duff (1975) wrote that, 'being thrown out of work seemed to alter a man's social relationships and to make him less accessible', although the relationships that most readily worsen may not be the immediate marital ones. The same authors, like others before them (e.g. Komarovsky 1940), claimed that the prior nature of the marital relation determines whether it will worsen or conceivably improve with unemployment. Since the unemployed person often appears to draw in on his or her family, as well as on his or her self, it may be more distant and diverse relationships that suffer. There are reports of feeling isolated from former work friends, of having to economize on social activities, and of being embarrassed about inviting others into increasingly shabby homes. Burghes and Field (1977) described one couple who had not had an evening out since they were married, apart from one occasion when friends paid for them to go to a dance. Cox and

Golden (1977) reported that the children of an unemployed worker on Tyneside would not leave their house at Christmas because the other children in the street would be bragging about the presents they had received. These specific cases, however, should be seen against the background of Daniels' (1974) finding that social isolation and missing company were felt to be the worse aspects of being out of work by only a very small minority of the unemployed.

Finally, with regard to the political attitudes and behaviour of the unemployed, there appears to be little systematic evidence. There have been reports, particularly from East London, of unemployed teenagers being recruited by the National Front, and bodies such as the Claimants Union attempt to create self-help amongst the unemployed. But the occasional dramatic political protest, whether from Denain in Northern France or Corby in Central England, appears to come from workers fighting the prospect of unemployment, rather than from those already unemployed. The prospect of the unemployed taking concerted and sustained action in an attempt to improve their lot seems no more likely now than it was in the thirties.

TENTATIVE CONCLUSIONS AND QUALIFICATIONS

What then can we conclude from the foregoing descriptive account of the consequences of unemployment in Marienthal, in the thirties more generally, and in the seventies? I am struck by the similarities rather than the differences. There may be signs of some diminution of severity of effects from one body of evidence to the next, but the phenomena reported appear to be the same rather than different in kind. It would be hard to deny that the financial and direct material hardships of unemployment have been mitigated somewhat since the thirties, but I would wish to defend the view that the psychological and social meanings of unemployment for the unemployed remain much as they were. Marienthal may have been an extreme case, but it was by no means an entirely idiosyncratic one.

For a discipline, social psychology, which is showing signs (cf. Jahoda 1979; Kelvin, in press) of correcting its neglect of this area, the working hypothesis that unemployment continues to bring material and non-material misery for the majority of the unemployed is a defensible and salutary starting point for attempting to describe and understand the lives of what is likely to be an increasing number of people in this country and elsewhere. At the moment, according to the Department of Employment's statistics, on any given day approximately 1 500 000 people in Britain who are officially regarded as both able and willing to work are registered as unemployed. The optimism of only a few years ago that the then recent marked increase in unemployment figures was a temporary reflection of a short-term economic 'dip' or 'trough' has dissipated completely. No economists, or even politicians, are predicting a return to markedly lower rates in the next year or two. The most common expert view now appears to be that the economic and political factors associated with widespread increases in unemployment in the industrialized world will remain in operation for at least some time to come. In addition, the development of micro-processors is likely to remove the need for many conventional manual and clerical jobs. As a result of both of these sets of pressures, predictions such as, '4 500 000 unemployed by 1990' or, '25% of the work-force out of work by the turn of the century' are now alarming rather than merely alarmist. Specific numbers and percentages necessarily have to be taken with a pinch of salt but the realistic assumption now seems to be that, short of radical economic and political change, a substantial, e.g. at least 5%, and probably considerably higher, level of unemployment is not a temporary evil but will remain as an inbuilt structural feature of life in Britain, and conceivably in other countries as well. Thus, if financial, psychological and social suffering are to remain the consequences of unemployment, the suffering will be continuous and widespread.

These tentative conclusions are far from precise. One important task of future research will be to refine and qualify them considerably. So far, for example, I have tended to write of 'unemployment' and 'the unemployed' as if there was no need to draw major distinctions within those categories. But feelings, problems and prospects are likely to vary, at least to some extent, depending on whether unemployment is the fate of a 16 year-old school-leaver, a 30 year-old engineer, a 45 year-old married woman, or a 59 year-old storekeeper. Length of unemployment is likely to be important, and it should be noted that most of the evidence cited so far has been derived from longer-term unemployed. Education and skills make crucial differences. Although white-collar, managerial and professional unemployment is by no means unknown (e.g. Wedderburn 1964), unemployment remains primarily a fate experienced by unskilled workers, with minimal education and qualifications. Again, age is an important source of variation. Unemployment is highest amongst over fifty-fives, and also higher than average amongst under twenty-fives, and the long-term consequences of having a substantial number of school-leavers discover that they have been educated for nothing but the dole are likely to be particularly unpredictable yet serious (Millham *et al.* 1978). The meaning and consequences of unemployment for males and for females are likely to be somewhat different. There is some suggestive evidence (e.g. Jahoda *et al.* 1933; Millham *et al.* 1978; Pahl 1978) that women cope better than men with the prospect and reality of unemployment. Yet, in part because many women desiring work outside the home do not register as unemployed, the extent, let alone the nature, of female unemployment has been inadequately studied. The employment prospects of certain racial and ethnic minorities differ from those of the white majority. Not only have the levels of unemployment generally been higher in this country for non-whites of West Indian, Asian and African descent, but when unemployment rose sharply in the mid-seventies, the unemployment rates amongst those racial groups rose markedly more than the general increase.

These then are some pointers to important qualifications that have to be made, and will have to be elaborated by further investigation, concerning the consequences of unemployment. An even more fundamental qualification might be borne in mind. Perhaps the claims I have made concerning the continuing financial, psychological and social disadvantages of the unemployed are untrue! Certainly many people appear to believe they are. Strikingly, Garraty (1978, pp. 251 – 3) who documented so carefully and movingly the misery of the thirties, wrote quite differently about the seventies, citing virtually no evidence whatsoever for his claims. He asserted that unemployment is no longer the psychological catastrophe that it was because unemployment benefits are so comprehensive and because the unemployed are unlikely to feel personally inadequate or hapless victims, since government is clearly seen as the cause of unemployment. As a result, unemployment has become a routine, in some cases desirable, feature of working life, there is considerable 'voluntary unemployment' because benefits discourage attempts to seek work, and the major adverse psychological reaction nowadays is merely fear of having to make some sacrifice in living standards. My own impression and experience is that such general assumptions and beliefs are quite commonly held, as are more specific ones, relating, for example to the overestimation of 'real' unemployment by unemployment statistics, and the existence of large numbers of welfare 'fiddlers and scroungers' amongst the unemployed.

I believe the evidence I have already reviewed seriously calls into question the more general assumptions concerning absence of material and non-material suffering. It is also not difficult to point to evidence that contradicts the more specific beliefs. The existence of unregistered, unemployed males and large numbers of unregistered married women and retired persons who would take paid work if they could obtain it, strongly suggests that official statistics under- rather than over-represent the magnitude of the problem. Numerous internal governmental inquiries as well as independent academic investigations have agreed on the effectiveness of the existing elaborate procedures for detecting fraud or abuse of social benefits (Field 1977) and have shown that the total amounts of money illegitimately obtained by the unemployed are minute, in comparison, for example, with the £500 000 000 that the Inland Revenue estimated was lost in 1975 to tax evaders, fiddlers and scroungers (Cox and Goulden 1977).

In my opinion, the interesting question to ask concerning the picture of unemployment painted, and challenged, in the last but one paragraph is not, 'Is it correct?', but, 'How widespread is such an erroneous view?' To the best of my knowledge, no systematic evidence concerning the general public's perceptions, attitudes or representations of unemployment are available. This may be an appropriate point at which to turn to a consideration of some of the implications of unemployment for future work in social psychology.

SOME IMPLICATIONS FOR SOCIAL PSYCHOLOGY

We must ask what contributions to the understanding of unemployment and of the unemployed might social psychologists help to achieve. But unemployment is not merely a 'social problem'; it is a strategic set of psychological, social, economic and political issues whose study is likely to illuminate many corners of social psychology not hitherto associated with unemployment. In conclusion, let us look at some of the ways in which those two slightly different sets of questions may be interwoven.

First, as we have seen, there remains a need for much finer descriptive studies of the consequences of unemployment for different sets of people in different circumstances. Important theoretical, as well as practical, questions will follow from attempts to separate the operation of material and non-material factors. There may be a case for initially adopting a very 'vulgar Marxist' stance, by assuming that financial position is *the* determinant of the experiences of the unemployed. The assumption would be made, not because one believes it to be the whole truth, but rather to see how far it will take one and how quickly it will break down. One likely limitation is implied by the ideas and research of Runciman (1966) and others on relative deprivation. That is, it may not be absolute loss or deprivation which is crucial, but rather deprivation relative to one's own expectations or relative to particular reference groups with which one compares oneself. That financial loss – whether relative or absolute – will not explain everything is implied by Jahoda's (1979) description, summarized earlier, of the non-financial losses accompanying loss of work. Nonetheless, an initial emphasis on money matters would be a healthy corrective for social psychology which has, by and large, totally ignored the economic realities relevant to so much of our behaviour and experience.

Secondly, again as we have seen, there is a need for the systematic study of widespread shared attitudes, or 'social representations' (cf. Herzlich 1973; Moscovici 1961) or ideologies concerning unemployment and the unemployed. It can be argued that the concept of attitude was introduced to social psychology by Thomas and Znaniecki (1918–20), in their investigation of Polish immigrants to the United States, in order to analyse shared belief systems with important social consequences, but that the subsequent study of attitudes has consisted of a gradual yet consistent individualization, and perhaps trivialization, of the attitude concept. Unemployment is one domain in which the original issues could be rediscovered. And if it emerges that there are indeed powerful social representations – or misrepresentations – of unemployment, a next question is how are they transmitted to the individuals who share them. Social representations should also be studied amongst the unemployed, to see if they accept conceptions of themselves common amongst the public at large.

Analyses of both the 'realities' and the representations of unemployment would surely throw light on a third set of issues, that some psychologists would regard as the central ones, namely the psychological states, and especially the self-esteem of unemployed individuals. In what respects is self-esteem lowered, and do they relate most closely to financial, psychological or social disadvantages? Are lowered self-esteem and a negative self-image related to attributing to self rather than others (cf. Eiser 1978) responsibility for loss of work; might an unemployed person with an internal locus of control (Rotter 1966) be more prone to lowered self-esteem? Is it helpful to reject the prevailing social representations? To what extent does lowered self-esteem contribute to explaining the apparent inability of the unemployed to organize themselves politically to object to their fate? Whether or not one expects the macro-economic and political miracles which might put an end to unemployment, could counselling for the unemployed help minimize some of the difficulties faced by individuals and families?

Kelvin (in press) assumes that self-esteem may not suffer as much damage in the future as it has in the past amongst the unemployed, in part because of their sheer numbers, but also because 'the work ethic' is changing and weakening. This last point raises an important fourth set of issues on which, up till now, the running has been made by writers other than social psychologists. Beynon (1973), Braverman (1974), Palm (1977) and others have documented the dispiriting, even degrading, nature of much industrial work and have argued for the lack of intrinsic satisfaction experienced by many workers. But others (e.g. Jahoda 1979) are sceptical of these arguments in part because of evidence (cf. Headlam 1978) that the supposedly alienated workers may actually be deriving satisfaction from their work. As we have observed, work appears to serve several important functions for the individual, and there remain many unexplored questions concerning the meaning and importance of work to individuals, and the ways in which family life-styles and relationships are structured by the work which family members do. Study of those deprived of work is likely to be one powerful approach to understanding these issues, and such an understanding in turn is likely to illuminate the consequences of unemployment.

Finally, at the risk of becoming messianic, it is possible to point to some even wider implications of unemployment for social psychology. Who are the most disadvantaged and underprivileged groups of people in our society? The poorly educated, the unskilled, the physically and mentally handicapped, the elderly, teenagers, blacks . . . They provide most of the unemployed, and many of the longer-term unemployed belong to 'the poor'. It will be impossible for social psychologists to study unemployment without getting involved in the study of poverty more generally. And to understand that, social psychology will have to come face-to-face with economic reality. Unemployment could be a powerful impetus to the development, largely from scratch, of a social psychology of economic life.

The realization that unemployment and its study could contribute a great deal to the development of social psychology should not blind us to the need for social psychology to make constructive contributions to the lives of the unemployed.

REFERENCES

Bakke, E. W. 1933. *The unemployed man*. London: Nisbet.

Beynon, H. 1973. *Working for Ford*. Harmondsworth: Penguin.

Braverman, H. 1974. *Labor and monopoly capital: the degradation of work in the twentieth century*. New York: Monthly Review Press.

Burghes, L., and Field, F. 1977. 'The cost of unemployment.' In F. Field (ed.) *The conscript army: a study of Britain's unemployed*. London: Routledge and Kegan Paul.

Cox, S., and Golden, R. 1977. *Down the road: unemployment and the fight for the right to work*. London: Writers and Readers Publ. Coop.

Daniel, W. W. 1974. *A national survey of the unemployed*, broadsheet no. 546. PEP. XL, London.

Eisenberg, P., and Lazarsfeld, P. F. 1938. 'The psychological effects of unemployment.' *Psychol. Bull. 35*, 358 – 90.

Eiser, J. R. 1978. 'Interpersonal attributions.' In H. Tajfel and C. Fraser (eds) *Introducing social psychology*. Harmondsworth: Penguin.

Field, F. (ed.) 1977. *The conscript army: a study of Britain's unemployed*. London: Routledge and Kegan Paul.

Garraty, J. A. 1978. *Unemployment in history*. New York: Harper and Row.

Gould, T., and Kenyon, J. 1972. *Stories from the dole queue*. London: Routledge and Kegan Paul.

Greenwood, W. 1933. *Love on the dole*. London: Cape.

Headlam, F. 1978. 'Unemployment, benefits and work motivation.' *Bibliographies in social research* no 4. Dept. of Sociology, La Trobe University.

Herzlich, C. 1973. *Health and illness: a social psychological analysis*. London: Academic Press.

Hill, M. J. *et al.* 1973. *Men out of work: a study of unemployment in three English towns*. Cambridge: Cambridge University Press.

Jahoda, M. 1979. 'The impact of unemployment in the 1930s and the 1970s.' *Bull. Brit. Psychol. Soc.*, 32, 309 – 314.

Jahoda, M., Lazarsfeld, P. F., and Zeisel, H. 1933. *Marienthal: the sociography of an unemployed community*. (First published in Britain in 1972. London: Tavistock).

Kelvin, P. In press. 'Social psychology 2001: the social psychological bases and implications of structural unemployment.' In R. Gilmour and S. Duck (eds) *The development of social psychology*. London: Academic Press.

Komarovsky, M. 1940. *The unemployed man and his family*. New York: Institute of Social Research.

Marsden, D., and Duff, E. 1975. *Workless: some unemployed men and their families*. Harmondsworth: Penguin.

Marshall, R. 1972. *Families receiving supplementary benefit*. London: HMSO.

Millham, S., Bullock, R., and Hosie, K. 1978. 'Juvenile unemployment: a concept due for recycling?' *Adolescence 1*, 11 – 24.

Moscovici, S. 1961. *La psychoanalyse, son image et son public*. Paris: Presses Universitaires de France.

Orwell, G. 1937. *The road to Wigan pier*. London: Left Book Club.

Pahl, R. E. 1978. 'Living without a job: how school-leavers see the future.' *New Society*, November 2, 259 – 62.

Palm, G. 1977. *The flight from work*. Cambridge: Cambridge University Press.

Pilgrim Trust. 1938. *Men without work*. Cambridge: Cambridge University Press.

Rotter, J. B. 1966. 'Generalized expectancies for internal versus external control of reinforcement.' *Psychological Monographs 80*, 1.

Runciman, W. G. 1966. *Relative deprivation and social justice*. London: Routledge and Kegan Paul.

Thomas, W. I., and Znaniecki, F. 1918 – 20. *The Polish peasant in Europe and America*, 5 vols. Boston: Gorham Press.

Warr, P. 1978. 'A study of psychological well-being.' *Brit. J. Psychol. 69*, 111 – 21.

Wedderburn, D. 1964. *White-collar redundancy*. Cambridge: Cambridge University Press.

Wedderburn, D. 1971. 'Unemployment in the seventies.' *Listener*, August 12.

Table of Contents of Psychology Survey, No. 1

Table of Contents of Psychology Survey, No. 2

Author Index

(Numbers printed in italics refer to the References at the end of each chapter)

Subject Index